SKI-RUNS IN THE HIGH ALPS

SKI-RUNS IN THE HIGH ALPS

BY

F. F. ROGET, S.A.C.

HONORARY MEMBER OF THE ALPINE SKI CLUB
HONORARY MMBER OF THE ASSOCIATION OF
BRITISH MEMBERS OF THE SWISS ALPINE CLUB

WITH 25 ILLUSTRATIONS BY
L. M. CRISP
AND 6 MAPS

The Naval & Military Press Ltd

Reproduced by kind permission of the Central Library,
Royal Military Academy, Sandhurst

Published by

The Naval & Military Press Ltd

Unit 10, Ridgewood Industrial Park,

Uckfield, East Sussex,

TN22 5QE England

Tel: +44 (0) 1825 749494

Fax: +44 (0) 1825 765701

www.naval‑military‑press.com

© The Naval & Military Press Ltd 2005

TO

MY DAUGHTER

ISMAY

HOPING SHE MAY NOT GO FORTH

AND DO LIKEWISE

PREFACE

IN 1905, when nearer fifty than forty, had I not been the happy father of a girl of seven I should have had no occasion to write this book. I bought, for her to play with, a pair of small ski in deal, which I remember cost nine francs. For myself I bought a rough pair, on which to fetch and bring her back to shore if the small ship foundered.

No sooner had I equipped myself, standing, as a Newfoundland dog, on the brink of the waves, ready to rescue a child from snow peril, than I was born again into a ski-runner.

Since, I have devoted some of my spare time to revisiting—in winter—the passes and peaks of Switzerland.

The bringing of the ski to Switzerland ushered in the "New Mountaineering," of which a few specimens seek in these pages the favour of the general public.

The reader may notice that I never spell "ski" with an *s* in the plural, because it is quite unnecessary. One may stand on one ski, and one may stand on both ski. The *s* adds nothing to intelligibility.

Nor do I ever pronounce ski otherwise than I write it. There is in ski the *k* that appears in skipper and in skiff. Though cultured Germans say *Schiff* and *Schiffer*, the *k* sound of ski is quite good Norse. It has been preserved in the French *esquif*, of same origin.

The *i* should be pronounced long as in "tree."

So let us always say *s-k-ee* and write ski for both numbers.

SAAS-FEE.
August 14, 1912.

CONTENTS

CHAPTER I

CHAPTER II

CHAPTER III

CHAPTER IV

CHAPTER V

CHAPTER VI

ILLUSTRATIONS

Ski-Runs in the High Alps

CHAPTER I

SKI-RUNNING IN THE HIGH ALPS

The different ski-ing zones—Their characteristics and dangers—
The glaciers as ski-ing grounds—The ski-running season—
Inverted temperature—The conformation of winter snow
—Precautionary measures—Glacier weather—Rock condi-
tions—Weather reports—Guides and porters.

IN a chapter like this, a writer on the High
Alps may well abstain from poetical or literary
developments. His subject is best handled
as a technical sport, and personal experience
should alone be drawn upon for its illustration.

Little more than ten years have elapsed
since men with a knowledge of summer mountaineering began to explore the Alps in winter.
Not only are the successes, which have almost
invariably attended the winter exploration of
the Swiss ice-fields, full of instruction for the
novice, but also the accidents and misfortunes
which, sad to say, ended in loss of life or limb,
have conveyed useful lessons.

In this chapter the writer has nothing in
view but to be practical and pointed. His
remarks must be taken to apply exclusively to the

2   17

Alps.   He has no knowledge of any other ski-ing field, and is conversant with no other experience but that gained in the Alps by himself and members of the Swiss ski-ing clubs, which count in their membership thousands of devotees.

It is necessary to distinguish the zones of meadow land and cultivated fields, forest land, cattle grazings, and rocks.

In the forest zone the snow presents no danger except, perhaps, in sharply inclined clearings where its solidity is not sufficiently assured either by the nature of the underlying ground or by the presence of trees growing closely together at the foot of the incline.

Above the forest belt the zone of pastures is a favourite ski-ing ground.   This zone is wind-swept, sunburnt during the day, and under severe frost at night.   As a general rule, it may be laid down that snow accumulated in winter on the grazings frequented by cows in summer affords a safe and reliable ski-ing ground, at any rate in all parts where the cows are in the habit of standing.   When in doubt, the ski-runner should ask himself: Are cows, as I know them, likely to feel comfortable when standing on this slope in summer?   If an affirmative answer can be given in a *bona-fide* manner, the slope is not dangerous.

Alpine grazing lands being selected for the con- venience of cows, they are almost throughout well adapted to ski-runners.   It is, of course, under- stood that gorges, ravines, and steep declivities will be avoided by Swiss cows just as much as by those of any other nationality. The ski-runner should leave those parts of the grazing alone on which a herd would not be allowed to roam by its shepherds.

The deepest and heaviest Alpine snows lie on the grazings, and the avalanches that occur there in spring are of the heaviest type and cover the most extensive areas. These are spring avalanches. They are regular phenomena, and it is totally unnecessary to expect them in midwinter.

Above the grazings begin the rocks. They are either towering rocks and walls, or else they lie broken up on slopes in varying sizes. In the latter case the snow that may cover them is quite safe, provided the points of those rocks be properly buried. As a rule, wherever there is a belt or wall of solid rock above a grazing (which is practically the case in every instance when it is not a wood), the loose stones at the foot of the rocks give complete solidity to the snow surface resting on them. The danger arises from the rocks towering aloft. If these are plastered over with loose snow, the snow may come down at any moment on the lower ground. One should not venture under such rocks till the snow that may have gathered in the couloirs has come down or is melted away.

Avalanches are a matter belonging more particularly to snow conditions in the grazing areas, but they need not to any degree be looked upon as characteristic of this area. Their cause has to be sought in the weather, that is in the rise

and fall of the temperature, and in the wind. There
is quite a number of slopes at varying angles, where
it is impossible that the snow surface should be
well balanced under all weather conditions, and
these are the slopes where mishaps do occur. The
easiest method to avoid accidents is to keep on
obviously safe ground, and it is also on such ground
that the best and most steady running can be got.

The glaciers of Switzerland are a magnificent and
absolutely unrivalled ski-ing ground.

The months appointed by natural circumstances
for ski-running in the High Alps are the months
of January and February. This period may quite
well be taken to include the whole month of March
and the last days in December.

There are reasons for excluding the first three
weeks in December, and the last three in April.

In night temperature, but in night temperature
only, the passing from summer to winter, upwards of 9,000 feet may indeed be said to have
fully taken place long before the end of the year.
This passage is marked by the regular freezing
at night of all moisture, and by the regular
freezing over of all surfaces on which moisture is
deposited by day. Still, the first fall of a general
layer of snow, which will *last throughout the winter*
on the high levels, may be much delayed. Till
that first layer has covered the high ground, the
ski-runner's winter has not begun.

The first general snowfall, if it mark the beginning
of the ski-runner's winter, does not yet mark the
setting in of the ski-running season. For a time,

THE WILDSTRUBEL HUT.

To face p. 2:.

which may extend from November to near the end of December, moisture proceeding from the atmosphere, that is rain and *vapours* (warm, damp winds), is not without effect at the altitudes which we are considering. Such a damp condition of the air and any risk of rain are quite inconsistent with ski-running. But everybody should know that if such risks must be taken throughout the winter by a ski-runner residing, for instance, at the altitude of Grindelwald, they may practically be neglected by a sportsman whose field of exercise is that to which the Swiss Alpine Club huts afford access.

There, from Christmas to early Easter, the only atmospheric obstacle consists of snowstorms, in which the wind alone is an enemy, while the snow entails an improvement in the conditions of sport each time it falls. The November and December snowfalls prepare the ground for running, and running at those heights is neither safe nor perfect as long as the process goes on. In January and February any snowfall simply improves the floor or keeps up its good condition. It may be taken that during these months the atmosphere is absolutely dry from Tyrol to Mont Blanc above 8,000 feet, and that a so-called wet wind will convey only dry snow. Any moisture or water one may detect will be caused by the heat of the sun melting the ice or the snow. It is a drying, not a wetting, process; it leaves the rocks facing south, south-east, and south-west beautifully dry, and completely clears them, by rapid evaporation, of the early winter snows or of any casual midwinter fall accompanying a storm of wind.

Such are the atmospheric reasons which help to determine the proper ski-running months in the High Alps.

There are others which are still of a meteorological description, but which are connected mainly with the temperature. We shall begin by giving our thought a paradoxical expression as follows : it is a mistake to talk of winter at all in connection with the High Alps. According to the time of year, the weather in the Alps is subjected to general rain conditions or to general snow conditions. Under snow conditions the thermometer falls under zero Centigrade, and the temperature of the air may range from zero to a very low reading; but the sun is extremely powerful, its force is intensified by the reflection from the snow surface. The temperature of the air in the shade is therefore no clue to the temperature of material surfaces exposed to the rays of the sun. The human frame, under suitable conditions of clothing and exercise, feels, and actually is, quite warm in the sun, a violent wind being required to approximate the subjective sensations of the body to those usually associated with a cold, damp, and biting winter's day.

This is a general characteristic of the Alpine winter, to which must be added an occasional, though perfectly regular, feature, namely, that the Alps may offer, and do offer every winter, instances of *inverted* temperature. This name is given to periods which may extend over several days at a stretch, and which are repeated several times during the winter months. These are periods during which the constant temperature of the air—that is, the average temperature by night and by day in the shade—is higher upon the heights than in the plains and valleys.

As a general principle, the winter sportsman may be sure that in the proportion in which he rises he also leaves behind him the winter conditions, as defined, in keeping with their own notions and experience by the dwellers on plains, on the seaside, or in valleys. When travelling upwards he reaches a dry air, a hot and bright light, and maybe a higher temperature than prevails in the lower regions of the earth which lie at his feet.

We said a little while ago that in January and February any snowfall improves the floor. In the preceding months the high regions pass gradually from the condition in which they are practicable on foot to those under which they are properly accessible to the ski-runner only. Time must be allowed for the process, and till it is completed ski-running is premature and consequently distinctly dangerous. The Alpine huts should not be used as ski-ing centres before they can be reached on ski, and one should not endeavour to reach them in that manner as long as stones are visible among the snow.

The distinctive feature of the ski-runner's floor is that it is free from stones and from holes. The stones should be well buried under several feet of snow, and the holes filled up with compressed or frozen snow before the ski-runner makes bold to sally forth, but when they are he may practically go anywhere and dare anything so far as the ground is con-

cerned, provided he is an expert runner and a con-
noisseur in the matter of avalanches. Of course, our
"anywhere" applies to ski-ing grounds only, and
our "anything" means mountaineering as restricted
to the uses to which ski may fairly be put.

The floor of the ski-runner is a dimpled surface
consisting of an endless variety of planes and curves.
It is a geometrical surface upon which the ski move
like instruments of mensuration that are from two
to three yards long. Snowfalls and the winds determine the geometrical character of the field upon
which the long rulers are to glide. This, the only
true notion of the ski-ing field, means that the *detail*
of the ground has disappeared. It presents a con-
tinuity of differently inclined, bent, edged, or curved
surfaces, all uniformly geometric in the construction
of each. Any attempt at ski-running upon this playground before its engineers and levellers (which are
snow and wind) have achieved their work in point of
depth, solidity, and extent, is unsporting and perilous.

The continuous figure or design presented by the
upper snow-fields of the Alps in January, from end to
end of the chain, is broken by prismatic masses, such
as cones, pyramids, and peaks, on the sides of which
the laws of gravity forbid the establishment by the
concourse of natural forces of snow-surfaces accessible
with ski. The runner who has been borne by his ski
to the foot of those rock masses—such, for instance,
as the top of Monte Rosa as it rises from the Sattel—
will continue his ascent as a rock-climber. He will
probably find the state of the rocks quite as pro-
pitious as in summer, and often considerably better.

To sum up, the characteristics of the ski-running season are: stability of weather, constant dryness of the air, a uniform and continuous running surface, windlessness, a constant body temperature from sunrise to sunset, at times a relatively high air temperature, solar light and solar heat, which must not be confused with air temperature and present an intensity, a duration most surprising to the dweller in plains and on the seaboard; last, but not least, accessibility of the rocky peaks with climbing slopes turned to the sun.

A real trouble is the crevasses. The ice-fields form such wide avenues between the peaks bordering them that a ski-runner must be quite a fool if an avalanche finds him within striking distance. But the crevasses are quite another matter. In summer the protection against falling into crevasses is the rope and careful steering between them. In winter mountaineering the ski, properly speaking, take the place of the rope. The longest traverses in the Alps have been performed by unroped ski-runners. At the same time, the usefulness of the rope, in case of an accident actually occurring, cannot be gainsaid, though it cannot be maintained that the rope, which has been known to cause certain accidents in summer, may be called absolutely free from any such liability in winter. Of the use of the rope we therefore say, "Adhuc sub judice lis est."

There are two golden rules for avoiding a drop into a crevasse: firstly, keep off glaciers or of those parts of any glacier where crevasses are known to be numerous, deep, long, and wide; secondly, if called

upon to run over a glacier that is crevassed, use the
rope, but use it properly—that is, bring its full length
into use, take off your ski, and proceed exactly as you
would do in summer by sounding the snow and crossing bridged crevasses one after another. It is absurd
to mix summer and winter craft; they are distinct.
When the rope is used under winter conditions, let
it be exactly according to the best winter practice.

If going uphill you find yourself landed on ice,
take off your ski and gain a footing on the ice by
means of the heavy nails on your boots. Never
attempt glacier work with unnailed boots or short,
light bamboo sticks. If any accident happens suddenly to your ski you are helpless and hopeless without nails; you probably will not have time to take
your climbing irons off your rucksack and bind them
on to your feet.

Accidents to ski generally happen when one is on
the move on difficult and dangerous ground. It is
absurd to expect that the difficulty or danger will abate
while you take off your rucksack, sit down, and strap
on your climbing irons. Remember that you are
on the move and that your impetus will carry you on,
if not immediately checked by nails gripping the ice.
That, too, is the reason why a short, light bamboo
will not do; it is a fine-weather weapon and quite the
thing on easy snows. On rough ground you want
something with a substantial iron point, a weapon of
some weight and strength which can support your
body and help in seeing you home should your ski be
injured. A good runner would never put his stick
to unfair uses, such as riding and leaning back.

If on going downhill you find yourself landed on ice, the essential thing is to be able to keep on your feet first, to your course next. A stout stick with a sharp point will then be sorely needed, and if you have been careful to fasten on to your ski-blades an appliance against skidding or side-slip, you will find it much easier to steer and keep to your course. On the whole, it is wiser on iced surfaces which are steep —and these are generally not extensive—to carry one's ski.

There ought to be an ice-axe in the party, but this ice-axe should be carried by a professional and used by him. Nobody can cut steps or carry safely an ice-axe without some apprenticeship, and this it is impossible to go through in severe winter weather.

The principal glacier routes of Switzerland have been proved over and over again to be free from any particular risk or danger arising from winter conditions. The *ratio* of risk is the same as in summer. Consequently, select the best known routes, which are also the most beautiful and ski-able. Take with you, as porters and servants rather than guides, men who have frequently gone over those routes in winter with some Swiss runner of experience. This is important, because many guides, particularly the most approved summer guides, are creatures of routine, and will take you quite obdurately along the summer routes, step for step and inch after inch. Now, this is wrong and may lead to danger. The ski-runner must dominate the snow slopes. His place is on the brow, or rather on the coping, not at the foot of the slopes along which the summer parties generally crawl.

When going uphill for several hours consecutively, as it is necessary to do in order to reach the Alpine huts, an artificial aid against slipping back is indispensable. When going uphill the ski support the weight of the runner and keep his feet on, or above, the snow. But they do not distinguish between regressive and progressive locomotion. The whole of the work of progression falls upon the human machinery. Under those conditions the strain put on the muscles by continuous or repeated backsliding is objectionable. The use of a mechanical contrivance is made imperative by the steepness of the slopes and their great length.

Another point is that when running downhill, say, from the Monte-Rosa Sattel to the Bétemps hut, it is never advisable to pick out the shortest and quickest route, which means the steepest run possible. High Alp ski-running demands the choice of the longest course consistent with steady progress and with an unbroken career along a safe line of advance. The watchword of the good runner will always be—at those heights and distances where so much that is ahead must remain problematical— move onward on curves, so as to approach any obstacle by means of a bend, admitting of an inspection of the obstacle, if it is above the surface, before you are upon it, and which, if it is the running surface which presents a break, even a concealed one, will prevent your hurling yourself headlong into the trap.

OBERGABELHORN, FROM DENT BLANCHE.

To face p. 29.

L.M.G.

The influence of wintry weather upon exposed and lofty rock pinnacles is practically the same as that of summer weather, but still more so, if such a paradoxical way of expressing oneself can be made clear. At the height of 10,000 feet above the sea-level and upwards the winter weather is glacier weather. This is not the weather that prevails in the depth of the Swiss valleys or on the Swiss tableland. The snow-fall upon the glaciers is not so great as one might expect. The snow that does fall there is dry, light, powdery, and wind-driven. Those characteristics are such that only some slight proportion of the snow driven across the glacier actually remains there. Most of it is carried along and accumulates wherever it can settle down—that is, elsewhere than on wind-swept surfaces.

The winter sun is so powerful that it very soon clears the high ridges from a kind of snow that is in itself little suited to adhere to their steep, rocky sides. Therefore the position is as follows: the ski-runner can gain access to the peaks with great ease. The so-called *Bergschrunde*, in French *rimaie*, are closed up, and the rocks towering above are practically just as climbable as in summer, with the help of the same implements too—rope, ice-axe, and if one likes, climbing-irons.

The start is made much later in the morning, but, on the other hand, one need not be over-anxious as to getting to one's night quarters by sunset. Running on ski at night over a course that has been travelled over in the morning, and therefore perfectly recognisable and familiar, is, in clear weather, as pleasant as it is easy. That is why the ascent of a rocky peak is, to my mind, an object which a ski-runner who does not take a one-sided view of sport will gladly keep in view.

The risk of frost-bite may be greater than in summer, in so far as the temperature of the air is much lower. But the air being, as a rule, extremely dry and the heat of the sun intense, the full benefit of this extraordinary dryness and of this heat really puts frost-bite out of the question in fine weather, provided rocks are attacked from the southern or south-west aspect, or even south-east. It is quite easy to wear thick gloves and to put one's feet away in thick and warm woollen material. But no attempt whatever should be made at rock climbing under dull skies, let alone when the weather is actually bad. It must also be added that bad health, exhaustion, indigestion, nervousness, and such like are, of all things, the most conducive to frost-bite.

The thermometer may mark in January, above the tree-line, and still more among rocks, as much as 40 degrees Centigrade at midday in the sun. This is not the air temperature, as in the shade the same thermometer will soon drop to zero Centigrade or less. But anybody who has experienced the wonderful glow of those winter suns on the highest peaks of Switzerland will be careful that he does not bring them into disrepute by visiting them when he himself is not fit or when they are out of humour. In any case, people who go about on ski with feet and hands insufficiently clad may well be expected to take the consequences.

The foregoing lines bring us quite naturally to consideration of the weather. The first principle to be borne in mind is that weather in the High Alps is quite distinct from weather anywhere else. The only authentic information at any time about the impending weather in the Alpine area is that given day by day by the Swiss Central Meteorological Office in Zürich. This report, and accompanying forecast, is published in all the important daily papers, such as the *Journal de Genève*, the *Gazette de Lausanne*, the *Bund*, &c. The figures are of less importance than the notes on wind, air-pressure, and the description in ordinary language which comments upon the more scientific data. Those reports should be consulted, and should be posted up by every hotel keeper.

Weather is not uniform throughout Switzerland. The driest area runs along the backbone of the Alps from the lake of Geneva to the lake of Constance, along the Canton du Valais and the Canton des Grisons. Chances of steady, fine weather are consequently greater in those valleys than elsewhere. The driest spot in Switzerland is Sierre. The High Alps, which are of most interest to the ski-runner, are also the part of Switzerland which presents the largest proportion of fine sunny days in the winter months.

The tableland, extending from the lake of Geneva to Bâle and Constance along the Rhine, and bounded on the south-east by the lakes of Thoune and Brienz, Lucerne, and the Wallensee, may remain for weeks together under a sea of fog, resting at the height of about a thousand feet above the surface of the ground. As long as those fog areas, which are generally damp and cold, are curtained from the rays of the sun, the canopy of fog acts as a huge reflector for the sun rays which impinge upon it from above. Provided there is no wind (and the Alps may be windless for days and weeks at a time) the rays, reflected back into space from the fog surface, heat very considerably the layers of air above, while the air imprisoned below remains cold. The winter snows themselves, by a similar process of reflection, generate a great deal of heat of the kind which a human body perceives, and in which the mountaineer is fond of basking.

The long Jura range, extending from the lake of Geneva to Bâle along the French border, shares in the Alpine climate, though in a somewhat rougher form.

The conclusion is that in Switzerland the weather conditions, to mention these alone, are extremely favourable to the ski-runner. In the matter of space at his disposal there are in Switzerland, on the slopes of either the Alps or the Jura, generally above the forest belt, three thousand grazings for cattle, every one of which is a ski-ing area. Only a very small number have hitherto been frequented by the ski-runner. Yet last winter three thousand pairs of ski were sold by one firm alone, and it is reckoned that the number fitted and sold last winter (1911–12) in Switzerland exceeds forty thousand.

Swiss guides hitherto have been trained and engaged only for summer work. Consequently their efficiency on ski is in every instance a personal acquirement, and their knowledge of their duties under winter conditions is simply consequent upon their summer training or derived from their own native knowledge of winter conditions, without the addition of any instruction. If one wishes to engage guides for winter work the best guarantee is that the guide belong to a local ski club, and should have attended, if possible, one or several ski courses before he is considered fit to accompany *amateur* ski-ing parties.

Another point is that guides in winter must be prepared to act as porters. It is in the nature of running on ski that the runner will hardly ever find himself in a position to call for individual assistance, and the routes he will frequent are of necessity routes which, from the mountaineering point of view, are easy and not suited to give great prominence to the qualities of a guide in the strict and recognised meaning of the term. What the amateur ski-runner particularly wants is a hardy and willing companion who will carry the victuals for him and is wise enough to employ his influence in turning the ski-runner away from any dangerous ground, and to pick out the best and safest lines across country. Guides holding a diploma should not be paid more for winter work than they are allowed to claim in summer under the established rates of payment.

CHAPTER II

WITH SKI TO THE DIABLERETS

First Ascent.—The Bear inn at Gsteig—The young Martis—Superstitions—The rights of guides.
Second Ascent.—The composition of the caravan—Odd symptoms—Winter amusements on the glacier—A broken ankle—The salvage operations—On accidents—My juvenile experience—A broken limb on the Jaman.
Third Ascent.—The Marti family—The Synagogue once more—An old porter—We are off.

T has been three times my lot to lay the flat of my ski across the brow of the Diablerets. This in itself would be of but little interest had not a trifling incident occurred each time which may be related with more animation than the ascents can be described.

1. In the month of January, 19—, at a time when the ascent of the Diablerets had not yet been attempted on ski, I marched early in the day out of the slumbering Bahnhof hotel at Gstaad, with a full rucksack on my back and rattled through the village on my ski along the ice-bound main street.

The sun had not yet risen when I knocked at the door of the Bear hotel at Gsteig and presented to the frowsy servant who appeared on the doorstep a face and head so hung about with

icicles and hoar-frost that she started back as though
Father Christmas had come unbidden.

When she had sufficiently recovered herself, I
inquired of her whether she knew of any man in the
village who would accompany me to the top of the
Diablerets. She looked so puzzled that I hastened
to explain that by man I did not mean a guide, but
any one who might be foolish enough to enter upon
such an expedition with a complete stranger advanced
in years. A mere boy would do, provided he could
cook soup and could produce a pair of ski with which
to follow his employer.

Two lads offered themselves ; the brothers Victor
and Ernest Marti, sons of an old guide. At first
they understood no more of the business than that a
gentleman had arrived with whom there was some
chance of casual employment. When I had made
my intention plain to them, they jumped at my
purpose with the eagerness of their age. They had
ski which they had made themselves, but was the
ascent possible ? Anyhow, if I wanted one of them
only, he certainly would not go without the other,
and when I tackled the other to see whether he would
not come alone, they might have been Siamese
twins for aught I could do to separate them alive.
They went to their mamma, who raised her hands to
heaven and would have put them into the fire to
rescue her darlings from my dangerous clutches.

In the end the boys, dare-devils much against their
wish, sallied forth loaded with ropes, ice-axes, and
other cumbersome paraphernalia, among which it
would be unfair to reckon their mother's blessings

and their father's warnings. Indeed, in their sight I was an evil one, bent upon sundry devilries in an ice-bound world. But for the halo thrown for them about my undertaking by the prospect of the beautiful gold pieces to be gained, they would rather have committed me alone to the mercy of the ice fiends.

Lusty of limb, though with quaking hearts, they had no sooner slipped on their ski than their fears were dispelled. They flew to and fro on the snow like gambolling puppies. Who would have thought they bore on their backs a pack that would have curbed the ardour of any ordinary person? They were already prepared in their minds to become Swiss soldiers a few months later, when they would carry, in equipment and arms, more than weighed their present guides' attire.

Guides, by the way, they were not, but hoped to be some day, when they were soldiers. I discovered that, meanwhile, besides working at the saw-mill, they played the part of local bandsmen. From Christmas Eve to New Year's Day they had shared as fiddlers in the mummeries, revels, and dances of the season. They had conceived thereby much thirst, as was soon made clear by the flagging of their spirits, and by the loving way in which they bent down to the snow, pressed it between their hands like a dear, long, unbeheld face and kissed it. When they were refreshed their tongues were once more loosened.

We were drawing nearer to the Diablerets. The overhanging rocks seemed to arch themselves threateningly over our heads, and if the young men

now spoke glibly, it was with a tremble in their
voices and about their renewed fears. It is not without reason that Diablerets and devilry are cognate
sounds in languages so distant from each other as
the Romance *patois* of the Vaudois Alps and the
gentle speech of the Thames Valley.

Like the remainder of Christian Europe, those
valleys shared once upon a time in the Catholic faith,
and this had wonderfully commingled the early and
earthly beliefs of our kind with the teachings of
Divinity. Free-thinkers in the Protestant sense of
the word, those boys, creeping under the shadow of
the cliffs up to the snowy vastness above, saw welling
up from the depths of their minds, as in a mirror, the
images of the strange beings with which the rude
fancy of the peasantry peoples those upper reaches of
the Alps which they call the Evil Country. But on
that day nothing came of those forebodings.

On the next morning, after a night spent in complete freedom from haunting ghosts, my boys hesitated
a moment before rounding the shoulder of the
Oldenhorn. The Zan Fleuron glacier opened up just
beyond. This was the known Synagogue, or meeting
place of the spirits. They dreaded to see what they
might see there if they turned the corner before the
arrows of light-bearing Apollo had scattered the night
mists of Hecate.

Suddenly the sun broke and poured forth in floods
upon a world springing up innocently from the folds
of sleep. My lads felt saved by glad day.

But, if they went through this first expedition
without suffering injury from the spirits, they were

less fortunate in their dealings with myself. They had allowed themselves to be drawn into a temptation for which they were yet to undergo punishment; namely, they had, for gold, disregarded the rules of the Bernese corporation of guides. It is a salutary regulation of that honourable guild that none who is not an officially certificated guide shall accompany alone a gentleman in the district. Now, a terrible thing had happened. Two young men, neither of whom was a certificated guide, had accompanied a gentleman in the district. Indeed, the mother of the boys must in the end be proved to be right in her mistrust. That gentleman had induced her boys to make light of the fundamental rule of local etiquette as to keeping off the Zan Fleuron beat entirely reserved for the spirits from All Souls' Day to Easter Sunday, and, in addition, he was getting them into trouble with the police.

One or two months later I was busily and peacefully engaged in my study when a member of the Geneva detective force was ushered in. I started up. What could be the matter?

The gentleman then explained politely that I was wanted somewhere in the Canton de Berne. What for? It could be no light matter.

Now I knew—by repute, rather than by personal experience—that justice in Berne is extremely rough and even handed. I said I would rather appear before a Geneva judge. On repairing to the courts, I was informed that the brothers Marti were summoned at Saanen for palming themselves off as guides upon an unwary gentleman of uncertain age

and feeble complexion. They had preyed upon his
weak mind and enthusiasm to drag him in midwinter
up to the top of the Diablerets, exposing his body to
grave risks, and his soul to the resentment of the
fairies, and thus indirectly infringing a privilege
which certificated guides alone enjoyed, to the
exclusion of the remainder of man and woman-
kind.

Reassured on my own behalf, I at once became
" cocky " and proceeded to prick that legal bubble
and take the guiding corporation down a few pegs.
I solemnly swore before the judge—in presence of
the clerk who took my words down with forced
gravity—that I had engaged Victor Marti as lantern-
bearer to the elderly Diogenes I actually was, and his
brother Ernest to act for me as crossing-sweeper over
the Zan Fleuron glacier, because I expected there
might be some snow, and it is bad for old men to
have cold feet.

I have since heard that the two boys got off that
time without a stain on their character.

I say that time, because this trouble is not the last
I got them into. But this is another tale, and will
appear hereafter.

2. My second ascent of the Diablerets was somewhat tragic—this, too, in January, and in pursuit of
the magnificent ski-run which one gets down the
Zan Fleuron glacier to the Sanetsch pass, and back
to Gsteig.

The brothers Marti were again with me. The
eldest was now a certificated guide, and had thus

acquired the legal right to take his brother with him when escorting strangers in the mountains.

On that occasion there were some strangers, mostly English, in the party. One of them was a young and able runner on ski, another was an elderly member of "the" Alpine Club, in whose breast a love for ski was born late in life, probably in the same years when I myself fell a victim to that infatuation. The third stranger of British blood need not for the nonce be otherwise presented to the reader than in a spiritual garb as a vision. He—or rather she—will appear in the flesh when a ministering angel is called for in the disastrous scene yet to be enacted, when the kind apparition will flutter down as unexpectedly as the goblins pop up through the soft white carpet, under which they have their homes in the comfortable cracks designed for them by the glacier architect.

This caravan went up the usual way, in the usual manner, above the Pillon pass. Near the end of the day, and at sunset, one of us was suddenly seen to curl up and roll in the snow. The next moment he was back at his place again, with his rucksack on his shoulder, ice-axe in hand, and with his ski under his feet, as if nothing had happened. Yet we had all seen him curl up and roll down. And here he was again, spick and span, like one of those tourists carved in wood which are offered for sale at Interlaken or Lucerne. The Marti brothers looked at me queerly.

They were, indeed, thankful I had got them unscathed out of the police court. In spite of parental advice, they had come again with me on that account. But this was beyond a joke. However, they went on, exchanging among themselves their own remarks, wondering whose sticks, ski, and rucksack would next be seen flying in opposite directions.

But nothing happened during the night. The next morning the brothers Marti, heading our column, wended their way carefully, as before, to the corner of the Oldenhorn, and peered cautiously round. It was still dark. From this place it is usual before dawn to catch a glimpse of the gnomes. They are impervious to cold. Being of an origin infernal in some degree, they naturally delight in the coolness of winter nights, and their eyes being habitually scotched by the flames that blaze in the bowels of the glacier, they much enjoy the soothing caress of the moonbeams.

On that morning—since there is a morning even to an evil day—the gnomes were still engaged in their after midnight game of skittles. They plant their mark on the edge of the glacier, above the cliffs which drop down clear on to the Derborence grazings. Their bowls are like enormous curling-stones hewn out of the ice. When the gnomes miss their aim—which in their love of mischief they like to do—the ice blocks fly over the edge of the rock parapet, and crash down upon the grazings. In summer the shepherds endeavour to meet this calamity by prayer. In winter it is of no consequence.

But what was of consequence is that we had no business on the glacier while the night sprites were still holding Synagogue. This the brothers Marti knew, and that woe was in store for us on that account. But all went well with us, to all appearances.

We left our baggage at the foot of the Diablerets peak, and, on our ski, pushed merrily along to the summit. We lunched, and enjoyed the view, like any ordinary mortals, ignorant of having challenged Fate.

Then down we went, curving and circling over the glacier, crossing unawares the place of the Synagogue. A gnome, crouching somewhere on the edge of a crevasse, lay in wait for us, hiding behind a heap of carefully hoarded curling-stones. The deadly weapons began gliding about. The brothers Marti were proof against them, being involuntary offenders. The head of the party could not be struck, being of the sceptical kind. The young Englishman jumped about, being ever safe in the air when the gliding missile came his way. But the member of "the" Alpine Club suffered the fate all were courting. His fibula was snapped.

Then nothing was seen but a man lying down in pain upon a beautifully white snow-field. The evil spot was clad in the garb of innocence. The sky spread above in a blue vaulted canopy, such as Madonnas are pictured against. One of the poor offending mortals lay low, expiating the fault of all. Would the sacrifice be accepted?

Yes. Amid the scene of temple-like beauty, charity—it might have been the Madonna or a simple Ice Maid—appeared in human shape amid the effulgence of midday, in the opportune costume of a hospital nurse.

With such help, the moment to be absolutely practical came. It was two o'clock in the afternoon.

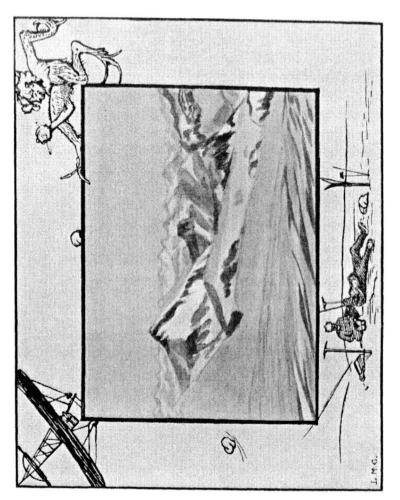

SPORT ON THE ZAN FLEURON GLACIER.

To face p. 42.

We were still on the glacier as high as we could be. Whether we retraced our footsteps or glided on, the distance was the same to Gsteig, where the Pillon and Sanetsch passes join together. Luckily the weather was fine, the air quite warm and still. I despatched Victor Marti, the better runner of the two, down the Sanetsch to Gsteig. His orders were to summon by telegraph a medical man from Gstaad to Gsteig, with instructions there to await our arrival, and to come provided with splints for the crippled man.

This young winged Mercury received another message to convey. It was to send forthwith a team of four men to the top of the Sanetsch pass. He himself was to bring back to the pass eatables, drinkables, and blankets. It was, indeed, impossible to tell whether we should not be kept out in the wilderness the whole night. In such places at that time of the year, the wind, in rising, might be attended by the worst consequences to human life.

We had before us many, many miles to be travelled over, across hill and dale, in deep snow, conveying on foot a helpless man, whom immobility would expose to serious risks while out in the open during the night hours.

Our messenger carried out his instructions with the utmost rapidity and punctuality. His ski carried him swiftly over many miles of snow to the wooded confines of the Sanetsch pass. He hailed two wood-cutters, and sent them straight up to the top of the pass, as a forward relief party. They got there some time after sunset, while Victor Marti continued on his way down into the valley to complete his task.

As for those left behind, they had in prospect a six-mile trudge before they could reach the pass. No question of continuing on ski. Our sister of mercy wanted them all to accommodate the wounded man. On the glacier the snow was not so deep that the hard, icy, under-surface could not support our footsteps, but as we proceeded lower our plight got worse. A ski-runner who, on deep snow, has to give up the use of his ski, is very much like a sailor upon a small craft in mid-ocean. Suppose the boat capsizes, the sailor may swim. But for how long? Similarly, a ski-runner bereft of his ski amid boundless, pathless snow-fields, may walk. But for how long? Snow is a good servant, but a bad master.

Most people who have not found it out for themselves do not know that snow gets deeper and deeper as you descend from the glaciers into the valleys. After we had reached the pass we would still have to climb by night down the Sanetsch gorge. This manifold task was about to fall to the lot of a party in which everybody, except one, was new to winter work. They were, besides, totally unacquainted with night conditions. The ministering angel dropped from heaven, too, was one who, strange to say, had never yet been sent to Switzerland on an errand of mercy. Besides, her task grew so upon her that the discharge of it made her more and more human, and in the end she experienced in herself all the inconveniences of being the possessor of a material body.

With the help of puttees we tied the inert limb to one ski. The other ski of the same pair supported the intact leg. We cut our ski-sticks into lengths, split them down the middle, and making crossbars of them we fixed the ski to one another. Thus was the stretcher or shutter made. We had nails, fortunately, and plenty of cord.

A stretcher, however, cannot be carried in deep snow up hill and down dale. We now required a sleigh. To build one we laid down on the snow, carefully and side by side, three pairs of ski, binding them together with straps, and thereupon we laid the shutter on which was tied the wounded man.

Would this improvised sleigh run on the snow? By means of his rope Ernest Marti yoked himself to the front of it. Head down, shoulders bent, he gave a pull. His feet broke through the crust of snow and he sank in up to the waist. To this there was no remedy. He would plunge at each step, and, recovering himself, breathless and quivering, he would start afresh.

Each time he got off the victim of our accident received a jerk that threw him back, for we had not the wherewithal to make a support for his shoulders. To obviate this very serious trouble, we fitted an empty rucksack to his back, and pulled tightly the straps over his shoulders and across his chest. The young Englishman and myself walked then on each side of him. Holding him by means of the shoulder straps, we checked the back thrusts to which he was exposed, and kept him upright from the waist.

Thus our caravan proceeded on its way, our pockets stuffed with the remaining bits of our ski, with which we might be glad to light a fire that night in some deserted shepherds' hut.

The charity dame walked alongside of us, cheering with her smile the sad hero of this melancholy adventure. What a picture it would have made if only one of us had had the heart to photograph it!

Night was creeping on. The snows turned dark and gloomy, still we were drawing near to the pass and had no sooner reached it than two burly figures rose up before us. They smiled, and laid hold of the guiding-rope which Ernest Marti, exhausted, threw to them. They had appeared in the nick of time to save us from spending the night up there. From that moment, turning to the north, we were able to continue to the top of the Sanetsch gorge without a stop.

The stars had long been glittering overhead when we were able to look down into the gorge across to Gsteig. The village was all agog. Lanterns were creeping about like glow-worms. Some appeared at time amid the woods, flitting from place to place like fire-flies. The other two men, ordered up by Victor Marti, now showed their lights quite near us. And then began the last stage in our salvage operations.

The Sanetsch gorge was as a vast, curved sheet of ice. Its northern exposure and the night air had done their work. It would not be possible to convey a man reclining on a stretcher down the steep windings of the mule path. The rescuing party soon hit upon the only practicable scheme. The patient was removed from his splints, poles, straps, and bindings, and set across the back of a powerful highland man. Ernest Marti took my Lucifer lamp and placed himself in front to light up the way. Two men stood immediately behind the human pack-mule. The group thus formed launched itself down into the gorge, each man depending for security upon the rough *crampons* driven into his shoe leather. All's well that ends well. The doctor was found waiting at Gsteig.

It is now his turn to take up the cue, but we do not vouch that he will satisfy the reader's curiosity, should we by any chance have left him with any curiosity to satisfy. I hope we may, because our third ascent of the Diablerets still awaits him.

This was not the first mountaineering misadventure I found myself mixed up with. Moreover, it was an accident, the memory of which I do not particularly relish. I am afraid I smarted visibly under it, and showed my personal disappointment. This may have conveyed to some the impression of some unfairness on my part.

Has the reader ever noticed how different is the attitude of the public mind towards accidents on land and on sea ? Why should mountaineering accidents be less sympathetically received than those befalling sailors ? It is, however, not unnatural that the sea should be more congenial, and command forgiveness by its grandeur. It teaches charity by the immensity in which it drops the cruel dramas enacted upon its surface.

When casualties occur in mountaineering, even those concerned appear to make efforts to single out somebody on whom to fasten the blame. Some people's vanity is bent upon discerning the wisdom, or unwisdom, of one or another of their companions. If a boat goes down a respectful silence is allowed to dwell alike around the survivors and those lost. But shall we ever, for instance, hear the end of the merits or demerits of each concerned in the accident that befell the Whymper party, in 1865, on the Matterhorn?

When a climbing party comes to grief, it is as an additional course for the menu of the *table d'hôtes*: a dainty morsel for busybodies, quidnuncs, and experts alike. The critical spirit grows ungenerous in that atmosphere. The victims of the Alp were tempting Fate; one knows exactly what mistake they made; so-and-so was altogether foolish in ——, and so forth. With such more or less competent remarks, the fullest mead of admiration is blended. This, too, be it added with the utmost appreciation of a kind disposition, does not go without some admixture of silliness.

I should prefer, even now, to leave all accidents in an atmosphere of romance. It is best to meet with them when one is young. The tender spots in one's nature are then nearer the surface, and the vein of chivalry more easily struck. The flutter and excitement of a rescue are then delightful. One would almost wish for accidents elsewhere than in day-dreams for the sake of dramatic emotion.

The accidents, however, arranged in the flights of my imagination were weak in one respect. They were egotistic. The brilliant part of a quixotic rescuer fell regularly to me. Let me give the reader

an instance from real life before I take him for the
third time up the Diablerets.

The thing occurred in a Byronic spot. In this
place in my book it will detach itself as a spring-
flower against the snow and ice background which
all these chapters have in common.

Was I in my "teens," like "her," or not quite
so green, or much greener? The question arouses
some vague twinges of wounded vanity. But I
consult in vain the tablets of my memory. They are
now as illegible in many places as old churchyard
stones. If I then believed I had grounds for jealousy,
I could not now trust myself to say with truth that
they were genuine.

My resentment fastened upon a rival. I withdrew
proudly to the recesses of the hills, as it is recorded
by romantic lore that even males of the dumb
creation are in the habit of doing when baffled in
desire and injured in self-esteem.

But as, a few days later, I lay lazily stretched out
at full length on the tender pasture grass of the Plan
de Jaman, viewing at my feet the scene of my sentimental *déconvenue*, I do not wish the reader to paint
for himself the picture of an angry bull pawing the
ground and snorting for revenge, though the number
of cows grazing about and the multitudinous tinkling
of the bells might well suggest such a classical
impersonation.

The view over the lake was pure, crystal-like
through a moist, shiny air. Rain had fallen during
the night over Glion and the bay of Montreux. The
long grass on the steep pastures of Caux was tipped

4

with fresh snow. It lay here and there in melting patches, and every blade of grass had its trickle of water.

Seated on my knapsack for dryness, I was comfortably munching some bread and chocolate when discordant and husky cries burst upon me from behind. The sound was more grotesque than pathetic.

On looking round there hove in sight a suit of fashionable clothes, which seemed to betray the presence of a man. They were mud-bespattered and stained green with grass. A scared and besmirched face stood forth from above them, marked with what looked like dried-up daubs of blood. From that dreadfully burlesque and woebegone countenance issued the affrighted Red Indian cries which had startled my ears. Dear me, how un-Byronic all this !

My feelings grew more sympathetic to that vision—and that, in a sense particularly exhilarating to myself—when in the soiled, distracted fashion-plate I recognised my successful rival. His language became immediately an intelligible speech for me, and when he blurted out a familiar name he won a friend, if not to himself at least to his plight, which was coming to me as a splendid opportunity. Too dazed to be aware of the true identity of his audience, he confessed to having lost his way with "her" that very morning on the Jaman grazings. Their house-shoes had literally melted away in the wet, slippery grass and been torn to shreds on the rocks. Famished, thirsty, exposed to the beating rays of the midday sun, his presence of mind had deserted him. They

FROM THE DENT BLANCHE, LOOKING WEST.

L.M.C.

To face p. 50.

had fallen together over a wall of rock. "Where, oh where?" shouted I.

The wretch could not tell. His mind was a blank. He had run thus far, but knew not whence, and looked round vacantly for a clue. Exhausted, he tumbled down upon the turf. To him it had fallen to do the mischief. I was to repair it. . . .

But was the repairing still within human power? My eyes travelled anxiously up and down the hangs of the Dent de Jaman. By what end should I begin my search? Had the accident occurred in the wooded parts screened over by a growth through which I could not see?

I began a systematic search at one end of the battlefield, as would have done a party of stretcher-bearers, Red Cross men, clearing the ground of the wounded and dead. I called out at regular intervals the name of the object of my search. No reply. Her companion looked on disconsolately from afar. An hour passed, two hours. Then at last, at one end of the wooded slope, hidden away in a gorge of minute dimensions, I came upon an apparently life-less figure partly reclining on a moss bank with a foot hanging out from a torn muslin dress over a running stream of snow water. The faint had lasted long. But for the tears in her dress she looked as though she had quietly fallen asleep. When I took her up in my arms, my touch seemed to re-animate her, evidently because it caused her some pain. Then she came back to life more fully, and gradually realised how the situation accounted for my presence. She was suffering from a broken leg. I carried her down to Les Avants.

The reader would expect to hear that this adventure bound together again the broken threads of love. Not so. The story did not end as in the case of a friend of mine who happened to be at the right moment in command of a column of artillery moving along the Freiburg high road.

A carriage and pair with several ladies in it was being driven up from behind. The horses took fright and bolted down a side lane. My friend galloped up, cut the traces of the horses with his sword, while the affrighted driver just managed to put on the brakes. On further approaches being made from both sides, it turned out that the carriage contained the material appointed by Fate to make a wife for him.

I believe that in my case so much emotional force got vent in bringing the work of rescue to a successful issue, that none was left over to nurse the flower of love to fruition. My personal feeling became as a part of my obligations to humanity. Dissolved into chivalry and quixotry, its subtle essence was lost in so broad a river and swept away to the sea.

3. It is not a far cry from the Dent de Jaman back to the Diablerets. At the end of March, 1910, I set out with Monsieur Kurz, of Neuchâtel, to be avenged on the ill-luck which had marred the January trip.

The name of Mr. Marcel Kurz will appear repeatedly under my pen in this volume. I made his acquaintance years ago on the occasion of a political speech. I was only too glad, after a night spent in public talk and conviviality, to throw off the fumes of

oratory and post-prandial cordiality. In this a lot of
keen young ski-runners agreed with me. Among
them was Marcel Kurz, son of Louis Kurz, the
eminent maker of the map of the Mont Blanc range.
He has since accompanied me on several expeditions,
the first of which was planned on that day, while
practising side by side Christiania and Telemark
swings in friendly emulation. Some of the photograph reproductions which adorn these pages were
made from snapshots taken by him. Not having yet
become acquainted with the Diablerets range in
winter, he accompanied me there in 1910 with our old
friends, the brothers Marti. These were *dienstbereit*,
which, being put in English, would read : Ready for
service, which guides and soldiers ever are.

But were they as free from their ancient fears as
they were willing to undergo fresh trials ? I might
well have my doubts when, this time, their father
expressed a desire to see me before his boys
acquiesced. The accident which attended our last
expedition had left its mark in the minds of the
people. The man with the broken leg had unfortunately hobbled about so long, on crutches, all over
the country side, that this sight had rudely shaken
the confidence which they were beginning to repose
in me, as bringing into the country fresh means of
earning a little money during the winter months.

The old Marti lady, particularly, whose heart had
no eye—if this is not an Irish bull—for economic
advantages that ran counter to the conservative
character of her domestic affections, watched me
wickedly from her doorstep, while her husband

interviewed me in the village street. Here we stood, with the villagers round us, looking a picture truly symbolic.

An old father, clothed in authority by his age and experience, the preserver of the traditions of the past in his house, as in the village community, and bearing within himself the true doctrine of the guiding corporation; his sons, with their minds in that half-open condition which is that of so many young peasants of the present day, when they may be compared, without thereby losing anybody's esteem, to oysters opening to the sunlight the shells out of which they cannot grow; the mother, anxious for those nurtured at her breast, the coming founders, as she hoped, of a domestic hearth like unto the old; a man from the outside, dropped maybe from a higher sphere, but disturbing the even tenour of their lives, and presenting in a new light to their awakening consciousness their sense of inferiority and perhaps of misdirected adherence to the past; lastly, the onlookers and passers-by, a homely throng, bearing witness, after the style of the Greek chorus in the village comedy.

I proposed to the old man that his sons should come again with me unhindered. We were a small party, and made up of such elements that there was but little chance of the last accident being repeated. But it had got to his ears that I had privately consulted with his sons as to pushing on from the Diablerets to the east over the Sanetsch and Rawyl passes. I had to confess that such was the intention of myself and of Marcel Kurz. Whereupon the old man held up his hands and his wife hurried to his side.

In the end it was decided that Ernest Marti should accompany me and my friend with provisions for one day only, and that on the next day the other brother and a porter would meet us on the Sanetsch pass. Unwilling to inquire at once what this porter arrangement might portend, lest the whole affair might be stranded on that inquiry, as a ship might do on leaving the stocks, we agreed to the suggestion. The conference broke up, each party being satisfied that it had gained one of its points.

Our ash planks carried us up without a hitch to the confines of the glacier. At the Oldenhorn hut, however, another of those sights awaited us which had made the brothers Marti feel queer. They of the Synagogue spent the witching hours of the next night in a drunken snowballing orgy. They pushed an enormous bolt of snow against the door of the hut during our peaceful slumbers therein. Never mind. We opened the window, got out through it into the snow, bored our way to the outside, and slipped down on to the ice. There was some spectral light in the air when we came out. The Oldenhorn battlements crackled and crepitated a little. When the sun lit them up from behind, it looked for a moment as if they were manned with a fringe of tittering monkeys. As I have said, there was a strange play of light in the air. But the snowballing might have been the work of avalanches. There is as a rule a natural explanation to be given of phenomena of this kind.

While the Oldenhorn pyramid glowed in the morning light, a veil of mist hung over the Zan Fleuron glacier. The mist in no ways interfered with our run. We flew like birds over the scene of the January accident. On the pass we sat down and waited. Victor Marti was to come up. But who was to accompany him up the pass, in the guise of a porter, with a further supply of provisions? We required no such thing as a porter—nor even guides, for the matter of that; but if I acted upon that view, the game was up. Local men would be slow in taking up the cry, the new cry: Winter mountaineering! So we looked for the expected two.

The mist still hung on the pass between us and the sun. Now and then the sun shone vaguely, as through cotton wool. When the wind broke the mist up in rifts a patch of blue would look down upon us benignly. At last, low down in the north, a black speck showed itself to our straining eyes. Then the speck divided up. There were two men, and something moving along close to the ground. This turned out to be a dog, dragging along a pair of ski. The dog got on very well on the hard frozen snow. But when about to leave the wind-beaten tract, he floundered and got no further. On inspection with my binoculars, the porter turned out to be none other than Father Marti, come to fetch his bairns. But we never quite knew why the dog was made to bring up an extra pair of ski.

The position was peculiar; the would-be porter could not cover the distance which separated him from us. We might have snapped our fingers at him and parodied the biblical phrase : " Thus far shalt thou come and no farther."

We preferred to push into shore on our skiffs and to parley. The old man declared he had come up to say the weather was bad. We looked round. Did appearances give him the lie? Kurz was sure they did. More cautious, because nearer the age of the old salt, I thought they might; but both boys promptly agreed with their father and the dog wagged its tail approvingly.

Kurz and myself began by making sure of the provisions. Then, by a few judiciously applied biscuits, we won the favour of the dog. Then we said that, rather than come down at such an early hour, we should spend the day in runs on the glacier, whereupon Victor Marti felt it would be his duty to do likewise. Ernest, in his turn, did not see why he should not spend, in our agreeable company, a day that was so young. The father winced, but consented.

Then I thought the juncture had come when I might propose to both young men to take full advantage of our new supplies of victuals and drink by spending another night on the heights. The family met again to " sit " upon the suggestion. Meanwhile I liberally paid old Marti for his trouble and took him apart to tell him that if the weather was really bad on the morrow, I should send his boys down. This arrow hit the mark. He was a perfectly honourable old man, true to the core. Turning to his sons, he told them that on no

account were they to come back home without their
" gentlemen." I hope, for his comfort, that he
realised that the " gentlemen " would not either
consent to be seen again in the valley without his
boys.

Anyhow, we spent a delightful day in ski-ing in
the precincts of the Synagogue, repaired at night to
our hut, slipped through the window, and spent a
night free from molestation. I deemed that it would
be wise to let the sun rise before *we* did. When it
did, it shone with wonderful grace and power. The
mists were scattered out of the sky and the cobwebs
cleared away from our brains. We entered upon the
trip which is described in the next chapter, and
during which my excellent young friends pushed on
steadily to Kandersteg, our goal, longing all the time
for the sight of the telegraph poles on which hung
the wires which would convey to their mother the
message of their safety.

CHAPTER III

FROM THE COL DU PILLON TO THE GEMMI PASS (DIABLERETS, WILDHORN, WILDSTRUBEL, AND KANDERSTEG).

The range—Ski-runners' logic—Itinerary—The Plan des Roses—Untoward experiences on the Rawyl pass—Death through exposure—The *Daily Mail* and Mr. Arnold Lunn's feat—House-breaking—On the Gemmi—Perspective and levels—Relief models of the Alps—My smoking den—Old Egger.

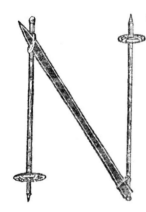 O visitor to Switzerland requires telling that a section of the Bernese Alps runs up to the Gemmi pass from the southwest. In this secondary range, the leading groups are the Diablerets, the Wildhorn, and the Wildstrubel. So far as the Wildstrubel and Wildhorn are concerned, the range separates the Canton du Valais from the Canton de Berne, but the Diablerets throw out a shoulder into the Canton de Vaud. From their summit the lake of Geneva can be seen.

Each of these large mountain clusters is linked up to its neighbour by a pass, running perpendicularly to the range. The Sanetsch pass is a dip between the Wildhorn and the Wildstrubel. Just as—in January, 1909—I had the pleasure of traversing the higher Bernese Alps between the Gemmi and Grimsel passes, it was, in March, 1910, my good luck to carry out in one continuous expedition the traverse of the nether Bernese Alps, beginning at the Col du Pillon and ending at the Gemmi and Kandersteg.

The summits of the Diablerets, Wildhorn, and Wildstrubel group do not exceed 10,705 feet in height. Singly, they have frequently been ascended on ski. But, to my knowledge, the ascent of all three had not yet been achieved as a connected and consecutive piece of winter work. My traverse having brought me much opportunity to fully realise the extraordinary quality and beauty of this high ski-ing ground, I do not hesitate to give here my best information on the route.

The route now opened out presents this capital feature, that the mountains along the top of which it lies are uniform in height and in conformation. Their general lineal development is straight; they arise steeply from their south-west extremities; they carry ski-runners down, on well-defined inclines, to their north-east extremities, which rest on the flat surface of high-lying passes.

No wise runner will attempt to run from the Gemmi end. By so doing he would be making light of the best rules of ski-ing, as well as throwing away the indications which nature herself gives him. From all three summits the larger and lengthier

MOVING FROM THE TOP OF THE FINSTERAARHORN.

To face p. 60.

glaciers stretch uniformly from south-west downwards to north-east, while on the opposite slope the mountains are precipitous and the glaciers short.

Not only will no wise runner attempt the trip from the Gemmi end, but he will also follow the rules of ski-runners' logic. The reader will notice that while summer tourists cross the Bernese Alps from north to south, that is from Canton Berne to Canton Valais, or *vice versâ*, from Canton Valais to Canton Berne, tourists on ski follow the range in its length, and will have nothing to do with its passes, as leading from one valley to another.

Indeed, a ski-runner must look a very paradoxical creature. For him, passes are just convenient, saddle-like depressions connecting the summits he has left with the summit he next wishes to attain. He will have no dealings with the valleys. He does not follow the path, say from Kandersteg to Louèche. That is all very well for mules. But he crosses, say, the Sanetsch and Rawyl passes, in the same way as a foot-passenger goes across a street from one pavement to the other. By so doing he knows no more of the actual pass-track than its width, say a matter of one to a few yards, as the case may be. This totally new conception of how to get about on the Alps from point to point is of great importance with a view to the military occupation of the High Alp passes and their defence in winter. I call it the ski-runners' paradox.

Gsteig is best reached from Montreux, on the lake of Geneva, or from Spiez, on the lake of Thoune, by availing oneself of the electric railway and getting out at the station of Gstaad; hence on foot or by horse-sleigh to Gsteig.

The hut, on the Tête aux Chamois, at the foot of the Oldenhorn, where the first night had better be spent, lies to the south-west from Gsteig, and is approached from the Pillon route. The approach viâ the Sanetsch pass necessitates the ascent of the Zan Fleuron glacier round the Oldenhorn. It is therefore much longer.

The map to be used, and to which all references in this book are made, is the Swiss Military Survey Map (Siegfried Atlas), sold to the public in sheets. A reprint covering the whole region may be bought at Gstaad, price 4 francs.

Cross the Reuschbach by a bridge, a little beyond point 1,340 (sheet 472). The chalets of Reusch will then be reached at Reuschalp, at the altitude marked 1,326 on the map (sheet 472 or 471). At Bödeli one should carefully avoid taking the path leading south, up to the Oldenhornalp. The situation of the Cabane des Diablerets is given on the Siegfried Atlas at point 2,487 (sheet 478). The line of access is plain from Bödeli. But strangers should not attempt to reach the hut in winter snow without being accompanied on the Martisberg slopes by some person possessing full local knowledge. The traversing of steep slopes, such as those which here run down from the Oldenhorn, is always dangerous.

Runners start from Gsteig and will do well to take with them one or both of the brothers Ernest and Victor Marti, young men and fair runners. Readers of the preceding chapter know that I have trained them in what little they understand about winter mountaineering. This little is quite sufficient to enable them to guide safely any party of able-bodied and fair ski-runners along the new route.

From Gsteig to the hut an average walker on ski may count five hours. The hut is comfortable enough for practical purposes, and can accommodate a large party.

On the next morning, do not leave the hut till daylight, and then, in three hours, one may reach the top of the Diablerets on ski, though these may have to be removed to traverse a part of the steep snow-fields resting on ice which run down the precipitous cliffs to the south. Runners with whom it is a point to run, rather than conquer hill-tops, may leave the summit alone. Wending their way round the Oldenhorn, they will at once face north-east and run down the Zan Fleuron glacier to the top of the Sanetsch pass. Use a compass, and run strictly east. Full north, full south, or south-east are equally pernicious. The snow may be crusted and windswept. But if it is dry, powdery, and smooth, the runner's joy will be inexpressible.

Our day—and so might yours—gave us a prospect of a very long run. We knew that we should not be able to make use of the Alpine Club hut on the Wildhorn, for a notice had appeared in the *Alpina* (organ of the Swiss Alpine Club) that this hut was badly overwhelmed with snow. Under ordinary conditions, provided one did not mind sweeping low down out of one's way to the north, there would be no reason why this hut should not be taken

advantage of to spread over two days the work
which on that occasion we did in one day, to get
from the Diablerets hut along to the Wildstrubel
huts. Without any waste of time, we pushed across
the Sanetsch pass, from the point marked 2,234
(sheet 481), on to the *arête* which runs due east
across the point marked 2,354.

If it is your intention to go as far as the Wildstrubel hut in one day, you ought to cross the
Sanetsch by eleven o'clock—an easy thing if you
left the Diablerets hut by eight o'clock. The line
to be followed leads down to, but keeps above, the
small lakes which are marked with the name Les
Grandes Gouilles, altitude 2,456. These lakes must
be left on one's right hand, and then make straight
for the Glacier du Brozet, above the words Luis de
Marche. Under ordinary winter circumstances, particularly late in the season, this glacier, which is
broken up to any extent in summer, will be found
to present a steep and hard surface most convenient
to ascend. When once the point 3,166 has been
reached, it will be unnecessary to complete the
ascent of the Wildhorn, though nothing could be
easier. Leaving the summit to your left at the
point 3,172, the descent on the Glacier de Tenehet
comes next to be considered. At that altitude you
should ski onward sharply to the north-east for a
while, then great care should be taken to proceed
downward gradually by taking a curved route, below
point 3,124 (sheet 472), full north-east, then east,
along the circular tiers of the ice.

Let me here remind the reader that the Wildhorn

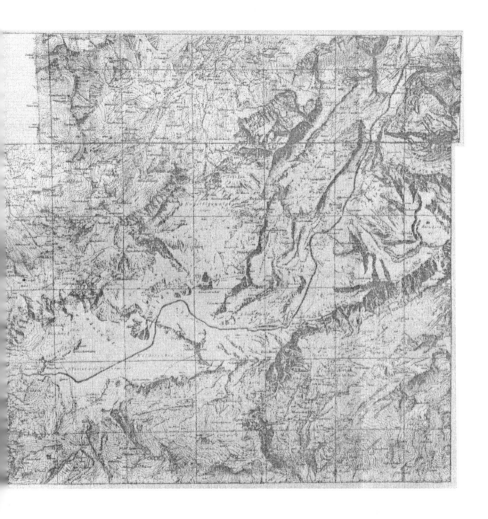

DIABLERETS—WILDHORN—WILDSTRUBEL—GEMMI PASS.

(Reproduction made with authorisation of the Swiss Topographic Service, 26.8.12)

To face p. 64.

hut is away far down on the northern slope of the Wildhorn, at the top of the Iffigenthal. Runners who wish to break their journey and spend a night there will beware of running down the glacier of Tenehet. They will cross the watershed to the north at the point 2,795, or thereabouts, and descend to the point 2,204, in the vicinity of which they will find the hut.

The course on to the Rawyl pass presents no difficulty to a competent runner. When under point 2,767, turn to the south, where the slope dips, and then again, when well under point 2,797, and the lake, turn to the north-east, so as to reach and keep on dotted curve 2,400. South or south-east would be irrecoverably wrong. In fair weather it will be unbroken pleasure, on condition that the runner is well led or is thoroughly conversant with map or level readings in a very difficult country. I reached the Rawyl pass by six o'clock.

The fairly level stretch along which undulates the Rawyl mule track is called the Plan des Roses, which sounds very poetical to cultivated minds, such as my readers always are. The Alps, and many other ranges in Europe, are studded with those appellations, whose delightful ring calls forth the fragrance and beauty of the rose at an altitude at which gardens are not usually met. Never did a summer rose grow or blossom naturally in most of the places bearing that pretty name—not even the Alpen Rose or the Alpine Anemone.

The imagination of some has seen in the name an allusion to the pink colour of the sky at dawn and at sunset. Alas, this too is a fallacy borne in upon us by the literary faculty. Monte-Rosa does not mean pink mountain.

Rosa (as in Rosa Blanche, above the Val Cleuson), roses, roxes, rousse, rossa, rasses, rosen (as in Rosenlaui), ross, rosso (as in Cima di Rosso), rossère, all mean rocks or rock. The Tête Rousse (above St. Gervais) would not be in English the Ruddy Brow, but the much more commonplace Rocky Tor, Ben, or Fell. All forms of the word go back to a common Celtic origin, whether they appear in Swiss nomenclature, in a French, German, Italian, or Romance form. This phenomenon is a good illustration of the manner in which the association of ideas by sound enriches and varies in time the very rudimentary stock of primitive impressions gathered in by the ancient Alp dwellers.

If the reader will think of Rhine, Rhône, Reuse, Reuss, Reusch, in the light of the foregoing explanations, he will hear through all those words the rush of water that is characteristic of Alpine streams.

I have lively recollections of the Rawyl pass dating back to the days of my boyhood. This pass is dear to me also as having served as an introduction to my young friend, Arnold Lunn. When he battled with the pass, on ski, he was probably little older than myself when I first fought my way through it on foot.

I was following the range in its length in the early, old-fashioned style, purposing to make my way from Sion, on the Rhône, to Grindelwald, by dipping in and out of the valleys; namely, first to

Lenk across the Rawyl, then to Adelboden, thence
to Kandersteg, then to Trachsellauenen, in the
Lauterbrunnen valley, hence to Grindelwald, over
the little Scheidegg—a regular switchback railway.

My walk over the Rawyl was marked by an
episode. It was late in the season—late in the
sense of the word in those days, when there was
no winter season to upset people's ideas. I reached
at night the Châlet d'Armillon, by hook or by crook,
along the precipitous Kaendle, and crossing mountain
torrents as casually as a squirrel would swing from
tree to tree, for those were the days of my *Sturm und
Drang Periode* as a mountaineer.

Nevertheless, when the Armillon shepherds pointed
out to me the heights of the pass shining pink in the
sunset with a fresh snow edging, my resolution
wavered for an instant. On I went, little dreaming
that thirty years later I should despise being seen
here at all, except in winter and on ski.

The job proved a serious one. Heavy snow lay
over the marshes and rivulets of the Plan des
Roses. The mule track was buried under wind-
blown wreaths. The moon rose and illuminated
a desolate landscape. A little rain, then snow,
began to fall, obliterating the moonbeams and my
own footprints behind me. Floundering about, I
broke through the thin ice that lay over the patches
of water imprisoned under the snow. Still I ploughed
my way forward.

Then, probably in the nick of time for my own
safety (else I might have spent the night up there,
being still young enough to show myself, in the

circumstances, obstinate unto folly), a guardian angel, whose assistance I certainly did not deserve, slily detached my brandy flask from around my shoulders and dropped it well out of my reach. When I discovered the trick, I took the hint and retraced my footsteps to the shepherds' huts at Armillon.

I believe they were more pleased than surprised. They sat down round the hearth, an open fireplace, with embers lying about on the ground. They handed to me a bowl of milk, a lump of cheese, a piece of rye bread as hard as a brick, and gave me a bit of goat's liver that was stewing in the pan in its own broth. They said their prayers aloud, standing reverently in the firelight; then the goats' skins were laid out flat on the ground. We lay on them all in a heap together, with our feet turned towards the fire. The last man threw the last chips upon it, pulled warm sheeps' skins over us, and laid himself down beside us.

The moon, high up in the sky by this time, shone placidly upon the pastoral scene. The air got sharper and more chilly. When we rose at dawn every blade of grass sparkled with frost.

I set out again up the pass in brilliant sunshine. My footprints were still here and there faintly visible. When they came to an end I made for the cross, marking the site of a rough stone refuge, then under snow. From here some faint footprints again became visible, turning down the gorge to the north. I made up my mind to follow them, for those who had made them were certainly moving in the right direction. After a while I saw a stick standing out of the snow. The footprints did not seem to continue beyond. On approaching, I found myself in the presence of the dead body of a mountaineer. Rumour will have it—for the scene of this mishap was visited shortly after, to lift the body—that I leaped aside at the sight, leaving marks on the snow which, graphologically interpreted, were seen to signify my dismay.

It was the first time that I had before my eyes an instance of death through exposure in the mountains.

On reaching the Iffigen Alp I reported the matter to the local authorities. From later information it came to my knowledge that there were two victims, the body of the second being covered up by the snow.

My other connection with the Rawyl pass is less gloomy, since I owe to the eccentricities of that pass one of my best young friends in England.

I was, a few years ago, standing on the platform of the railway station at Gstaad, when an English vicar, whom I took pleasure in instructing in ski, brought me a copy of the *Daily Mail*, in which a whole column was literally flaming with the exploits of two English runners who had crossed the Rawyl a few days before. That sort of description we generally call " Journalese," and let it pass without correction. It would be an ungracious act on the part of climbers, who seek out deliberately so many hardships, to wince at the touch of the voluntary kindness that almost kills.

The true account of what then took place appeared

in the columns of the *Isis*, the Oxford under-
graduates' organ, on January 23, 1909. There
Arnold Lunn expresses himself as follows :—

"I spent five winters in climbing from various
centres, before—in the winter of 1907–8—I first
tried cross-country work. With three ladies and
my brother, I visited the Great St. Bernard and
spent New Year's Eve in the Hospice. Next day
I was thoroughly walked out by two plucky Irish
ladies, and had just enough energy left to reach
Montana on the following afternoon. I had previously arranged with a friend to cross the mountains
to Villars, a four-day trip, but on arriving found that
he was unable to go.

"I was introduced to Mr. W., who had only been
on ski three afternoons, but volunteered to come.
We left next morning at 4 a.m., climbed for eight
hours up to the glacier of the Plaine Morte, and then
separated. Mr. W. went on to the hut and I climbed
the Wildstrubel alone, from the summit of which
I saw a beautiful sunset. The solitary trudge back
over the glacier at night thoroughly exhausted me,
and I narrowly escaped frost-bite in one of my feet.
At Lenk that night, 6,000 feet lower down, they had
40 degrees of frost, and the cold in the hut was
almost unbearable. We did manage to get a fire
alight, which proved a doubtful blessing, as it thawed
the snow in the top bunk, forming a lake which
trickled down on our faces during the night in inter-
mittent showers. The next morning our blankets
were frozen as stiff as boards. Even the iron stove
was sticky with frost.

DESCENT INTO THE TELLITHAL, LOETSCHENTHAL.

To face p. 70.

I. M. C.

"Our natural course led over the Wildhorn, a delightful ski-run, but though Mr. W. throughout displayed wonderful pluck and perseverance, his limited experience prevented our tackling the long but safe Wildhorn. So we took a short and dangerous cut down to Lenk, following a track which crossed several avalanche runs. We raced the darkness through a long hour of unpleasant suspense, and won our race by a head, getting off the cliff as the last rays of light disappeared. A night on the Rawyl would probably have ended disastrously.

"The remaining two days of the expedition were comparatively uneventful, but we were dogged by an avenging Providence. A telegram miscarried, and a search party was organised to hunt for our remains. The guests at Montana spent a very pleasant day with ordnance maps in attempting to locate the position of our corpses, and were not a little disappointed when they learnt that the search party had found nothing but our tracks. The net result of the expedition was a bill for £20 for search parties, plus hospital expenses, as one of the guides had been frost-bitten."

Arnold Lunn's performance in bringing down safely to Lenk a companion encumbered with ski in places fit for the use of climbing-irons only, at that time of year, was conclusive as a proof of his sportsmanlike qualities, as it was a bold and unexpected line to take. For that reason I found it necessary to reflect upon his daring in the *Gazette de Lausanne*, which had quoted the English press, lest it should unwittingly lead my young countrymen into dangerous undertakings. Arnold Lunn and myself made friends over the correspondence which ensued between us. A better companion and a fairer knight to joust with in Alpine tourney it would be, I believe, difficult to meet.

Now, it might be well to return to the Plan des Roses, whence, still north-east, and then upwards on the Rohrbachstein glacier to the Rohrbachhaus, whose roof was plainly visible at sunset, we strolled peacefully and unconcernedly along.

In connection with the Rohrbachhaus, the brothers Marti, for the second time, had an encounter with the Bernese police courts on my account. It was my evil influence that brought them to that comfortable but closed house. I need not say that I carefully kept out of the mischief that was brewing by lingering behind to admire the view by moonlight.

With an ice-axe they dealt a well-directed blow upon the lock. Before this " Open Sesame " the door gave way. We gained admittance to a kitchen, well stocked with fire-wood; a dining-room, with preserves, tinned victuals, and bottles of wine in the cupboards; a vast bedroom, furnished with couches, mattresses, sheets, blankets, eiderdown quilts! Quite an Eldorado, but, for my young friends, another step on the downward path to the prisoners' dock!

The police of Berne had a watchful eye on the Rohrbachhaus. Though I did promptly send the culprits to make their report in the proper quarter, to ask for the bill and pay for the damage done (which precluded any civil action being brought against me), the Court at Blankenburg tried them for house-breaking on the Procurator's charge. But this business was happily purely formal, as the *bona-fides* of the house-breakers was not questioned. The offenders were spoken free, on condition that they paid the costs of the official prosecution. This part of the bargain was passed on to me to keep, which I did cheerfully. Indeed, the whole transaction appealed to my sense of right in the administration of law. There was no doubt in my mind that we had broken into a private establishment without leave, and even without actual necessity. The establishment was, of course, there for the use of such as ourselves, even without consent, on an emergency. But the weather was good, the night still and clear, our health excellent, and there was an open refuge within short ski-ing distance. It is true that on foot we might have been totally unable to reach it.

Those who do not wish to run the risk attending the forcible bursting of locks in order to get shelter at the first hut had better move on, in the quiet of night and with an easy conscience, to the open hut, which stands a little further on, and reach it by lantern light. They may, however, make previously an appointment with the caretaker at Lenk. He will then come up, weather permitting, and open the Rohrbachhaus.

I need not dwell on the pleasant night we spent in the beds of the Rohrbachhaus. Stolen joys are

sweet, and even may, as in our case, be well
deserved, or at least well earned—a way of putting
it which leaves morals uninjured. Our first day
had been heavy, but had afforded two magnificent
runs on glaciers and on slopes abutting to passes,
each covering about four miles exclusive of curves,
which, of course, being purely voluntary as to their
number and scope, cannot be calculated.

Ski-running parties spending a night in one or
the other of the two Wildstrubel huts will find
themselves on the next day surrounded by as fine
and as varied a country as they may wish for.
Whatever line they choose, there is but one that
should absolutely be avoided. This, they know
already, is the Rawyl pass, whether winter tourists
wish to go north to Lenk or south to Sion. The
outlet of the pass to the north is best described
as a most precipitous and ice-bound region. The
southward descent is dangerous quite as much,
owing to its great complication amid rock, ravine,
forest, and watercourse. Runners should divert
their ambitions well away from those gorges. The
best way to Montana and Vermala lies over
the Glacier de la Plaine Morte, and thence to
the south.

Runners proceeding from the huts and wishing
to follow in our footsteps, in order to reach the
Lämmern glacier and the Wildstrubel, will run
down the slopes leading to the Glacier de la
Plaine Morte (map, sheet 473). They will glance
at the Raezli glacier tumbling down to the north-
west, between the Gletschhorn and the Wildstrubel

(west-end summit). Hence they will steer a straight course to the east, along the centre line of the Glacier de la Plaine Morte, and then turn to the north-east towards the Lämmernjoch, a pass to the east of the Weststrubel, on a ridge, which is steepish to reach, though usually well covered with snow. From that point to the top of the Weststrubel there is an additional rise of about 120 metres, say 400 feet. The view from this Strubel is worth the additional labour, and it also gives one the satisfaction of having reached the last of the highest points on the Diablerets–Wildhorn–Wildstrubel route. The height of the Diablerets is 3,222, of the Wildhorn 3,264, and of the Wildstrubel west 3,251 metres. But this satisfaction, like that which may have been got from ascending the Diablerets and the Wildhorn, may, in point of time, be too dearly bought.

It is quite sufficient to direct one's course straight from the Lämmernjoch on to the higher reaches of the Lämmerngletscher, which open up beyond the Lämmernjoch to the north.

Runners should not plunge full east straight down the glacier. Such a course would be attended with much danger, as a line of crevasses runs across the glacier roughly from south to north. A careful runner will map out for himself a " circumferential " route, which will bring him round that dangerous part, by descending the slopes of the glacier which are beyond that spot to the north. Then, by turning to the east, one enters the lower reaches of the ice, when one faces the extensive building of the Wildstrubel Hotel on the Gemmi pass, about 3 miles ahead. The best way off the glacier on to the Lämmernalp is on the north side of the gorge, in which the glacier tails off, though I found it quite convenient to reach the Lämmernboden (see map) by means of the slopes which run down to it on the southern side of the stream.

Our route leaves completely out of account the Gross-strubel (3,253 metres), which rises above Adelboden and the Engstligenalp. This summit does not belong to the traverse I am now describing. There are quite distinct expeditions to be made to either or both Strubels from Adelboden or Kandersteg. If from Kandersteg, one should go and spend the night at the Schwarenbach Hotel, on the Gemmi road, go up the way we have just described for the descent, and return *viâ* Ueschinenthal. The Kandersteg guides know all about this run, which is much to be recommended to the expert.

There are three long, flat strips on the run from the Wildstrubel huts to the Schwarenbach Hotel *viâ* Gemmi. The first is the Glacier de la Plaine Morte (about 3 miles), the second the Lämmernboden (about a mile), the third the Daubensee (about a mile).

The run from the Daubensee to Kandersteg requires no particular notice. It begins at the spot where the Lämmernboden turns to the north, within 800 yards or so of the Wildstrubel Hotel on the Gemmi pass. The run on the Daubensee, then to the Schwarenbach Hotel (one should not pass to the right, east of the summer road) affords excellent ski-ing. Then, on the rush down to the Spitalmatten, with the Balmhorn and the Altels towering to one's right, will be met some of the best ground of the whole trip, the slopes being throughout beautifully exposed to the north. The gorges to the east should on no account be entered. The course runs straight north on the west side of the valley, till the upper bends of the summer road are met on the shoulder which drops down to Inner Kandersteg, at the entrance of the Gasternthal. The slopes to the west of the woods on the shoulder are periodically swept by avalanches. Look carefully whether the fragments lie on the ground, and whether the rocks above, whence they start, are bare of snow. If so, you may proceed among the fragments. If otherwise, take to the road and walk.

The whole distance travelled over during this expedition, starting from Gsteig, is, measured on the map, about 40 miles to Kandersteg. We had with us ropes and axes, but never used them. In point of fact, I should consider that expeditions upon which a use is foreseen for the axe and the rope are not, strictly speaking, ski-ing expeditions. Ski-ing, by definition, excludes the use of rope and axe, though one should be provided with them when having reason to fear unforeseen contingencies.

The levels are as follow :—

At Gsteig: 1,192 metres (3,937 feet).
On the Zan Fleuron glacier : 2,866 metres, being a rise of 1,674 metres.
On the Sanetsch pass : 2,221 metres, being a fall of 645 metres.
On the Wildhorn glacier: 3,172 metres, being a rise of 951 metres.

On the Rawyl pass : 2,400 metres, being a drop of 772 metres.
On the Lämmernjoch : 3,132 metres, being a rise of 732 metres.
On the Gemmi pass : 2,214 metres, being a drop of 918 metres.
At Kandersteg : 1,169 metres, being a drop of 1,045 metres.

From this table of levels, the general public, if there is any in mountaineering topics, may draw a conclusion and a moral.

Have you ever looked at a model relief map of the Alps ? As one of the general public, you may not be aware that the relief is artificially forced. It is intended to amaze by the steepness of the declivities and the terribly sharp angles at which the ridges of the peaks meet in the air and terminate into a threatening point.

The designers of those otherwise beautiful and attractive models wish to heighten the impression which you are accustomed to receive when you look up to the Alpine peaks from some point below. The laws of perspective bring then those peaks nearer the perpendicular. By an optical delusion, which is full of scenic effect, they tower aloft. The designers of Alpine models run after poetical and picturesque effects. They very naturally do not wish to show you in plaster Alps far less formidable than those which agreeably overawe you in nature. They add from 10 to 20 per cent. to the angles of declivity, deepen the valleys and pull out the mountain tops like putty. They thus show you the Alps in your own natural perspective, as a painter does on his canvas. But the whole thing is fallacious.

I should feel called upon to condemn the process

as a downright black lie if there was not enough snow on those models to paint the lie white. Look at the Matterhorn from Zermatt and then look at one of those paper-weight models in stone which are sold for a few francs in the local bazaars and which are cut according to scale. You will be surprised to see how really flat the Matterhorn is. I advise every one who intends to climb it to first make a careful study of a paper-weight model. It is most re-assuring.

Now this is exactly what an Alpine ski-runner does or should do.

There is in the vestibule of the University buildings at Geneva, on the first floor, a magnificent plaster model of Switzerland, true to scale. Each time I cast my eyes upon this model I more fully realise how exactly the author's execution of the relief, based on science, corresponds with the runner's conception, based on experience. In its own un-varnished language, the model says : " By me know the Alps, and by them know thyself and be modest, thou hast not done so much after all."

So the general public may now understand why the runner sees the Alpine world in his own perspective. The real reliefs are printed on his mind. A summer tourist, who instead of fitting foot-rules to his feet, pegs or stumps along, can with difficulty enter into the runner's notion.

Orographic conformation and questions of exposure are ski-running matters. The runner studies the *relievo* in the light of two or three truisms resting on experience, which are as conditions determining the rational use of ski and assuring the pleasure of the runner.

1. The runner aims at rising rapidly, because he cannot draw from his ski a full measure of pleasure except from the moment when the ski cease to be the means of carrying his weight uphill, and become merely a means of velocity.

2. While rising as abruptly as he possibly can, the runner seeks out—for this tiresome operation is seldom avoidable—the declivities whose exposure marks them out as unsuitable for a good run down. No wonder. It is not to his interest to throw away, as it were, good slopes by employing them for work uphill. Now, steepnesses turned to the south, south-west, and west, afford poor running, viewed, of course, in their generality.

Here meteorology—or, in plain English, weather—is more important than geography, because warm winds, whether they blow soft or wild, beat upon those faces. When not actually dangerous, such defective slopes are convenient for rising to the high levels. The runner who knows how to take advantage both of meteorology and orography shows himself possessed of an advanced knowledge of his craft.

3. The best running hills are those whose gentler slopes are exposed north and east. The winds from those quarters are not warm winds, though they too have their own way of spoiling the snow. At any rate, the sun—which has even in winter powers for mischief—is too low on the southern horizon to interfere with the powdery condition of snow facing north. But there is not much gained in mapping

ON THE TOP OF THE FINSTERAARHORN.

To face p. 80.

out one's tour in the manner indicated if one is landed for the descent on abrupt, though northern or eastern, slopes.

So now draw your moral and conclusion Will it not be that you should walk round and round a large relief model of the Alps when planning your winter excursions? This you could easily do if some kind patron of Alpinism would provide you in London with a copy, cast in metal for durability, of the Geneva plaster relief.

Would the reader like to know, after this long lecture, how I take the refreshment, and smoke the pipe—in my case it has always been a cigar—which I should like to offer him now? He is welcome to my den.

I scoop out the snow, in the manner of dogs, to the depth of 2 feet, or thereabouts. I lay my ski across the cavity thus formed. Pressed close together, they roof in about one-third of the opening. I put my feet in the hole, wrap them up in my empty rucksack, bend my knees and sit on the ski. Before me, on the snow shovelled up with my hands in the shape of a tray, I display the contents of my larder. Then I plant my sticks behind me, one supporting each shoulder. Thus, my armchair, dining-room, and table are all ready. I wait upon myself, as is usual at lunch, and when the time has come for the blissful smoke, I lazily stretch my legs across the empty table and lean back, looking into immensity through the puffs. When the time comes when I should like a nap, I find that the sticks at my back invite me to recline by gradually giving way. I lay

6

them flat on the snow, spread my cloak over them and, thus comfortably padded, I pull my cap over my eyes, and try hard to convince myself that it is a cold midwinter day. The smoke ceases to rise, the cigar end drops and—— This is all vanity no doubt, but is mine not better than that of many a wiser man?

Old Egger at Kandersteg, who received me with a cheery handshake on completion of the trip described in this chapter, had seen me start about a year before on my traverse of the Bernese Oberland. He expressed satisfaction at seeing me again, though with another companion, and said he thought we had been rather long. But when I told him that another trip had been thrown in, as well as my companion changed, he insinuated with a smile of great intelligence that we had had time to grow very thirsty. It was, he said, a grand thing for Kandersteg that it had been at the beginning of the first trip and at the end of the second. So he would drink our healths. And we honoured him likewise.

CHAPTER IV

THE SKI-RUNNER OF VERMALA

Vermala—The mysterious runner—The Plain of the Dead—
Popular beliefs—The purification of the grazings—A
haunted piece of rock—An awful noose is thrown over
the country-side—Supernatural lights and events—The Babel
of tongues—The Saillon and Brigue testimonies—The curé
of Lens and his sundial—The people's cure—The Strubel—
Chauffage central—Did I meet the Ski-runner of Vermala?
—My third ascent of the Wildstrubel—A night encampment
on the glacier—Meditations on mountains, mountaineers,
and the Swiss—How to make *café noir*—Where to sleep
and when not to—Alpine refuges—The old huts and the
new—The English Alpinists and the Swiss huts—The
Britannia hut.

HE sheet 482 of the topo-
graphical atlas of Switzerland
assigns the name of Vermala
to the *mayens* in Canton Valais,
situated above Sierre, at an
altitude of 4,500 feet or thereabouts. Swiss *mayens* are
places where grass is grown
that can be mown and on
which cattle is grazed in
autumn.

About 600 feet higher there is in the forest a

clearing, with a south-west exposure, in which the
Mont Blanc range, framed in fir-trees, presents itself
in the distance to the appreciative eye as a beautiful
background to a picture of loveliness. If the bare-
ness of the map is to be trusted, this spot was not
yet inhabited in 1884 when the topographical survey
was made.

The map is right, and yet it is not quite right.
There were at that time no ordinary dwelling-houses
in the clearing, but people of ordinary mind held
that the Ski-runner of Vermala, whose presence
on the country-side was at that time exactly known,
had his home somewhere in those parts.

From afar curious people would point out a
rocky platform planted with beautiful, well-spaced
firs amongst which it would be pleasant to bask
in the sun in winter. But others were rather taken
up with the peculiar apparitions which at night were
seen there skimming the rocks in a sinister play of
light. The map marks the place with a broken line,
between Vermala and Marolire, right above Praz-
Devant.

It was said that in earlier times the mowers piled
up their hay at the top of the clearing in one or
two *mazots*, or rough barns, set on short posts, four
in number, planted in the ground and crowned with
flat stone disks. But that hay had an unwelcome
way of catching fire, consuming the *mazots* as well.
Nothing was left but the stones. So the peasantry
gave up this unlucky storage ground.

At present no other mystery hovers about this
spot than that which these recollections call back

to mind. The Forest Hotel occupies the site. The sun holds divided sway in summer with the coolness of the woods, in winter with King Frost. Here conventional tourists embrace at a glance the most marvellous piece of Alpine scenery—from Monte Leone and beyond, to Mont Blanc—that human eye can long for, such, that had Byron known of it, he would have sent his world-sick Manfred to contemplate it from Vermala.

The sweetness of this name would have rung as true to the poet's ear as, in the Italo-Celtic tongue, it rings to the ear of the rough mountaineer. Would you not, for a while, when reading on the map names of such romantic harmony, forget that they are mere geographical terms? Let us personify those place names. Do not Vermala and Marolire spell out as tunefully as the classically tender and melodious Daphnis and Chloe?

But then there might be a risk of forgetting that there is not a halfpenny worth of love in this story. It is a homespun yarn, woven by rustics in ignorance and fear, and would fall very flat on the ears of civilised mankind, but for the curiosity roused by that consummate sportsman whose humours shine through the woof of the story.

Whence did he come? Who was he? Nobody ever knew.

He had already disappeared from the country when a more enlightened generation ceased to look upon him as a true ghost. There arose a class of minds which ran to the opposite extreme and held him to be a superman of the morrow. In the end he was

described as the Ski-runner of Vermala, when some
acquaintance with the new implements called back
popular imagination within the bounds of reason.
Then the glamour that had gathered around his
memory at last faded away.

The terraced plain of Crans on which there is now
a golf course was not then much frequented. The
whole district was held to be inhospitable. The
Wildstrubel mountain group, which fills up all
the space between the Rawyl and Gemmi passes,
bore a redoubtable reputation. It was still more
feared for the Plaine-Morte and the glacier of the
same name, which spread as a counterpane over his
feet. Both the plaine and the glacier were reputed
abodes of the souls of the dead. Poor souls perishing with cold in the cracks! Dante's idea of an
ice circle in hell harks back to the rustic belief
that souls serve their term of purgatory on the
Plaine-Morte and come down on certain sacramental
nights to visit the living and receive additional
punishment from the contemplation of the evil
deeds they have left behind them to work themselves out.

In summer, the Valaisan peasant would not
venture upon the Plain of the Dead, had he not first
sought the protection of the Holy Virgin and saints.
In winter he doubts not that the Plain of the Dead is
reserved for the evil ones by the holy Powers that
be. As soon as the first winter snow turns to white the
brown, sunburnt slopes of the upper grazings, these
are laid under the ban by the piety of the villagers, if
not by the Church.

Who knows, say the vintners of Sierre, what is going on there ? Assuredly, nothing of worth, while the sun draws its daily course slowly on the horizon from the Equinox of autumn to that of spring. Thus an alarming scientific fact has become a nursery ground for fond popular beliefs.

We should easily sympathise with the credulity of those big children if we would but imagine our own state of mind, did we believe we had positive reason to fear lest the sun which had ripened the last harvest might not return in spring to ripen the next, after we had exhausted the garnered crops of the former year. And in what mood would we see the shades of night enfolding us this evening, if we did not rest more confidently in the hope of dawn than in the arms of sleep ?

It is under the influence of motives of that kind that the inhabitants of the populous villages thrown as a belt round the plateau of Crans Mollens, Randogne, Montana, Chermignon, Lens, and Icogne— were quite prepared to go into the forest to pick up their allotment of firewood, and even to pilfer that of their neighbour. But, so long as their herds and flocks—when the sun rises again full east and sets again full west, which is the signal for the raising of the ban—have not been solemnly escorted to the grazings by the priest with holy water and sprinkler, they will not be seen ascending to the beats whence they retreated in the autumn. And if any do visit those desecrated spots before they have again been hallowed, even the boldest miscreants undertake the venture with a sense of insecurity, knowing full

well that, for the pure-minded, they are committing
sheer blasphemy.

The God of winter is still a God for heathens in
the eyes of those people. Nor should this call forth
any astonishment. "How beautiful upon the
mountains are the feet of him that bringeth good
tidings." If so, how much more awful than elsewhere must appear there those of the arch-fiend!
He alone is of a nature sufficiently proof to fire to
make his home in ice with impunity. His followers
alone are sufficiently witched to share in his
privilege.

Therefore, when the rumour was spread that a
supernatural form haunted the Vermala woods, it
needed but little comment before it gained credence.
Everybody was pretty clear in his own mind as to what
kind of person he must be, and none needed to
question others to know that they thought exactly
the same thing.

As might be expected, poachers, chamois hunters,
and wood-cutters, people with uneasy consciences—
because they steal wood or game, and because their
occupation makes them particularly liable to mistrust
each other and to meditate on the Evil One—were
among the first to believe a story so much in keeping with the trend of their own thoughts. They
could even bear witness to its truth.

They had uplifted their eyes, at night, upon a
shade so pellucid that the moonbeams shone through
it. The shade stole away among the trees like the
wind, with a slight rustling of the snow. Then, in a
hollow lane leading from the Mayens de Lens

towards Chermignon, they had come across strange
marks which were not those of game, such as hares,
foxes, or badgers. They were not either the marks
of any hoofed animal, whether it be a four-footed
beast or even the dreaded biped. Those marks soon
seemed to join together into tracks that flung themselves like huge ribbons all over the country-side.
But, of all those who would, none was able to follow
them out. Never had impressions like these been
seen on the snow, of which it was impossible to say
whether the being who made them walked backwards or forwards. Some said he was a creature
mounted on a wheel or riding on two. Others said
he was a serpent crawling on his belly, so unbroken
was the track and so much did it keep winding
about.

However much it seemed to roll away in every
direction and to stop nowhere, a few bold spirits
determined to follow its course. They forthwith
found themselves plunging and diving in such deep
snow that, breathless and shivering, they gave up the
chase, feeling numb at heart.

From that moment the public mind was made up.
No creature in mortal shape, no flesh could ever
have marked the face of the snow with this
labyrinthine coil. To wind up this clue of thread
one must either fly like a bird, or blow like the wind,
or be favoured with the malediction of God. This
last explanation being of all the most clear, and the
most creditable to the piety of the largest commune
in the Canton du Valais, it was accepted by the
municipal council and the clergy.

In the spring—the next to the great disturbance
—the melting snow blotted out the dreadful spoor,
the alarm it had caused and, of course, the Runner,
for want of his element.

As soon as they dared, people hurried up to the
Vermala rock. There they found the remains of
a new and unexpected kind of habitation. The
drooping branches of a mighty fir appeared to have
been pinned to the ground by frost, consequent upon
the piling of snow upon their extremities. Then
snow had been piled up higher and higher around
the tree, embedding other branches as it rose,
which were cut away from the trunk, except at the
top, where they stretched out in the form of a snow-
covered dome. There had thus arisen a pyramid-
shaped dwelling enclosed in walls of ice, for the snow
had clearly been brought to transparency by the
application of heat from within. And thus was
explained that wonderful effluvium of light, the
shimmer of which looked so sinister from afar. It
is even said that some children picked among the
tufts of green grass which here and there began to
grow about the floor of the abandoned hut, pieces
of a yellow amber-like substance which shot forth
sparks bathed in a soft purple radiance, when seen
by them in the darkness of their own homes.

No wonder that people spoke of Vermala in fear-
some strains! What a pity the most beautiful spot
in the country was haunted!

In the ensuing winters, things went from bad to
worse. People ceased visiting the plateau de Crans
for pleasure. Do you fancy, they said, that strangers

L.M.G.

ABOVE RIED, LOETSCHENTHAL.

To face p. 90.

henceforth will ever set foot upon this ground, unless
it be for their sins?

So much tribulation turned the feebler heads.
Folk no longer understood each other aright. They
got confused over names. Those who called La
Zaat by its name were rebuked by those who called
it La Chaux Sei, and those parties both fell out with
the supporters of the name Bellalui. No one was
quite clear about the identity of Petit Mont Tubang
and Grand Mont Tubang. They were in a mist as
to Petit Mont Bonvin and Grand Mont Bonvin.
Everybody confused one and all of these with the
Tonio de Merdasson. In short, the mind of the
country-side was muddled, now that all eyes saw
double when they looked in the direction of
Vermala.

Old men, however, stiffened their backs and spoke
in firm voices above the new Babel of tongues.
They said it had always been known before their
time and would ever hereafter be manifest, that the
crest that is visible from Lens is the brow of Bellalui,
and they clinched the matter with the reminder that
when Bagnoud the mayor built his new house, he
called it Bellalui after the mountain.

As it happens, it was at Lens that the meteoric
personage once more called attention to himself.

Truth to say, though there was no one who did
not expect his return, there was nevertheless a
general shudder when Jean Perrex who had gone to
Saillon, brought back the news that "he" was
known to have brought out of the stable the horse
which had lately been bought with a new cart, to

show visitors over the country. "He" had put the
horse to the cart without collar, traces, or bridle.
Without whip or ribbons, he had driven to St. Pierre
de Clages. He had tied the horse to the church
door. Then he had sat down on the grass at the
foot of the Norman tower, between the beehives of
the curé and the wasps' nest that is there sunk in the
soil. Nobody could say how and when they had
seen him. It would have been useless to ask what
he was like. But it could not but be he, since the
abandoned horse and cart had been impounded, and
the church was now sinking more rapidly than
heretofore.

The most convincing testimony, however, was that
of Claudine Rey. Her brother was in the habit of
walking out with a girl who had a situation in a
hotel in Brigue. One night he had clambered up the
wall to the terrace, when the moon suddenly grinned
through the clouds. Then, instead of the girl he
was to meet, whom should he see there to his right
in the arbour but "him" in the shape of a dwarfish,
wizened wiseacre, clutching in his right hand a
death's head, and with the fingers of his left running
rapidly along the lines of a book of charms!

When, on St. Martin's eve, this account was given
to the worthy curé of Lens, who had gathered about
his hearth some of his parishioners to crack in goodly
company the arolla nuts roasting in the ashes, the
dear old man shook his head; his mind was running
on the words "Get thee behind me, Satan."

Then a gentle scratching was heard on the panes
of the closed window. The gathering looked that

way and most turned pale. The first snow of the coming winter was swirling and whirling against the glass, borne on the soughing wind. And the bluish purple light poured forth from the wells of memory into the sockets of their eyes.

The curé came out with his guests on his way to trim the church lamp. A thin layer of snow covered the village lanes. He cast about him furtive and mistrustful glances. The pure white carpet was as yet unsullied by footprints. Would " he " come ?

Now this curé was a bit of an astronomer and a clerical moralist. He took every care of the sundial of his church tower and had adorned it with an inscription, in two expressive lines :—

" Le temps passé n'est plus, l'éternité commence.
Pensez-y donc, mortels, et pensez-y d'avance."

That night he stared at it. The piece of advice was as good as ever. But the involutions of the meridian mean curve, drawn with such careful exactness on the stone and painted with such a light hand in the gayest colours, struck him now as being the exact counterfeit of the ribbons on the snow. Was he not breaking away from his ordinary piety in accusing his church dial of taking after an unChristian pattern ? Surely, he was wronging his dial. And the good curé kept poring over the unholy coincidence, in so far at least as his mind could find time to spare for meditation upon matters of paramount importance.

On the morning of St. Martin's Day, the village showed itself to be all in a tangle of loops. The

diabolical spoor went in and out round every house.
The figure eight of the sundial had thrown off
innumerable copies upon the ground. The bells
were tolled in vain. To no purpose did the chimes
peal. In vain did the most Christianlike of all suns
that ever poured its kindly light upon Lens, kindle
the most reassuring smile upon the wrinkled stones
of the old tower. Not a single parishioner was bold
enough to spurn with his foot the cabalistic loops
that embraced the bosom of Mother Earth in their
oppressive grasp. Not a child dare step across them,
not even to go and dip his fingers in the holy water
at the church door.

The most thunder-struck was the curé. A trucu-
lent pentagram in red chalk was displayed all over
his distich, surrounded by a double circle that
looked like a green fairies' ring designed in moss
upon the church tower.

As for the good men of the largest *commune* in
Canton Valais, they bethought themselves of a day
of fasting, the natural remedy for their orthodox
faith to point out. But there was a sign against
that too. The pewter pots and mugs of the village
tavern appeared that morning all set up in a row
upon the railings of the churchyard gate, upside
down. They would have to be fetched and brought
back to their proper place. The hardiest commoners
were summoned. They took heart from their thirst.
The general anxiety was soothed by such an obvious
way of drowning care.

The frequenters of the forests, whether they were
honest day-labourers or night-birds, knew alone,

beyond all doubt, the identity of the mischief-
maker. For them the prime mover in the big upset
was none other than the *Strubel*, about whom the
village elders would still relate, in the dim light of
the evening fires, dreadful stories of an ancient
stamp, such as suggest themselves in the woods after
dark, when the old tree stumps are phosphorescent
and glow-worms come out of their retreats to set up
their tiny lamps on the edges of the rocks.

Of all creatures born of local lore the Strubel was
to them the nearest in kin. When the north wind
blows the Strubel races from crest to crest, from the
Gemmi to the Rawyl, and from the Rawyl to the
Gemmi. Up there his long white shock of hair
streaming in the wind, and upturned by the gale,
spreads as a plume across the sky. The tumbling
folds of his beard fill the precipitous ravines. A hail
of icicles rattles out of his roaring breast. The rush
of his huge body, soaring amid snowflakes and in
glacier dust, awakens the slumbering elements. At
night the Aurora Borealis gathers in streamers
around his brow. At dawn and at sunset a diadem
of snow-crystals sets a many-coloured band about
his hoary head. He flies, and his feet do but tip
the top of the peaks, and his stature rises aloft in an
immense upward sweep. In a blue-and-white transparency, such as one sees in glacier crevasses and in
pure ice water, the spring of his sinuous limbs uplifts
him to the confines of atmosphere and firmament.

Such is the poetic picture of the dread being which
the shepherds still worship secretly, far down in the
recesses of their primitive hearts. And it is he

whose image the antics of an enigmatic ski-runner revived for several winters, as our story shows, under the low and gloomy roofs of the white-hooded chalets.

There is an evening hour, when, after cooking and partaking of the day's last meal, the family gathers round the domestic hearth. Then the last embers are fanned into a congenial flame. The dying light of the hearth kindles anew the memories of a bygone age. Is the time near when these will die out for want of fuel, as the flame of that hearth when the family goes to bed? But why should we link any melancholy after-thought with their well-earned rest? The thought of the reward granted to their toil pleases one's moral sense. Yet he who, like me in this chapter, uses figments of the past as a page decoration, cannot but regret that such picturesque elements should be gradually, but surely, vanishing for ever from the face of our modern world.

The accepted idea is that things have progressed. So they have. A nice hotel crowns the Vermala rock. At night real electric light of industrial origin has taken the place of the fantastic rays of old. There is a *chauffage central*, fed with colliers' coal, and stoked by porters who never could produce heat without matter and on terms that were not commercial. Now people dance at Vermala, they have music at night, they lounge about in smoking-jackets, and, when all is said and done, I am one of those who most enjoy the new situation.

Did I ever meet the Ski-runner of Vermala? I should have a vague fear of being caught prevari-

cating should I answer either Yes or No. Truth
sometimes dwells in half-way houses.

I was staying at Vermala last winter. The glacier
de la Plaine-Morte, and the ascent of the Wildstrubel, were objects which a young man of my party
kept steadily in view. It was his second winter holiday in Switzerland. A much-travelled man, he
had camped out in Persia, and endured thirst and
hunger in some of the most God-forsaken spots of
the globe. How would he fare in the Wildstrubel
country? A man may have done very well in sandy
deserts and yet find himself out of his depth in snow.
He had ski, but would they do as much for him on
these charmed snows as a camel's spreading feet had
done in the desert?

So we set forth late one morning, after paying
the usual penalty to the photographic fiend. So
great an honour conferred by a number of fair
women inspired us with proper pride. It was a
most strengthening draught to harden us against
the trials that might be in store, but it also worked
so insidiously as to cause us to overlook the wise
saw of the most bourgeois of French fabulists:
" Rien ne sert de courir, il faut partir à temps,"
which, topically rendered, might mean : " A man
who has started late need never hope to make
up for lost time when going uphill on ski."

The glacier de la Plaine-Morte lies at the altitude
of 9,500 feet approximately, measured at the brim, or
lip, which we had to overcome before we could dip
down to the surface of that shroud of the dead. We
were setting out for it from the altitude of 5,500 feet,

7

and allowing for unavoidable " downs " that would break the upline, we had quite 5,000 feet of vertical displacement before us.

At whatever hour of the day we might have started we had that much to ascend by sunset, if we wished to reach the Hildebrand hut in comfortable circumstances, and so the true bourgeois spirit would have us do. Had we been in military mood we should have borne with the dictates of punctuality. Unfortunately we had received attentions that had raised us beyond ourselves. We chose to trust our elation to bring us on over the ground. But the 5,000 feet we had to ascend would not grow less. The sun would not delay its progress. The ups and downs would not smooth themselves out, however much gentle pressure our planks might bring to bear upon them. The refreshing compliments we had stored up would not check the flight of time.

All too early Night put in a punctual appearance upon the scene. She found us, indeed, sailing gently along the shroud of the dead, but far from the place prepared to shelter weary Alpinists.

We seemed to be in for the same adventure as a friend of mine who spent the night wandering on the glacier during a wind and snowstorm. The dead then might almost have been moving under their shrouds in every direction. He did not lose his way, but was impressed by solitude and by the weirdness of the shifting snows, let alone the fatigue that loosened his limbs. He confided to me quite lately how odd he still thought it that he did not go off his " chump."

Anyhow, Mr. B., my present companion, decided that he saw something happy in the situation, the beckoning finger of a friendly fate, that would guard us while we spent that January night on the open glacier. The air was still and clear. The cold might be keen, but not sharp, though somebody since would absolutely have it that the thermometer marked that night at Vermala 2·2 Fahrenheit.

As Mr. B. was anxious to view this escapade as a fit counterpart to his nights in the Persian desert, the situation could be accepted with equanimity. He was possessed of the true romantic spirit. Poor man! He was afflicted with much thirst. I had, unfortunately, nothing better to offer him than the carefully worded expression of my regret that he had not been able to get himself fitted up, before he left Persia, with some of the valuable water compartments of his Bactrian camels. So by ten o'clock we laid ourselves demurely down on the angular glacier moraine, pretty confident that long before the hour struck for the sun to rise, we should be anxious to roll the shutters away from the Palace of Dawn.

On the contrary, when the sun stepped out of his car upon the glacier and, at the most reasonable hour of eight on the clock, knocked us up, we were still reclining in our *alcôve*. Shall I say that we found at our bedside shaving water and a cup of tea? No, for this would be a really undue elongation of truth. But we saw the " boots " busy lighting odd scraps of paper and slipping them into our shoes to soften the frozen leather. We thanked him and were about to tip him when he took fright and flew away upon a sunbeam, leaving behind a pot of blacking and an electric brush.

If I ever did set eyes upon the Ski-runner of Vermala, it was during that night, nor could it have been in a better setting than on the Plain of the shrouded Dead. In fact, in the supposition that he is a person that never existed, the glacier de la Plaine-Morte would cry, out for him.

Glaciers are legion, but there is only one glacier de la Plaine-Morte.

Measured with tape, its size, as our readers have learnt in a preceding chapter, would come out at a few miles.

Sir Martin Conway, in his "Alps from End to End," comes nearer to conveying a correct impression, because he measures it by the standard of his own mind.

Those who have in any weather entrusted themselves in winter to that ice cup scooped out of the top of lofty Alpine battlements, may alone imagine in its true character the Alpine world as it was in those dim and distant days, when half Europe would have been too small to hold the glories of the Plaine-Morte in its pre-historic stage of being.

Since last year (1911), a cable railway runs passengers up from Sierre to Montana-Vermala. Some day, perhaps, the railway may be taken 5,000 feet higher. It would then pass the place where we spent the hours of our mystic night, alternately watchful and asleep, taking in the immense charm that flowed in upon us, and seeking in short terms of slumber rest from our meditation.

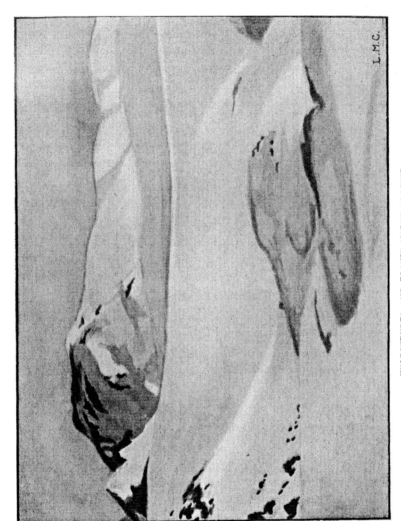

WILDSTRUBEL AND PLAINE MORTE GLACIER.

L.M.C.

To face p. 100.

The *amateurs* of mountain scenery whom the rail may bring up here will not be so single-minded about it as we were.   They will look for something else to lie upon than a gritty stone bed.   They will allow a wooden barrier to intercept the pulsation of nature on its way to their souls.   They will not catch in full the gracious calls which pass in the stillness between heaven and earth, and roll in harmoniously upon the mind, as a sonorous shore echoes the beat of the waves.   My young companion, more restless because the situation was so overmasteringly novel, looked around for distractions which I needed not. I have often stood, or lain, like that, looking from the outside upon the play of life in which I otherwise bear my faint part.   I like to withdraw from the stage of the company directed by Messrs. Time and Space in which we are, with as much humbleness as the master dramatists could be with pride, composers, actors, and managers of some small theatrical contribution.   I am then doubtful whether I feel some approach in me to the lotus eater's frame of mind, or whether I rejoice in the overflowing energy of the superman.

There is a deep meaning in the Gospel passage that shows us the Son of man being led upon a hill, and upon a temple pinnacle, that He may be tempted by the sight of those aspects of the world which it was His mission to forswear, combat and finally to overcome by the spirit and succumb to in the flesh.   It is on pinnacles such as these that we may behold ourselves.

Let us see.   Is he who learns his philosophy by

conversation with the mountains not at once a lotus
eater and a superman ?   He acquires from them
a firm conviction that—

"Il mondo va da sè.
Le monde se fait lui-même ; "

which apophthegm breathes the spirit of abdication
and is a source of weakness for him.

On the other hand, the conscious personal power
by which he overcomes the savage forces and the
blind puttings-forth of might by Nature, does mark
him out as instancing in himself human courage,
a well-created *physique* and some superiority.

When his energy is excited, he caresses the
illusion that he could crush his fellow beings, if he
thought it worth doing. But his dignity forbids.
His fellows need have no fear, for there is some
taming effect in his haughtiness. The loftiness of
his spirit lames his hand for battle against those in
whom he hardly recognises his like.

He cannot take the affairs of men so seriously that
he would whip up in himself the ambition to take
after Napoleon or Cæsar.

When he is in lotus-eating mood, the Rubicon is
really too big a thing to be crossed lightly.

When he is in his superman's temper, the undertaking is indeed so small that it is not worth while
that such as he should be bothered with it.

The Swiss, as a people, have shown in a high
degree that such is the mental composition of a
true mountain race. Left for six hundred years to
their unbroken line of development, they show in

the successive layers of the formation of their national mind the stages of the process.

They first won in the Alps, by arms, sufficient room for themselves, and set round their borders a ring-fence of impassable pikes. Then, turning to supermen, they fought the battles of others, for the sake of war, despising power, and moving untempted in the domains of kings.

In the nineteenth century, the reflective mountain spirit gained hold on them. They held war as an immoral pursuit and ceased from being mercenaries. But their contemptuous loftiness remained. Without despising their former glory they, as it were, drew into themselves and drew themselves up at the same time.

They have become the typically lotus-eating neutral nation in Europe, supermen still in a way and armed to the teeth, but with swords ever sheathed and with bayonets ever resting in the scabbard.

In their national life the Swiss practice political self-education, and would do so rather than seek the means of making their influence felt among nations. The Swiss are but a small and insignificant nation, but their history shows that, disillusioned of mere strength, they passed to the consciousness of a moral identity.

They became self-centred, and liked to keep aloof from other people's affairs. They formed the conclusion that—

" Le monde se fait lui-même.
Il mondo va da sè ; "

and, in the public life of Europe, assumed the part of spectators and political moralists.

For Napoleon, a mere village or two were a sufficient stake for which to set Europe ablaze. With material means, he built up a political society that soon crumbled away. Had the French been by temperament lotus-eating supermen, would they have followed him? They too would have answered him with the words—

"Le monde se fait lui-même.
Il mondo va da sè."

The victories of fourteen years could not make a Buonapartist Europe.

What subsists of the Superman's adventure? It had been just as well for him, had he stood on the edge of the glacier of the Plaine-Morte, withstanding temptation, though he had thereby shorn Elba and St. Helena of their title to fame.

The bent of the mountaineer's mind is turned inwards, towards the education of self. As a superman he pits himself against nature, to man he is kind and just. He is the lotus-eater who would forget the things, the seeking after which would turn him away from self tuition.

He is a kind of Marcus Aurelius who does the share allotted to him in the common task, and then withdraws into his higher self, preserving a kindly interest in those who have built up no such upper chambers.

That sort of man is not an adept at self-sacrifice, because sacrifice is the opposite of education. If he

entirely gave himself away, he would have no inner
garden left to cultivate, and in which to plant his own
vine and sit under his own fig-tree. But if you need
not expect him to die for you, or live for you, neither
does he expect you to do the like on his behalf.
Mountaineers are known to help each other when
their lives are in danger in cases of Alpine peril.
In self-love they practice self-reliance. "Exercise
thyself" would be their motto.

Why? because the mountaineer believes in his
Creator and looks upon His work as a good piece of
work, the quality of which the creature has to justify
in itself.   So in the end should the mountaineer
perish at the hands of the forces of Nature which he
has, by right of spiritual conquest, transformed into
moral values for the world, with him it is a case of
invicto animo vicit moles.

While I was thus trimming the lamp of my
thoughts Mr. B. contrived sundry little amusements
for himself. He brought out of his bag an extremely smart dressing-gown and bedroom slippers.
He arrayed himself in the former and dressed his
feet in the latter. Then he smoked the few cigarettes
he found in his pockets.   Then we shared the frozen
sandwiches that were left over for our evening meal.
When those occupations were exhausted, it might
almost be described as a fortunate factor in the situation that his thirst would not depart from him. How
to slake it became the main concern that whiled
away the long hours of the night for the sleepless
Londoner.

The problem was as follows : being given snow *ad*

infinitum and a very fair quantity of ground coffee
beans, how to produce a refreshing and fortifying
beverage whose supreme quality consists in being
black, hot, pure, and strong :—

> " Noir comme le diable,
> Chaud comme l'enfer,
> Pur comme un ange,
> Fort comme l'amour ; "

but which, under the circumstances, would be valued
principally for its quantity.

The improvised cook looked about him for a coffee-
pot. He found nothing in his bag that would do.
But there was in mine a small tin pot which had re-
sided there from time immemorial. It was somewhat dented with age, and bore many signs of the
hardness of its lot, though its office was of a quite
amiable description. It carried about my smoked
glasses and sundry silk veils. I liked to have these
by me—though I personally never use them—because
they often came in conveniently to relieve from the
glare of the sun those tender-skinned representatives
of the fair sex who insist on not making sufficient
preparations to go over glaciers. The pot contained
also some cotton wadding, tintacks, pins, and such
like necessaries of hut life. With regret I poured
these forth upon a dry patch of ground, and committed the pot to the mercies—whatever they might
be—of the would-be cook.

Some time later our camping ground was wrapped
in a sheet of light. I looked round. My friend had
done wonders. He had scooped a nice square hole

in the snow and planted in it our lantern, in which he had stuck and lit one of our tapers. The light from the taper had suddenly flashed upon the scene through the transparent wall of snow. Then some of the coffee was poured into my tin pot, and this was placed on the top of the lantern and lumps of snow were heaped upon the coffee.

Then began the labours of Hercules. The snow in the pot melted very properly, but that which walled in the stove would do likewise. It either fell in and smothered the lantern below, or else fell from above and put out the taper.

All night long the cunning of the young engineer was kept devising means of meeting every fresh emergency. Anyhow, at every watch in the night I was kept supplied with a few mouthfuls of hot coffee.

So well did this suffice that, on striking our tents at eight o'clock—*façon de parler*, for we had between us but one dressing-gown to take off before revealing to an astonished world the effectiveness of our Burberrys—we gave no thought to the Rohrbachhaus, but made our way straight to the Wildstrubel, between the Raezli and Lämmern glaciers.

Once more the popular notion that to allow one's self to fall asleep on an open glacier is to court an awakening in the other world, had been effectually dispelled. Provided one is clad to perfection in weatherproof material, with chamois leather under-wear over the usual woollen undergarments, one need have no fear as long as the air is still and free from falling snow.

On the contrary, in a violent snowstorm and with a heavy wind, nothing but an actual place of shelter can afford sufficient protection. For all that some people will push their dread to the most ridiculous extremes. I met, not very long ago, a young German, an otherwise doughty lad, who, rather than spend the night in one of the extremely comfortable Concordia huts on the Aletsch glacier, preferred, after coming up on ski the whole way from the Loetschenthal, to reach Rieder Alp in an exhausted condition, at much greater risk than if he had stopped on the way.

It is reported by de Saussure that the dread with which the men hired by him in Chamounix to ascend Mont Blanc looked forward to the night which must unavoidably be spent on the glacier des Bossons, was the main difficulty he had to contend with in keeping up their *morale*. No sooner had they reached the spot marked out for pitching the tents, than they dug for themselves an underground recess and buried themselves therein, as though they expected a hail of bullets to pepper them all night. Yet, they had hardly been herded together for half an hour, when such a terrible epidemic of heat broke out among the huddled pack that they dribbled out one after another, saying they preferred a fair battle with the elements to such a process of extinction.

The history of the construction of Alpine huts enables us to trace the progress which public opinion has made since. The first huts were simply caves, walled in on the open side with a rough stone dyke, and on the floor of which was strewn some straw, while a few utensils and a stove lay about, all higgledy-piggledy, with some logs of fir or pine wood. They were dirty, damp dens.

Now, such ill-conditioned refuges have been given up as an absurd and rudimentary conception of our forefathers. They sought a well hidden away nook. We choose the most exposed spur of hill that is near our route. We build on high, preferring places exposed to the full fury of the blast, and we erect wooden houses that appear too fragile to resist the violent onset of the storm fiends. But such refuges as these are dry and airy, the snow has but little chance of choking them up. The light shining through the windows when a party is gathered therein after dark, is as a mast light on ships anchored at sea.

The stored-up wood keeps dry. The emergency provisions that a party may leave for the next—a party perhaps less favoured—do not rot away. And when the sun shining upon those lofty mansions lights up the yellow or brown pine wood, a sense of near comfort and of coming security pervades the weary traveller's breast and warms the cockles of his heart.

This progress has to be paid for in the form of a light tax levied upon the traveller to defray for the Swiss Alpine Club some portion of the expense incurred in keeping the huts in order and regularly supplying them with fire-wood. The original characteristic of the huts, which were intended to be mere emergency refuges open gratis to all, has somewhat suffered in this respect from the new policy. Visitors are now requested in most of them, by an appropriate notice, to deposit their contribution in a receptacle fastened to the wall. This may be the most convenient way of collecting the money due. But it means that sums of money—not inconsiderable in the opinion of any one badly in want—are left for rather long periods in uninhabited premises which are far from being inaccessible.

It has happened that cash-boxes have been rifled. A less objectionable way of managing this little piece of business is surely within the resources of civilisation. It is not justifiable that any other premium than wholesome exercise and natural beauty, should be held up as an inducement to make an excursion on the glaciers of Switzerland.

While here on the subject of huts, the awkward position which their great multiplication of late years entailed upon the British clubs, may be suitably laid before the reader. As the huts of the Swiss Alpine Club became more and more frequented, questions of preferential rights of admission came to the fore. It was obvious that non-Swiss clubs, able to grant terms of reciprocal admission to the Swiss, must obtain for their members, in the Swiss huts, preferential rights over Alpine clubs who were so by genuine profession and yet had no local habitation in the Alps or elsewhere in which they might hope to offer hospitality in their turn, as an acknowledgement of hospitality received.

Consequently, when notices were put up in the Swiss Alpine Club huts, which number now from seventy-five to eighty, showing what clubs enjoyed a right of admission on the score of reciprocity, the absence of any and every English club struck the eye. English visitors were then able to realise that they had been drawing benefit from the hospitality provided—for all and sundry, it is true—by a large body of private persons in Switzerland. In spite of every desire to remedy this situation by contributing to the expense of building and maintaining the Swiss huts, English climbers could not obtain a definite *locus standi*, for want of being able to come under a reciprocity clause. Even at present it would be idle to hope that English clubs may be quoted by name, beside the Swiss, French, German-Austrian, and Italian clubs. But the following arrangement was come to, on the initiative of English climbers, and with the concurrence of the Swiss Alpine Club:—

1. A committee was formed in London, of an administrative character, to serve as a rallying point for Englishmen who might wish to enter one of the sections of the Swiss Alpine Club. The members recruited in that fashion for the Swiss club formed an association of British members of the Swiss Alpine Club, which is recognised by the Swiss club, but has no corporate existence within that club.

2. The new association, which now numbers little less than 400 members, started a subscription with a view to providing the Swiss club with funds sufficient for the building of a first-class hut on the Klein Allalin Horn above Saas Fée, at the expense of £800. This hut was built by the care, and will

remain under the administration of, the Geneva
section of the Swiss Alpine Club. It was completed
and inaugurated this year (1912).

The Britannia hut deserves particular mention
in these pages, because it has been contributed to
by the ski-ing clubs of Great Britain, on account
of the first-rate opportunities it offers for ski tours
in the High Alps. It occupies a central position
in the Mischabel range which, from the top of
Monte Rosa to the glacier of Ried that rolls down
from the Balfrin to within 4 miles of St. Niklaus,
is one of the finest ski-ing fields of Switzerland.

The Strubel.

CHAPTER V

THE BERNESE OBERLAND FROM END TO END

The Oberland circuit—My appointment with Arnold Lunn—An
Anglo-Swiss piece of work—An unbelieving public—Switzer-
land and Britain—Geographical—Practical—We start from
Beatenberg—The Jungfrau ice-slabs—New Year's Day at
Kandersteg—In the Gasterenthal—On the Tschingelfirn—
Foehn-effects on the Petersgrat—The Telli glacier—The
Kippel bottle-race—A church door—Theodore Kalbermatten
—The Loetschen pass—Burnt socks—Roped ski-ing—The
Concordia breakfast-table—Why we did not ascend the
Jungfrau—The Concordia huts—The Grünhornlücke—On
snow "lips" and cornices—An afternoon snooze—The Fin-
steraarhorn hut—A guideless party—Ascent of the Finsteraar-
horn—Our next pass—A stranded runner—The Grimsel—
Home life at Guttannen—Our sleigh run to Meiringen—A
comparison of winter and summer work—Memories and
visions—Table of levels—How to form a caravan—The pay
of the men—Side-slip and back-slip—Future railway facilities.

HIS is the Oberland "circuit." We
left Beatenberg on December 31, 1908,
passed through Interlaken, went on to
Kandersteg, crossed the Petersgrat to
the top of the Loetschenthal, traversed
the Aletsch glacier between the Jungfrau
and the Concordia hut, ascended the
Finsteraarhorn, reached the Grimsel
hospice, and came back to Interlaken
and Beatenberg, where we were again
comfortably quartered on the night of
January 8, 1909.

This traverse was made into an event and marks a date in the history of Swiss mountaineering. The telegraph and news agencies announced it far and wide. It was the object of press articles and flattering references in most countries in which interest is taken in mountaineering feats. It has been lectured on, and related in periodicals over and over again.

The reception given to a trip of this kind obeys the laws of pictorial perspective. Maybe, however, shorn of the benevolent element so kindly contributed by the public, our expedition is still worth describing in its true relief, in the light of the impressions of the two explorers who carried it out.

This expedition, the first of its length at such altitudes at that time of the year, was an Anglo-Swiss piece of work. It was performed in company with Arnold Lunn.

We met by appointment at Beatenberg, which his father was then opening up for the first time as a winter station. Arnold Lunn is as keen a mountaineer as was ever born under the skies of Britain. His poetic and adventurous mind is endowed with an exceptional facility for imaging forth in words Alpine scenery, and for communicating to others the manly joy which overtakes him in such scenery. He has the soul of a propagandist and missionary. He is a striking example of how, with climbers, performance goes before propaganda, unless one would belong to those who are deservedly marked out as hangers-on to the exploits of others. There are only too many such loitering about the Alps nowadays.

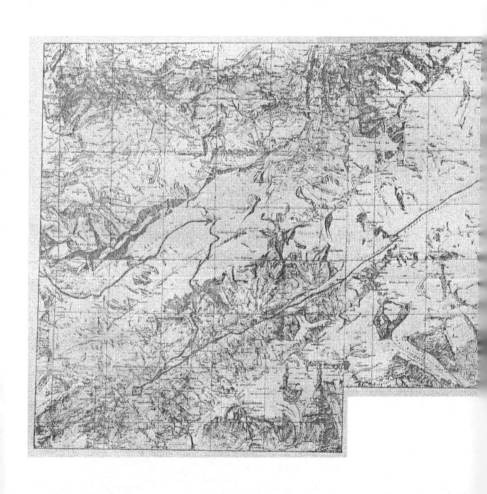

KANDERSTEG—FINSTERAARHORN—GRIMSEL.

(Reproduction made with authorisation of the Swiss Topographic Service, 26.8.12.)   To face p. 114.

Can there be a more noble spectacle than the
sight of one, who having met young with an
extremely serious accident in climbing, which to all
appearance, and according to cool reason, should
confine him to the part of an armchair propagandist and pen-wielding missionary, yields again
to the irresistible call of the Alps, and ascends the
Dent Blanche in spite of the lameness consequent
upon the accident in North Wales in which his
right leg was broken in two places, under such
conditions that it has continued ever since to be a
source of daily suffering?

Last winter, on the Eiger, battling with a terri-
fying snow and wind storm, my lame friend was
three times thrown out of his steps. He had with
him Maurice Crettex, one of the most powerful
rock and snow men, I believe, of the present day
among Swiss guides. The situation would have
been frantically impossible but for him. But what
a picture! Two men, side by side, one, all physical
strength and professional devotion to duty, the
other, all spiritual energy and moral force.

It is particularly gratifying that a Swiss and an
Englishman should have been united in showing
to ski-runners that the way across the Bernese
Oberland was open from end to end and that the
most magnificent mountain scenery that ever
wasted its sweetness upon the desert air was awaiting them. These were spectacles for which I was
quite prepared, having already moved, like many
of my country men, amid the glories of High Alp
winter scenery, ever since some of the sections of

the Swiss Alpine Club (that of Geneva leading
the way), had instituted for their members and
friends, the expeditions known under the name of
Grandes Courses d'hiver.

It is, however, one thing that the Swiss should
favour such expeditions, and quite another thing that
strangers to Switzerland should entertain the idea.
I understand that when the first accounts of my
winter ascents of the Aiguille du Chardonnet and
the Grand Combin were read, in London, in the
pages of the Alpine Ski Club Annual, there came
upon the lips of many competent readers a smile
which partly betokened admiration—which I certainly did not deserve—and, partly, incredulity—
which I certainly expected in some measure.

Even in Geneva I had at first some hesitation
in making known my Bagnes–Entremonts–Ferret
circuit.   When I did make up my mind to send
an extremely short and compendious notice to the
Journal de Genève, the editors let my scrap of
paper lie six weeks before they printed it.   It was
unkind of me to laugh in my sleeve while this
long pause lasted.   I did not fare much better
after my ascent of the Dent Blanche.   I slipped a
word about it into a local but widely read halfpenny
paper, to whose information people "in the know"
are wont not to attach much importance.   In fact,
some busybodies had already forestalled my note
with a few warning lines to the effect that any
attempt to cross in a consecutive trip the Pennine
Alps, in January, from Mont Blanc to the Simplon
pass, would be too hazardous to prove anything but

fatal. And here was a gentleman who not only had got from Bourg St. Pierre to Zermatt, but asseverated he had ascended the Dent Blanche.

Some of my colleagues in the Geneva section, desirous of protecting the good name of their club, and anxious to exonerate one of the older and more respected members from any charge of senile self-complacency, explained gravely that it was a printer's mistake, and that surely I had written Tête Blanche in my hastily scribbled manuscript note.

The reader must be told at this juncture that the Tête Blanche is an insignificant little bump of snow on the Col d'Hérens, of which those good colleagues of mine, with their knowledge of my climbing powers, could well trust themselves to say that I might have reached its summit, without putting too great a strain on my powers. Even now, another of my young disciples, Marcel Kurz, whose circuits on ski in the Bernina and Mischabel districts may be followed in two of the maps appended to this volume, writes me that he is pleased to hear of its approaching publication, because it may conduce to the enlightenment of disbelievers, across isolated specimens of whom he still occasionally comes.

Arnold Lunn, too, has met with ultra-sceptical folks, and a boastful trait has been read by some into his ardour.

For my part, I am content to look upon our mountaineering fellowship as a pleasant little incident in the history of Anglo-Swiss relations. These I much

take to heart. There is every reason in the world
wherefore they should be frequent, numerous, and
close. Sometimes, in the flush of after-dinner
speeches, I have spoken of the Swiss as the
navigators of the Alps and of the English as the
mountaineers of the sea. There is some similarity
in the risks incurred.

It would be a truism—in fact the repetition of a
truism—to say how English climbers of the middle
of the nineteenth century helped the Swiss in introducing into mountaineering the wholesome element
of risk. " On ne fait pas d'omelettes sans casser des
œufs."

It should not be hidden from the present generation of English climbers, however, that the
example of their forerunners has perhaps been more
thoroughly taken to heart in Switzerland than
among themselves. There is hardly a family or
friendly circle in Switzerland that does not count
one of its members in the ring of those whose life
was sacrificed for love of the Alps.

The motives for associating here Swiss and
English in my mind are not solely sporting. It
has hitherto been little realised how much Swiss
neutrality and national integrity are one of the
bulwarks of the freedom of Britain's movements in
Europe.

Every effort is being made to join Switzerland
more closely to the economic system of central
Europe. In a century in which economics are
considered to offer a more effective political weapon
than the open use of military force, the tighten-

ing of the ties of fellowship between two nations, neither of which can possibly aim at political encroachments upon the other, may usefully serve to counteract a less innocent set of tendencies. What with military roads, tunnels, and railways, the Alpine barrier between the Baltic and the Mediterranean is being worn very thin.

It needs, probably, no further insistence to show that sentimental Anglo-Swiss relations may be attended by practical consequences of some immediate utility. In this network of associations an important function devolves upon winter mountaineering. The English have no sporting winter. They have already, in ·large numbers, adopted the Swiss winter as what they want to supply home deficiencies. May this continue and an ever wider bridge of Swiss and British ski be thrown over the Channel. That this book, among others, might serve this purpose was one of the motives that impelled the writer when he put together, for publication in England, such accounts as that which follows.

At first sight, the title I have given to this chapter may appear exaggerated. But it will not bear out any such unfavourable construction, if the reader will charitably recollect that he has already travelled with me from the western extremity of the Bernese Alps, visiting from end to end the Diablerets, Wildhorn, and Wildstrubel range, as a prelude to this excursion beyond the Gemmi to the east.

Geographically and technically the euphemistic

title of this chapter is not without excuse. The
Oberland is theoretically taken to include not only
a western, but also an eastern wing, on to the
Galenstock and Dammastock. Popularly, the name
Oberland is understood to apply to the great range
which is cut off on the east by the Grimsel and
Haslithal, on the west by the Gemmi and Kan-
derthal. Classical literature agrees with the popular definition, the main point about which is, for
ski-runners, that between those two depressions
there is no pass that does not lead across glaciers.

The Oberland shows, between its extreme points,
two parallel rows of peaks. The northern row overlooks the lakes of Thun and Brienz. The southern
row overlooks the valleys of Loetsch and of Goms
(in French Conches), leading up to the Furka pass.
Of those parallel rows the northernmost, facing
somewhat to the west, comprises the Blumlisalp
and the Lauterbrunner Breithorn. The southern-
most, drawing to the east, culminates in the Bietschhorn and Aletschhorn, and includes the summits
which, under the names of Wannehorn, Galmihorn,
&c., look down upon the glaciers of Fiesch and
Oberaar, while the northern row, curving round the
Lauterbrunnen Valley from the Breithorn, is crowned
by that magnificent cluster overlooking both Schei-
deggs : the Jungfrau, Mönch, Eiger, Wetterhorn,
&c., with the Schreckhorn and Finsteraarhorn somewhat in the rear.

Between those two rows a high glacial basin takes
the form of an elongated trough. From distance
to distance this trough shows transversal lips (cross-

bars or threshholds, if one so prefers to style them), which are the upper Tschingel glacier with the Mutthorn hut (9,700 feet), the Loetschenlücke, with the Egon von Steiger hut (10,515 feet), the Grünhornlücke, between the Jungfraufirn and the glacier of Fiesch (10,840 feet), and at length the Oberaarjoch (10,800 feet), between the Oberaarhorn to the north and the Oberaar-Rothhorn to the south. One sees from the figures quoted that those glacier passes all reach to an altitude exceeding 9,000 feet. The top of the arc—to speak like Euclid—would pass over the Finsteraarhorn at an altitude of 14,035 feet.

This high level is, in the opinion of Sir Martin Conway, who followed it in his journey through the Alps from end to end, the very finest snow-field in the Alps. It passes at the head of the greatest ice stream, and is sufficiently remote from the Italian border to escape the unfavourable influence which the Rhaetic, Lepontine, and Pennine faces of the Alps have to endure from the hot atmospheric currents and inordinately violent action of the sun.

"Two things were necessary for the success of this trip," says Arnold Lunn in one of his printed accounts; "good weather and immunity from accidents. We could reduce the chances of accidents to a minimum by a careful scrutiny of our kit, and we could reasonably expect fair play from the weather by judiciously choosing the moment to begin our attack, though, of course, the weather is always the most fickle factor in determining the success of an expedition.

"As regards kit, I carried two pairs of gloves, one made of reindeer skin lined with sealskin, the other a thick pair of woollen gloves, a woollen scarf, a silk scarf, and a woollen helmet. A spare suit of underclothing and two pairs of stockings completed the list of extra clothing. I wore laupar boots and goat's-hair socks on my feet, with a pair of crampons in my sack for rock and ice-climbing. And here, incidentally, let me remark that the ordinary crampon-nails which are fixed into the sole of the boot soon spoil laupars. The only practical kind are those which are sold in summer to be strapped on under the boots.

"I think I have at last found the ideal ski-binding for mountain work. It is made by a Geneva firm, and was given me by Professor Roget. It never gave any trouble; it was strong and tough. It did not vary in tightness with the tempera-ture, and, most important of all, it could be put on and taken off at a moment's notice. This is really essential, as one may meet with short stretches on which it pays to 'take up one's ski and walk.'

"I tried, for the first time, a pair of sealskins, and found them answer admirably. They reduced the labour of climbing by 20 per cent., weighed hardly anything, and could be taken on and off without any trouble. An extra ski-tip, a pair of Canadian rackets, 'climber's guides,' maps, &c., completed our kit."

My intention was to use Kandersteg as a start-ing-point, to land on the high level, at 9,000

KANDER GLACIER.

feet, by means of the Kander glacier gradient, to go
down to Kippel, in the Loetschenthal, by the Petersgrat; to pass through the Loetschenlücke, to drop
thence into the basin formed by the Aletsch *névés*
(the Jungfraufirn and Ewig Schneefeld of German
maps); to rise again to the Grünhornlücke, to skid
down upon the *firn* of the Fiesch glacier, to over-
top this network of ice-mountains by the ascent
of the Finsteraarhorn, to go round the Finsteraarhorn group on its south side, to return to the north
as far as the Oberaarjoch, to descend the Oberaar
glacier to the Grimsel hospice, to follow thence
the posting road and to enter Guttannen as knights-
errant, mounted and spurred—that is, in our case,
on trusty ski and shod with nailed boots, the attire
in which we would leave Kandersteg.

Thanks to the absence of any unpleasant incident, thanks also to a most obligingly long spell
of unbroken weather, the precautions we had taken
enabled me and my companions to carry out this
programme without interruption and without incon-
venience. The "stripling," Mr. Arnold Lunn, gave
proof of remarkable staying powers. Though our
Bernese porters seemed at first to believe that they
were being "let in" for harum-scarum adventures,
by which they discreetly hoped the party might be
brought to a standstill after a few hours' march,
before it could run its head, beyond hope of escape,
into the dangers of this raid, they laid no visible
claim to being wiser than ourselves. They proved
themselves to be good and reliable fellows to the
end, and came out of their trials with beaming coun-

tenances, grateful for the lessons they had received in High Alp ski-running.

We got into training at Beatenberg, where a snow-fall delayed our start for three days, if three days spent on the running slopes above Beatenberg may be looked upon as a delay. Then, one morning, the sun, bursting through the snow clouds, showed us the great peaks of the Oberland looking down on a scene newly painted white. Our hopes rose high, and making our rucksacks proportionately heavy, we skied down to Interlaken, losing a bottle of whisky on the way. Carefully laid on the top of my pack, with its nozzle looking out upon the world, it flew out, on Arnold's calling a sudden halt, and broke its nose against the wall by the roadside. Thus was our expedition christened straight away, as a launched ship that leaves the stocks.

On reaching Kandersteg, the gossamer banner of ice-dust blowing off the Blumlisalp showed plainly enough that the gale from the north, which had brought the fine weather, was still in full swing. My sympathy went out to any young men who might be then battling up there with the raging wind, for at Christmas and New Year's tide the Alpine huts are much visited by holiday-makers. Indeed, I saw later from an account published in the Swiss periodical *Ski*, by Mr. Tauern, and by Mr. Schloss in the Alpine Ski Club Annual, that those gentlemen were actually at the time on the Aletschfirn. They had hoped to ascend the Jung-frau. Under the circumstances the prospect lost its charm.

As I write, the Jungfrau has not yet been ascended in winter. The Swiss papers gave out last year that my young friend Fritz Pfeiffer had succeeded in reaching the top. It was a misapprehension. Within two hundred yards of the ice-cap that crowns the Jungfrau, Mr. Pfeiffer, who was accompanying an officer of the St. Gothard troops, was compelled to fall back before the heap of slabs of solid ice, with which the combined action of wind and sun had strewn the way. On these the two distinguished mountaineers were unable to gain footing. The slabs slipped away from under their feet, or bore them down in such a manner that they could not have had better toboggans. Toboggans, however, were not the thing wanted, nor even such trays or pieces of board as children are fond of using, for the sake of amusement, in sliding down grass slopes nearer home.

The formation of these ice-slabs on exposed summits of suitable shape opens up an interesting, and as yet unsolved, question in the history of natural phenomena. What clearly happens is this. Snow, driven by a tearing wind, falls against an ice buttress. Then the sun shines with all its winter power upon the snow that sticks to the rugged ice. Exposed to the action of two physical agents of great force, namely, to the heat produced by the sun and to the impetus of the wind sweeping now with perhaps still greater violence across a clear sky, the amorphous but plastic mass is cut up and divided by a process which may be compared, though the analogy is merely superficial, to what happens to dough in an oven when a hot blast is driven through it. The dried-up dough breaks up into flakes.

When I first came across that winter phenomenon —I have never met with it in summer—I was led to compare those piled-up ice-slabs to the stone slabs of like shape and size which lie on the bare crests of so many mountains. The supposition lies near that these, too, may be due to some combined action of pre-existent heat and supervening wind impetus, in those geological ages when we have a fancy for imagining that the still plastic earth-crust was blown about in huge billows by the liquid and aerial elements.

Be this as it may, I hope I may never be uncharitable enough to desire, for ski-ing parties, an encounter with those ice-slab pyramids.

The caretaker who in winter keeps watch over the Schwarenbach Hotel had just come down to join in the New Year festivities. He announced that there was on the heights a fresh layer of snow 30 inches deep. Stoller, a guide of some reputation, whose advice we applied for, was of opinion that we should put off our departure till the 2nd of January. The advice might be sound, but I did not like it because I knew how badly the men I might be about to engage were likely to spend their time on New Year's Day. As a matter of fact, when we did enter the Gasternthal, we found nothing like the amount of snow that we were told would impede our way. From Stoller, who had just returned from a week's engagement to teach the rudiments of ski-ing to a Swiss club, we heard that all guides with first-class certificates were away climbing, and that he, having only just returned, would not be available. We engaged three men, under his advice and under that of Egger, for whom Arnold Lunn had a valuable letter of introduction from his father. One of these men had a guide's certificate, the other two were porters.

I took three men because I wanted to carry sufficient commissariat for six days, which the raid was supposed to last, with a margin in case of a check being put on our progress by a change in the weather or some accident that could not be foreseen. I hoped to force my way through without touching any inhabited spot before we reached Guttannen. We went down to Kippel, because our progress was so smooth and easy that it would have been a pity to sleep in a chalet at Guggi just for the pleasure of not stopping in a decent hotel.

None of our men had been beyond the Aletsch glacier. This I did not mind, having previously gone over the whole route in summer. Provided those men carried their loads from hut to hut, we should be satisfied.

Arnold Lunn says in the *Isis* that we arrived in Kandersteg just in time for a fancy dress ball, and aroused considerable curiosity as to what we were supposed to represent. At dinner he sat next to a man who, lost to all sense of local colour, had come dressed as a nigger minstrel. This was on New Year's Eve.

Next day we pottered round Kandersteg, one of us receiving much useful advice as to how to fix on his ski, from a lady who was under the quite pardonable impression that she was addressing a novice, while the other was considered enough of an expert to instruct another lady who had the good taste not to be so sure of her own knowledge.

We left Kandersteg on the morning of January 2nd. As usual in those early starts, we had plenty of time, the five of us, to try and find out of what stuff each and every member of the party was made. It was my first expedition with Arnold Lunn. I was entitled to think he would take my measure as curiously as I was about to take his. Two of our men turned out to be quite satisfactory, but the third was destined to become the butt of our satire I am not prepared to say that he had spent New Year's Day in those excesses which I dreaded, because I have since been told by old Egger that Adolf—as we shall agree to call him—was in bad health when he undertook to serve us. Whatever might be the cause, whether excusable or not, he showed himself throughout in the colours in which he is painted—maybe somewhat to the amusement of our readers—by Arnold Lunn and myself.

Those who mountaineer for sport are very much like schoolboys, or they become schoolboys for the nonce. The printed records of mountaineering are to a great extent records of the kind of humour that overgrown and elderly boys—if I may so describe those of us who have gone through public school-life and wish to preserve some of its characteristics in a sphere where these may be as harmless to others as comforting to themselves— would be expected to cultivate.

For us, in the course of a constant fellowship of seven days, Adolf soon represented quite a definite and rather objectionable specimen of the human kind. We found him lazy, slow, clumsy, ever ready to take undue advantage. Some one, who had evidently made a close study of political types, dubbed him the Socialist, and the title stuck. For my part, anxious to secure for him a place among types ranking in a higher class, I placed him, under the name of Thersites, in a gallery of classical portraits in which I allotted to Arnold the part of fiery Achilles, and to myself that of the worldly-wise and cunningly cautious Ulysses.

Our course lay up the Gasternthal, one of the wildest and most impressive valleys in the Alps, utterly desolate in summer. From its rugged floor rise some of the sternest precipices in Switzerland. On our way we had plenty of time to examine the superstructure of the shafts which were then being driven through the floor of the valley to ascertain the depth of the gravel-bed that formed it. Our readers may remember that, in 1908, the Italian workmen engaged in excavations on the north front of the Loetschberg tunnel were suddenly overwhelmed by an inrush of water, gravel, and mud. The progress of the boring was stopped till it could be known to what extent it would be necessary to divert the tunnel, in order to keep in hard rock.

It is a bit of a reflection upon the forethought of engineers—and geologists—that, before working their way from beneath across Gasternthal, they had not sunk that shaft which was now to supply them with an information that would still be opportune from the engineer's point of view, but which was belated in regard to safeguarding human life.

Three hours after starting, we reached a rustic *café*, or summer restaurant, which we discovered it was Adolf's summer occupation to preside over. It was a pretty place with a fenced orchard about it, whose trees now stood out barely from amid the coverlet of snow which contributed to enhance the attractiveness of the spot. But a dreadful doubt crossed our mind. Was Adolf a *bona-fide* mountaineer or was he a professional tavern keeper?

On reaching the doorstep of his property, he angrily dropped to the ground his burden, produced the key of his cellar, and contrived to give us the impression that he expected us to call a halt of some duration and indulge in the delights of his Capua. We were suddenly confronted with the thought of the temptation put by Circe before wary Ulysses and his simple-hearted companions. Thersites, as a mental picture, was outdone. The vision conjured up before us was that of five days to be spent in plenty in this winter-bound Abbey of Thelema. We would empty the larders. We would clear the bottle shelves. We would rifle the cigar boxes, under the watchful, but encouraging eye of this male Circe, who would fill his pockets with sweet-scented coin, instead of bruising his shoulders

GASTERNTHAL.

To face p. 136.

any longer with that dreadful pack. We commend the trick to those who may have the face to play it on the public. Nothing is easier. Switzerland is full of those concealed Canaans flowing with milk and honey.

Shortly after leaving Adolf's pavilion, a bend in the valley disclosed the ice-fall of the Tschingel glacier. The moraine up which we had to pass came into sight. It was three in the afternoon—and we had distributed some of Adolf's packages amongst the other two guides—before we caught our first glimpse of the sun, which flashed out triumphantly behind the Hockehhorn, only to disappear in a few minutes past the Balmhorn. A steep slope of snow led from the moraine to the glacier.

Out of laziness, we did not fix up our ski with carrying straps. We might have paid dearly for the mistake, as a sharp wind caught us half-way across, and a dropped ski would have taken hours to recover. It is always wise to have at hand in one's pockets the short straps which serve to tie together the ski at each extremity, and to make use of them whenever one has to carry ski across an unskiable piece of ground. It is also better to be provided with ski-slings wherewith to carry them across both shoulders. The wind is the ski-runner's treacherous enemy. When you are on your ski it may drive you out of your direction, and when you carry your ski it may try to wrench them from you and blow you off your balance by weighing upon them.

The last three hours of our walk lay along the

névé of the Tschingel glacier, a snow valley bounded
on the north by the cliffs of the Blümlisalp, on the
south by the gently rising Petersgrat.

" The last lingering rays," writes Arnold Lunn,
" faded from the snows, but the sunset was soon
followed by the rise of the full moon, a moon undreamt of in our English skies, so bright that I
read with ease a page of my note-book. Those who
have only seen her ' hurrying with unhandsome
thrift of silver ' over English landscapes have little
idea of her real beauty. Before we reached the hut
we had been climbing fourteen hours uphill, loaded
with heavy sacks. Yet such was the mysterious
fascination of the moonlit snows that we made no
attempt to hurry. Again and again we stopped, lost
in silent wonder.

" Straight ahead, the Jungfrau, backed by the
slender cone of the Eiger, rose above a sea of
shadows. The moonlight slept on her snowy
terraces, steeping in silentness her cliffs and
glaciers, and revealed the whole as a living monu-
ment of incarnate light. A hut stood in a *cirque*
of snow. Here the wind had played strange havoc,
torturing the billows and cornices into fantastic
shapes. Anything more weirdly beautiful than the
glancing sheen of this hollow I cannot conceive.
Its colour could only be compared, if at all, to the
fiery blue of Capri's grotto."

The writer of the above lines, whom we shall not
tire of quoting in this chapter, does not overpaint
the picture. What could be more beautiful, more
entrancing, than the Tschingel terrace, by moon-

light, in the middle of winter? Standing on a balcony little less than 10,000 feet high, we were able to read our maps, after ten o'clock at night, as plainly as at noonday.

To the furrowed and broken ribs of the Blümlisalp clung several small glaciers, suspended in the couloirs like swallows' nests in the eaves of a ruined castle. The sharp pyramid of the Eiger shone beyond the white cupolas of the airy Jungfrau, as though they had been the distant walls and minarets of an Oriental city. The snows about us were alive with a smooth and soft radiance. The sky was transparent, and as yet hung about with light veils. Silver clouds fluttered about the peaks, and when they floated into the moonlight from behind them, they flashed forth like fishes when the sun plays upon their scales. Layers of purple and crimson haze rested upon one another along the horizon. The play of light and shade upon the black patches and white spots of the visible world showed them, according to whither you looked, wreathed in smiles or puckered up in frowns. Buttresses, cliffs, abysses swam in a bluish mist, in which the twinkling rays of a million stars danced as sparkling dust.

It is a law of this world that what is unbecoming —τα ου δεοντα of Greek comedy—must ever come to underline and show off the most beautiful sights by giving them a contradictory background. For Arnold and myself, the last three hours of that day were spent on one of the most beautiful walks we can remember. But Adolf had been completely knocked up long before. During the self-same last

three hours he experienced a great desire for sleep,
and the burden of his refrain was not, " How grand!
How beautiful!" but "Very, very tired!" Sometimes he dozed; sometimes he half uttered swear-
words, which issued from his throat like stones
rattling down a mountain gully. I had to send one
of the other men to his help. Whether we shouted
to him Thersites or Circe, or the Socialist, he
cared not. What went to his heart, and as it
were broke his wind, was that we had left his tea-
house far behind and would not take him back across
the beloved threshold. A miserable Alpine hut
awaited his tottering footsteps. He staggered
through the doorway and collapsed on the mattresses, sleeping at last when to sleep was decent.
What was it to him that every curve in the swelling
snows, every crag and buttress of the Blümlisalp
cliffs was lit up by the mellow rays of the mountain
moon ?

Of the night spent in the Mutthorn hut nothing
need be said, except that it seemed to us a perfect
night. At 5.30 the alarum went off, and, if Arnold
Lunn's story be trusted—and it must be, in the
absence of any other accountable person, as I was
asleep at that moment—the ring of the bell was
accompanied by an ill-sounding German epithet.
A guide stumbled to the door, threw it open, and
muttered in more parliamentary language : " Abscheu-
liches Wetter." Arnold says—and I must trust him
in this again, for I was still asleep—that a sense
of sickening disappointment, such as climbers know
so well, fell upon the waking inmates of the hut,

a definition which must be taken to exclude Adolf
and myself. Arnold stepped outside and discovered
heavy grey clouds blowing up from behind the Eiger,
sniffed a gust of south-westerly wind, laid his finger
on sticky snow, and, in thus feeling the pulse of the
weather, became aware of a high temperature.

He says : " We sulkily despatched our breakfast
and started up the slope leading towards the Petersgrat. Suddenly Professor Roget caught sight,
through a gap beyond the Blümlisalp, of the still
lake of fog hanging quite undisturbed over the plain
of Switzerland and above lake Thun. I should like
to say that he gave a cry of surprise, but, alas ! the
professor has his emotions under strict control, and
was content to rapidly communicate to us his
analysis of the apparent bad weather. These un-
auspicious phenomena were merely local disturb-
ances, which would vanish after dawn. The westerly
breeze was only a glacier wind, the grey clouds only
the effect of the intense solar heat collected the day
before and blending throughout the night with the
cold air from the snows. As long as the *Nebelmeer*
remained undisturbed, no bad weather need be
feared. Every sign of evil actually vanished an
hour after sunrise."

On the Petersgrat we could fancy ourselves on the
top of the globe. We were standing on the highest
point of a curved surface, shaped like a balloon, and
on all sides it seemed to fall away into immensity.
Beyond, rose in gigantic outline the summits of the
Alps and, still further, in long sinuous lines curving
in and out of sight, the Jura, the Vosges, and all

that distant girdle that hangs loosely about the out-
skirts of Switzerland. The winter fog filled up the
intervals. Afar, there was not a breath of wind,
not a whirl in the air.

The phenomenon that alarmed my party was that
which is well known under the name of *Foehn*, a
phenomenon which may assume almost any dimensions, sometimes general enough to embrace the
whole of the Alps, and sometimes so closely circum-
scribed that you might almost compare it to the
motion in the air produced by a small top spinning
round on the palm of your hand.

The phenomenon is as follows : Masses of air of
varying density and temperature are pushed up the
Alps and are dropped down, as it were, upon the
other side. Or else, as this morning on the Peters-
gat, it is a layer of hot dry air formed aloft that
forces its way down, in corkscrew fashion, on a given
spot, through the nether air.

With us the phenomenon lasted an hour and was
as a water spout in the middle of a still ocean. The
universal quietude of the elements impressed itself
again upon the spot on which we stood, doubting,
like Thomas, but ready to believe, if a sign would but
be given. By 8.30 the sun gilded gloriously the
whole Pennine range, towards which our eyes were
eagerly turned.

As we reached the sky-line, that distant host of
old friends greeted us beyond the morning shadows,
but what held us most was the wonderful pyramid
of the Bietschhorn. The sharp-shouldered giant,
sprinkled with snow from head to foot, through

which showed his jet-black armour, stood forth before us, as within reach of the hand, strangely resembling the view of the Weisshorn from above Randa, but how much grander in his winter cloak with jewel-like crystals!

This second day was to be a day spent in idling down glacier slopes and in lounging above the forest zone of the Loetschenthal. We knew now that we could count on the sun till its proper time for setting in the evening. We knew that on his decline and fall the moon would take his place, as the night policeman succeeds the day policeman upon the common beat. The winter God was full of gentleman-like consideration. The rules of meteorology might have been purely astronomical and mathematical for any chances we might see of their being upset by the weather fiend.

The snow was hard and crusted as we entered upon the southern slopes of the Petersgrat. After forty minutes running, or thereabouts, the guides advised us to take off our ski while we descended the steep bits on the Telli glacier. The fact is that those men were not quite sure of their ground. I asked the party to proceed in close formation and to move with studied care till we should reach the bottom of the Telli glacier, considering that it would be wiser to cope with any difficulties it might put in our way than to ski down the Faffleralp, as to whose condition in winter I had not the faintest indication. The ordinary summer route might prove dangerous from avalanches. On the Telli glacier, the hardness and comparative thinness of the snow layer cemented to the ice, allowed of crevasses and depressions being easily recognised. It would be a piece of summer mountaineering in midwinter, and to this, for safety's sake, there would be no valid objection.

I kept my people close in, to the eastern edge of the glacier, so as to pass under the buttress on which were supported the masses of snow over which I would not ski. The descent of the deep gully proved the right solution to our difficulty and procured for us for some twenty minutes the distinct pleasure of being thoroughly occupied with a serious job.

A run over some extremely broken ground, then some cuts and capers in a wood led us to a chalet, where we decided to have a feed and a rest.

"This confession," says Arnold Lunn, "lays us open to the scorn of those who imagine that mountaineering is a kind of game, the object of which is to spend the minimum of time on a peak consistent with reaching its summit. Our party fortunately belonged to the leisurely school that combines a fondness for wise passiveness with a strong dislike to reach one's destination before sunset.

"Thus understood, mountaineering on ski is the purest of all sports. The competitive and record-breaking elements are entirely eliminated. Those who go up to the hills on ski are then actuated by the most elemental motives, the desire to explore the mountains in the most beautiful of all their aspects, and to enjoy the most inspired motion known to man.

"To me the ideal form of ski-ing is cross-country mountaineering. One thus approaches nearest to the methods of the pioneers to whom mountaineering meant the exploration of great ranges, not the exhausting of all possible climbs from one small centre. Nothing is more delightful than to penetrate into the remote Alpine valleys in the winter months. The parasite population that thrives in summer on the tourist industry has disappeared. One meets the genuine peasant, 'the rough athletic labourer wrestling with nature for his immediate wants.'

"Those who travel first class and stop in the best hotels do not know the real Switzerland. It is in the third-class carriages and small inns that one sees the most characteristic types. Nothing is more enjoyable than to escape for ten days from conventionality and dress clothes, wandering, kit on one's back, from club hut to club hut, and descending at rare intervals to remote recesses in winter-bound valleys."

The conclusion of this is that neither of us could describe in strenuous language the lazy afternoon we spent on the upper fringe of the woods above Blatten and Ried. We had a quiet repast, smoked our pipes, or cigars—and watched the shadows creeping up the Loetschenlücke. Having heaps of time, we sailed down to Kippel, as merry as finches, piping like blackbirds, and as fresh as new-laid eggs. Would we have been in such a happy predicament if we had not been on narrow boards about six and a half feet long and half as many inches broad, of Norwegian origin, which were used primarily as a means of crossing deep snow, and have lately been adopted as an aid to winter mountaineering?

The hotel we landed at was quite an ordinary eating

and sleeping house of the ugly type which too often disfigures Swiss villages. How is it that dwellers in the Alps who, when left to themselves, show such good taste in the plainness of their dwellings and in their primitive church architecture, are, when they build for townspeople, such utter strangers to the most spontaneous suggestions of the artistic instinct?

At table we chanced to have as neighbours three members of the Swiss Alpine Club, whose native language was the Germanic. They were on their way from the Grimsel and had just completed that section of our route upon which we were to enter on the morrow. We sat with them after dinner, and here fiery Achilles behaved most wisely. With high hopes he went quietly to bed at a reasonable hour. Then Ulysses, seeing his opportunity, thought he would like to unbend for a while. He sat up with the Swiss party and sacrificed to good fellowship a few hours of rest and the contents of a few fragile flagons.

As midnight came on, the moon suddenly peeped indiscreetly upon the carouse, showing through the casement a seductive vista of most beautifully slanting slopes round the foot of which roared the river Lonza. Cunning Ulysses, beside himself with a naughty idea, sent the empty bottles flying through the window. Immediately the blood of the young Swiss was up. They rose, strapped on their ski in a trice, and down they went along the slope to the bank of the Lonza. The bottles were by then floating on the swirl of the stream. But, in the case of each pursuer, a timely Christiania swing brought him round up the bank again. There was a swish, a spray of snow, and three young men were saved to fight again for their country.

On returning to the hotel, they and I found a jolly old villain in possession of the tap-room. He was in the early stages of inebriation. Seeing from the costumes of the party that he had to do with town-bred mountaineers only, he drew from the depths of his imagination the longest bow that was ever harboured by a genuine mountaineer in his armoury. With him the humour was transparent. But it is not always so, unfortunately. Some of the Swiss peasantry, brought into contact with the foreign *clientèle*, are in the habit of being so pampered by sentimental, gullible people that they quite overstep the bounds of any liberty that may be permissible in resenting such treatment.

On the whole, the winter life led in the high Swiss valleys is not altogether wholesome. When they are visited in summer, the people are seen in the busiest time and appear in the most favourable light. The domestic establishments of the hotels, and the few individuals who benefit from the presence of strangers, such as mule drivers, casual dealers in cut flowers, in carved bears and rock crystals, are merely para-sitic and as temporary features in the landscape as those whose passage called them into being.

The evils inherent to winter seclusion are more serious. This old man was an example, for he could be seen there day after day, spending his time in idle talk and throwing into the till his earnings of last season.

But stop: is Ulysses acting up to his reputation

for wariness in moralising at the present moment to a weaker brother's detriment? Has he forgotten that on the next day, Monday, January 4th, the little company turned out into the night at six o'clock without him? Was it a fair excuse, that, on the eve, he had engaged Theodore Kalbermatten to carry his kit for him to the next hut?

Having once more sworn allegiance to his usual beverage, milk, the best friend of the young and the old, he marched out last, but in good order, to join the troop over which he held command. As the dawn broke he found them waiting for him before a church in the Upper Loetschenthal, built six hundred years ago. Arnold had time to examine it. He says:—

" The church door was carved by the hand of some long-forgotten genius, carved with a delicacy of execution surprising in this remote corner of the Alps. We stopped for breakfast in some cheese-making chalets high up in the valley. Here we exchanged some remarks on cows and kindred subjects and gently chaffed the cheese-makers on the proverbially high stature of the men of Ried. But one realised throughout the barrier which one could never pass. We could form little or no conception of the world as seen through their eyes. To them these mountains must seem a waste by-product, an inexplicable freak on the part of the Creator. They regarded us and our ski with that amused tolerance that everyone extends to those idiosyncrasies which are not personally annoying.

" This rugged conservatism is nowhere so accentuated as among those who are shut off by mountain barriers from the 'sick, hurry, and divided aims' of modern life. Theirs is the spirit so gently satirised in Utopia. These things they say pleased our forefathers and ancestors: would God we might be as witty and wise!

"For six hundred years their forefathers had worshipped in the little church we had passed, sheltered by the hills from all breath of modern scepticism, apparently undisturbed by the thought that beyond them existed spirits who recklessly doubted the priest's control over the economy of nature in such modest details as harvest rains. The Loetschenthal still possesses the strange pathetic beauty of those secluded Catholic valleys whose inhabitants seem to live a life as old as the hills themselves, and in which one poor priest and one little church stand forth as the only help, the only symbol of the world outside, and of ages not absolutely prehistoric."

Arnold Lunn relates that after leaving the chalets he had an amusing talk with Theodore Kalbermatten, whom I had engaged to carry my sack up to the club hut. A fine-looking fellow, he showed a touch of that not ungraceful swagger which one notices in many guides and in which Lunn rightly sees nothing more than the unsophisticated pride that humble and well-meaning men take in the achievement of good work. But business is business. Lunn says very wittily that the conversation concluded with the inevitable production of a card, coupled with the caution that, though there were many Kalbermattens, there was but one Theodore Kalbermatten.

Anyhow, we were soon great friends with Theodore. The day was indeed long enough—like the glacier on which we were wandering—to make and undo friendships several times over. Circumstances lent themselves so well to mere strolling—think what it is to be able to cross the Bernese Oberland without once having one's foot brought up against a stone— that we pressed our pace no more on this third day than on the preceding. We might have been Egyptian sages walking up and down in conversation outside the porticoes of Thebes with the hundred gates. Had we been told that what we stirred up with our ski were the burning sands of Africa which we mistook for Alpine snow, because our eyes were under the spell of *mirage*, it would have been ungracious on our part to pretend to know better, so much did we long for the coolness of the evening, for sea breezes and the dew at dusk, as Arabs might, returning upon their tired steeds to the secrecy of the oasis, after a raid in the desert.

All said and done, we found that we had spent twelve hours in reaching the summit of the Loetschenlücke pass. Arnold's poetic gift found at every step fresh sustenance. He had discovered the *beau ideal* of a pass. " It was," he says, " the only opening at the head of the valley, visible, with the whole length of the glacier, during the entire day. For twelve hours a little gap backed by blue sky told of a wonderful new world that we should see from the summit. Above us we caught sight of our goal, the Egon von Steiger hut, bearing the name of a Swiss climber who perished on the Doldenhorn, and built in his memory. This is the real ungrudging spirit of mountain lovers, the attitude which Mummery sums up so well. ' The great mountains,' he writes, ' sometimes demand a sacrifice, but the true mountaineer would not forego their worship even though he knew himself to be the destined victim.'

" We had the whole day," says Lunn, " to reach the hut, and without being lazy, were wise enough not to hurry, and, indeed, there was no temptation to rush on. The time was all too short to take in the wonders of the Anen glacier on our left, the stern beauty of the Sattelhorn cliffs on our right. Slowly the distant ranges climbed higher into the sky. Peacefully the morning merged into the afternoon, and the afternoon into the evening. We paused below the final slope to watch the glow creeping down the snows of Mont Blanc. Even the guides were impressed by the strange stillness, as—

> ' Light and sound ebbed from the earth,
> Like the tide of the full and weary sea,
> To the depths of its own tranquillity.'

" I shall never forget the tantalising suspense of that last slope. For twelve hours a little strip of blue behind the sky-line had been an earnest of the revelation that was awaiting us. For some six hours we had been faced by this same long slope in front and above. Now only a few yards remained. We took them at a rush. At sunset exactly, the sky-line was beneath our feet and in one moment were set forth before us, backed by the Finsteraarhorn, the ' urns of the silent snow ' from which the

greatest of all the Alpine glaciers draws its strength.
The rays of the risen moon mingled with the ebbing
twilight and lent an atmosphere of mystery to our
surroundings. For the moment we were no longer
of the earth earthly, for the moment the Loetschenlücke became a magic casement opening into perilous
snows ' mid faery lands forlorn.'

" Thus what, seen from a distance, was obtrusively
—almost offensively—a pass, wore a peculiar fascination for that very reason. It grew upon the
imagination with the magic of those corners one
has only turned in one's dreams."

Like the historic gap between the Mönch and
Jungfrau, it led to the solitudes of the Aletsch,
which Lunn had never seen save as a white streak
from distant ranges. Like all good mountaineers,
who have usefully wasted hours over a map in keen
and eager anticipation, he now could dwell with
gladness upon the reality of the mental picture
elaborated long ago, while contemplating certain
white spaces on an old copy of the Siegfried map.

But the inevitable anti-climax that dogs the flight
of all poets was awaiting us. " On this occasion it
took the form of the club hut stove, and a more
effective bathos has never been devised. Amongst
the torments of the damned I am sure the smoking
stove holds a proud place." Some of last summer's
moisture had remained in the pipe. Our fire might
have been of green wood and wrung from us copious
tears.

" The guides for the space of some half-hour,
wrestled and fought and prayed, Kalbermatten

meanwhile keeping up a running conversation with his favourite saint. Adolf, with a wonderful sense of the fitness of things, chose the moment when supper was on the table to put in a belated appearance. His contribution to the evening's work was a successful attempt to burn my thick socks," writes Lunn, righteously indignant.

The temperature outside the hut was 8° Centigrade under zero on arriving and, very naturally, somewhat colder inside. At the Mutthorn hut we had noted 9° Centigrade under zero in the evening and 10° in the morning.

Our expedition unfolded itself from day to day with the monotony and exactitude of a scroll. On the 5th, by seven o'clock, an hour before sunrise, we were again on the slide eastwards. The lie of the land was nasty. Most of us turned a somersault or two, a performance at which those will not be astonished who have come down in summer from the Egon von Steiger hut to the Gross-Aletsch-Firn. Then badly conducted parties are daily watched from the Concordia huts, with no little curiosity. They flounder about till they are often heard calling for help, or seen disappearing in a crevasse, from which moment they are entitled, under the rules of the game, to a search party.

In his diary Lunn says that the Aletschhorn had shoved its head in front of the moon. The solitude was almost oppressive. " Never have I so realised the weakness of the cry that the Alps are played out and overcrowded. True, some thousands of climbers have explored their inmost recesses ; but substantially they are little changed from the peaks that looked down on Hannibal:—

> " ' Die unbegreiflich hohen Werke
> Sind herrlich wie am ersten Tag.'

And on a winter night one feels more than ever the insignificance of such trifling excrescences as club huts and mountain inns. The parting *genius loci* has, perhaps, been sent with sighing 'from haunted hill and dale'; but I strongly suspect that these white solitudes of eternal snow are still visited by the court of the Ice Queen."

To tell the truth, I rather hope that the feminine section of that court leave the Aletsch severely alone, for our remarks that morning would have stood trimming. Why? Because, fearing concealed crevasses on the Aletsch-Firn, we roped. It was a miserable experiment. At rapid intervals Adolf sat down, in the rear, of course, as he never could do anything else but tail. Four sudden jerks, and four more bold ski-runners bit the dust. At times, somebody in the front of the train followed suit, an inspiration which necessitated a rapid swing on the part of those behind. We swung, of course, in opposite directions, and the tangled skein that ensued was enveloped in a mist of snow with a few oaths darting about. No wonder, for such evolutions "excyte beastlie and exstreme vyolence," as Lunn found it expressed in his mind, so elegantly stored up with classical quotations, and we rapidly came to the conclusion that there was "a good deal to be said

L.M.C.

CONCORDIA PLATZ.

To face p. 149.

for being dead," oh, much more than for roped ski-
ing with Adolf.

Ski-running on a rope is only possible if every
member of a party is a steady runner. I, for one,
have always found its utility limited to providing
a merry, rough-and-tumble entertainment, such as
the Wiggle-Woggle, the Whirling Pool, and such-like
helter-skelter performances in which 'Arry delights
to jostle 'Arriet.

Meanwhile the quotation runs that :—

> "The hunter of the East had caught
> The mountain turrets in a noose of light."

But its author was in far too sulky a condition to
appreciate a sunrise.

By nine o'clock, with our troubles well ended, we
were all comfortably seated on the rounded edges of
the famous breakfast-table, an erratic stone in the
centre of that wonderful ice *quadrivium* marked on
the maps as Concordia Platz, in which the stone
in question expresses the altitude in four figures
(2,780 metres). Carpeted in the purest white, surrounded by pyramids in the best assorted white
marble architecture, set out with flying buttresses
and domes in jasper, jade, and sapphire, the Concordia Platz did not betoken the symmetrical
designing power of man, but perfect harmony in
the work of Nature's agents—sun, snow, rock,
and ice.

What a perfectly beautiful city for the dead, these
precincts and temple whence the handiwork of man

was absent! And what a number of graves were
laid under the pavement of this cathedral! Think
of the tears shed for the many who came here, impelled by the desire to behold in this world a
habitation pure enough for angels, and whose
human strength gave way before the resistance
opposed by the cruel guardians of this blissful
abode !

During breakfast we discussed our plans. Our
eyes were fixed upon the Jungfrau, partly because
we had vaguely talked of the tempting ascent, but
still more because, having come up here with ice-
axes, regulation ropes, and ten-pronged climbing-
irons, it was quite plain that a serious ascent entered
into our programme. If I may put it frankly, pure
adventure was not the purpose that brought me on
the Concordia Platz. I wished to put to the test of
reality, in the highest mountain rink of the Bernese
range, the theory forced upon my mind by observations and experiences elsewhere.

I had learnt conclusively much that was new and
interesting about winter conditions in the forest
zone and on the denuded grazings that rise above
them. The comparatively easy slanting and horizontal expanses of the ice-covered parts of the Alps
had yielded some positive information to the winter
pioneers now visiting them for the first time. Now
I wanted to know, with ever-increasing accuracy,
how those huge spurs of rock and ice that are
thrown up into the sky from the glacier region behaved in winter. Hitherto they had been looked at
and their condition judged from a distance. Con-

clusions come to in that manner were extremely unfavourable to their accessibility. One might, moreover, safely say that no scientific men had subjected the winter Alps to the same scrutiny as, in the years following the middle of the nineteenth century, made Agassiz, Desor, the Englishmen Tyndall and Sir John Lubbock, famous, and so many more whose hard and shrewd thinking about the physical complexion of the Alps has met with general acceptance.

In a humbler sphere, too, among men in daily contact with the Alps, such as guides and chamois hunters, there was till lately an absolutely ineradicable belief that the Alp peaks would oppose almost insuperable obstacles to those bold enough to grapple with them under winter conditions.

But neither scientific scholars nor practical men could exactly say why this should be the case. It was one of those vague impressions or beliefs which are more imperative in proportion as actual first-hand knowledge is scantier.

Most would tell you, when pressed, that in January the High Alps could not but be found smothered in the most stupendous quantities of snow that the frightened imagination could body forth, and that in those masses rock peaks and ice domes would be buried alike.

Once more, on the Concordia Platz, the notion I had formed as to the comparative scarcity of snow on the flanks of the leading summits of our Alps— those exceeding 10,000 feet—was about to be reported upon and tested by impartial eyes.

Our three Bernese guides could barely trust the
testimony of their own eyes. They expected to see
a Jungfrau embedded in snow from head to foot,
stuffed out to a shapeless mass, bolstered out as with
the seven petticoats of a Dutch *belle*. On the contrary, the Bernese Maid was more slim than they
had ever seen her in summer. Almost entirely free
from snow, she turned towards us a shoulder as
smooth, bright, and pure as that of a Greek goddess
that might have been clad in a close-fitting suit of
silver armour. One of my men who saw her again
last summer (1911), one of the two hottest recorded
since 1830, found her less free from snow than she
appeared on that January day, when she was actually
melting away under the perfect downpour of solar
rays towards which her face was turned.

Thus was an important doubt set at rest by the
testimony of practical men. It would have taken
us half the day to cut steps in the sheer ice that
stretched from the Roththal Sattel to the very top.
The near completion of the railway from Grindelwald
to Jungfraujoch will make it quite easy to institute
a series of regular scientific observations on this
interesting subject.

So far as we were concerned, after five days of sun
and inverted temperature it was out of the question
for us to attempt the top slopes of the Jungfrau at
that hour of the day. It was tacitly agreed to aban-
don it for the Finsteraarhorn. The same causes
which turned the snow slopes of the Jungfrau to
ice and rendered them impracticable would dry the
rocks of the Finsteraarhorn, clearing them from the

excess of snow which the winter winds might have piled up there. So we pressed on towards the Grünhornlücke, past the Concordia huts, ski-ing leisurely downwards on the Aletsch glacier.

The reader may easily picture to himself how much our ski were in tune with the wonderful surface over which we were passing.

"These rollings of *névé*," relates Lunn, "are almost unique in the Alps. On other glaciers one's attention is diverted to the surrounding peaks. But, as some one says, on the Aletsch the boundary mountains form an insignificant cup-lip to the glacier itself, which, to my knowledge, may be compared to the same on the Plaine-Morte only. The Oberland peaks, which from Grindelwald or Lauterbrunnen exhibit such a wonderful wealth of design, are comparatively tame from the basin of the Aletsch. When we think of the Jungfrau we always think of her as seen from the pastures of the Wengern Alp. Seen from the Aletsch she is not particularly striking. One's whole attention is focussed on the broad, silent reaches of snow. From the Loetschenlücke, from the Jungfraujoch, from the Grünhornlücke, three vast ice streams flow down towards the Concordia, rightly so named, for, there, irresistible forces blend silently in perfect harmony and move downwards without a break."

By three o'clock in the afternoon we passed by the huts which now form quite a township on the rocky spur which supports them. There is the Cathrein Pavilion, a regular little mountain hostelry, the new Swiss Alpine Club hut, and the old hut. Stowed away under the rock the ancestral hut of all might betray its site to curious Alpine antiquaries.

We could have walked straight into the township on that day, the rocks being dry and swept clean of snow, the effect of the sun only, as I can easily prove by the testimony of Mr. Schloss who, with his party, had to take refuge in the Swiss Club hut during the storm that had raged in the last days of December. He says : " We rammed the ski into the snow at the foot of these rocks, expecting to reach the hut, some 50 metres above us, in a few minutes. But the storm made the passage up the narrow path hewn out of the rock wall very unpleasant. It was covered with ice and snow, and the wind, blowing in furious gusts from the Jungfrau snow-fields, threatened every moment to hurl one or the other of us down on to the glacier below." Let the reader take warning.

From the Concordia Platz we started up steep slopes to our next pass. But were they so steep ? and did we climb at all ? There is in words a forceful though conventional mendacity. In language the most honest catch themselves playing the part of gay deceivers. Did we have any occasion during that week to draw one laboured breath from our tranquil breasts ? Restful and vigorous, we led the æsthetic life.

As on the previous evening, there was a tantalising interest, the same eagerness to look beyond the sky-line into the new world of snow. This time the pass revealed the Fiesch glacier and the great pyramid of the Finsteraarhorn. " Professor Roget," writes my young friend, whose fancy I like to tickle by

appearing before him in the *rôle* of an old cynic,
" having been here before, exhibited no indecent
haste, and so I had some time to myself in the
pass. The guides—to them also the country was
new—were moved to unwonted enthusiasm on seeing
the Finsteraarhorn. They said, ' Eine schöne Spitze,
die müssen wir morgen machen.' "

Indeed they might on the morrow. There it
stood before us such as three times already I had
climbed it in summer. A photograph would hardly
show the difference in the seasons. The Finsteraarhorn could be ranked in the same category as the
Combin de Valsorey and many others 12,000 feet
high and upwards with rocky sides falling away to
the south and west. Whenever they had a northern
slope whereby they were accessible in summer, I had
found that by that flank their top could be reached
in winter with the help of ski and ice-axe judiciously
blended, and that, on the other side, they would
regale the tourist with the gymnastics of a scramble
as diverting as in summer.

It was about two in the afternoon when our party
assembled on the lip of the Grünhornlücke. This
substantive, which has before now enjoyed our
favour, I do not employ as a mere literary phrase.
Let me say why.

High Alpine passes are like funnels up which the
wind sweeps the snow. Most passes I describe in
this book being parallel to the main range of the
Alps, are most susceptible to winds blowing from
the south-west and to north-easters. When the
wind blows from the south-west the snow driven

up the inclined funnel overlaps to the north-east
and forms an overhanging lip in that direction.
After a time intervenes a gale from the north-east.
It drives up snow under the curve of the lip and
fills the bend as with plaster. A time comes when,
that space being filled up, the new snow is rolled
up over the lip and then bulges out in a hanging
cornice towards the south-west. That in its turn
gets reversed, and so forth throughout the winter.
On passes, therefore, cornices are not fixed. They
shift from one side to another of the sky-line.

This may constitute a serious danger, either
because the lip is curled over above you, and then
you may have to break through it or even bore a
tunnel, as when a waterpipe, in order to be carried
up through the projection of a roof, is led straight
up a wall and an opening pierced to take it above
the roof. At other times it is easy enough to get on
to the lip, because the outside edge of it bends down
away from you. But then the difficulty is how to
get off the lip on to the chin below. Here again,
if you go carelessly forward your weight may break
off the edge of the lip. You will fall with it, through
the open space underneath, on to the lower level.
Or else you may have to jump, or let yourself down
by means of a rope if the distance is too great or
the landing surface too steep or too slippery or too
near an abyss for you to be sure of getting a safe
foothold. It is sometimes the wisest course to dig
one's way down, as on other occasions you may have
dug your way up. These are the minor incidents
that attend every kind of mountaineering. But they

are much more frequent, and sometimes a cause of
real peril in winter, because overhanging hems of
snow may be met with, even in the zone of the
grazings, where the snow is usually very deep and
much tossed about by the contrary currents of wind
resulting from the extremely broken character of the
country.

High glacier passes are, on the whole, pretty free
from cornices because the wind has free play so near
the altitude where all land ceases. Geography is
very much simplified from 9,000 feet upwards. You
would be easily convinced of it if, on a relief
model, you sliced off all the pieces rising above
9,000 feet and separated them from the remainder
of the model by slipping in a tray under them at
that altitude. That is why the High Alp ski-runner
is much less concerned with avalanches than his
less ambitious brother who confines himself to lower
and more complicated regions. The reader will now
understand better why Lunn and myself are so perpetually "lounging, strolling, idling" in this raid.

It was actually only two in the afternoon—let us
say it again in the light of these observations—when
our party assembled on the lip of the Grünhornlücke.
We looked back towards the Loetschenlücke, once
more a mere dent against the sky, and contrasted our
easy journey with the long, laborious tramp which is
there the lot of summer trippers over slushy, soft
sticky snow. How often had I worked my way
toilsomely, with wet feet and perspiring brow, over
these extensive fields when they were mud-coloured
and a vast network of puddles! Yet the temperature

throughout had been delightfully mild! Our party
lay down on the summit of the pass as comfortably
as on a hot Sunday afternoon, the members of a
boating party on the Upper Thames might choose to
land on a dry and elevated part of the bank—but,
alas! in our case quite shadeless—to boil the kettle
and lay the table for afternoon tea.

At 11,000 feet above sea-level we lay about on the
white dry floor and enjoyed a prolonged siesta, and
thought how unlikely all this would seem when we
should relate it.   But when the sun had set behind
the Aletschhorn, the change was instantaneous. We
had now to go down slopes facing east, whose surface
glazed immediately.   Our ski seemed alive, and
skimmed over the glaze like swallows skimming the
surface of a lake.   We had plenty of room in which
to break our speed by curving in uphill and bending
down and round again.   I could indulge to my heart's
content in my favourite amusement on such slopes,
which, when you present the broadside of your ski
somewhat upwards and sideways to the concavity of
the surface, let you down at varying rates of speed
while you describe a spiral line to the bottom.

In this case the foot of the pass was indeed the
bottom, but it was also the top of the Walliser
Fiescher Firn.   Like arrows from a hidden bow, we
shot along the path of the moonbeams and came
to a standstill at the foot of a dreadful black rock, on
the top of which the rays of the sun, before parting,
had lit up as a beacon the windows and chimney-
pots of the Finsteraarhorn hut.   We left our ski
well planted in the snow and scrambled up with

our packs. This hut once stood on the Oberaarjoch, till it was removed thence and rebuilt in
its present position. The trials of transport may
account for its being somewhat loose in the joints.
It is not weather-tight, and the snow on the roof
—in summer I have known it to be rain—trickles
through in large drops, sometimes on the clothes set
out to dry on strings all round the stove pipe and
sometimes on the noses of the sleepers in their berths.
I understand that the trickle of water on one's
cranium is one of the most terrible tortures a man
can be subjected to.

Anyhow we had climbed a thousand feet, taken
perhaps the wrong way up, the whole in very good
time to allow Adolf his usual extra hour for joining
us round the flowing bowl of hot soup.

"As we were sitting down to supper," says Lunn,
"a party of some six or seven Swiss came in." They
had just completed the ascent of the Finsteraarhorn,
and were not a little pleased to find the stove lit and
water on the boil. We had noticed on arrival that the
hut had the appearance of being inhabited, and on
looking round had soon caught sight of its denizens
slipping and stumbling merrily down the shoulder of
the Finsteraarhorn. A look at the hut guest-book
also told us that it had been lately visited by two
Norwegians.

"That night in the hut we were a merry party.
The Swiss belonged to the class that in England
divide most of their time between watching football
matches and playing billiards. They made one realise
how much the higher life of a nation was stimulated

by a prevailing love of mountains. For mountaineering is essentially the people's sport. Climbing tends more than any other sport to break down artificial barriers between classes. Snobbery is seen in its true proportion against a background of mountains. The wealth of enthusiasm which mountaineering inspires among the artisan classes of Switzerland is a permanent asset to the nation, lifting all those who come into contact with the hills out of their narrow ambitions. Shelley felt this truth. The great peaks, he writes, have a voice to repeal large codes of fraud and woe. One had only to look at these Swiss to feel how their lives were coloured, their ideals raised, their views broadened, by their love of their native mountains."

Lunn likes to speak of the Swiss parties he meets as being " guideless." I do not know to what extent this epithet may convey a clear meaning to others. It hardly does to me. What is a guideless party? Unless it means a party who undertakes, without the assistance of a professional guide, one of the ascents for which such a guide is authorised by a binding tariff to claim payment, the expression is wanting in point. There is nothing particularly noteworthy in this, that the natives of Switzerland should explore and climb the mountains of their country without the assistance of professional fellow-citizens. These form a class which has been instituted to serve two purposes : (1) To provide them with an additional economic asset ; (2) to give strangers confidence in exploring the Alps.

Guides seek from their employers certificates of

good conduct and utility. Many of the latter have acquired a taste, in those documents, for sitting, as it were, at the feet of their guides as though the positions were reversed. Indeed, it would be more natural that the guides should give certificates of ability, daring, and endurance to the amateur mountaineers whom they have in their charge. Under such altered circumstances a guideless party would be a party in possession of a certificate to the effect that they had gained sufficient proficiency in mountaineering to hold a licence as guideless parties. Till things are so arranged, the epithet is bootless.

Many young Swiss solve the difficulty by going through the official course of training laid down for professional guides, in the persuasion that should they, or the party they are with, meet with an accident, it would not be possible for either the guiding corporation or public opinion to fairly lay any blame at their door. There was assuredly no reason why the young men whom we saw on that day should have been expected to meet with an accident because they had no paid bystander.

" Luxuries had long been devoured, but even soup has a delightful flavour in a club hut. And no one can really understand the charms of tobacco who has never smoked in a club hut at the end of a good day's work. The mountain pipe has a flavour undreamt of in the plains. Even some horrible hay-like production purchased in Adolf's inn seemed inspired with ambrosial flavour."

On this 6th day of January it was to be our turn to ascend the Finsteraarhorn. For the first time in

11

our trip this verb is an apposite term. It meant
work, and our Socialist undertook to prove it. He
first of all swallowed up on the sly the last contents
of our pot of honey. If I wished to be nasty, I should
say that he got himself tied at the end of the rope
because he had calculated selfishly that he would be
dragged up and, being first and lowest on the rope
when descending, he would be held up by us.

This little piece of reckoning did not miscarry. Wise
Ulysses was too good natured to let it be seen that he
" saw through " this little plot ; fiery Achilles was of too
powerful a build to mind a little extra weight, and the
other two Bernese guides were such excellent fellows
that they gave no sign of how much they suffered in
their pride on account of their colleague.

" For once in a way," says Lunn, " the guides were
punctual. I think Professor Roget was the only one
in the party who did justice to the breakfast. A
seasoned mountaineer of thirty years' standing, he
can eat stale bread and tinned meat at 6.30 in the
morning with the calm persistency of the man who
realises that food is a sound insurance against cold
and fatigue. But we were all glad to turn out of the
hut, which we left at 7.15 a.m. The first signs of dawn
appeared before the moon had set, a somewhat unusual phenomenon. Such a sunrise—though one
misses the more dramatic change from the darkest
night to the day—is accompanied by an almost
unique depth of colouring. Two hours above the hut
the sun shot out from behind the Oberaarhorn, I
should like to add, like a stone flung out of a sling."

The simultaneous presence, morning and evening,

BREAKFAST ON THE FINSTERAARHORN.

To face p. 163.

of sun and moon at opposite ends of the sky, was
one of the most interesting pictorial features displayed before our eyes. I am not aware that painters
are ever likely to succeed in reproducing the cross
light effects we witnessed, silvery and cold at one
extremity, golden and warm at the opposite extremity,
meeting on that endless expanse of neutral white,
and shot throughout with the azure of the sky.

The Finsteraarhorn proved itself as accommo-
dating as the Jungfrau was rebellious: for one and
the same cause, as already hinted. The rocky *arête*
stood up like a lace ruff above its shoulder, as fine as
if it were wrought in muslin, and offering everywhere
an easy hold for our hands. It was free from snow
and from ice, owing to the constant action of the
sun's rays percolating through the superimposed
layers of dry air. Where there was any snow there
was so little that we could hardly have expected less
in summer. The *arête* was warm to our touch.

On reaching the breakfast place, we looked
anxiously at the sweep of the uppermost span into
space. Not a suspicion of any wind blowing up
there. The last two hours of the six afforded a
delightful scramble along the edge of that very
impressive cock's comb. For an hour and a half
more we climbed up alongside steep snow slopes,
down which we saw the most alarming ski tracks I
have ever beheld.

By one o'clock our ropes were thrown as a noose
all about the top of the Finsteraarhorn, the giant of
the Oberland. The Socialist hung on to the end of
the rope like a scorpion's sting; Achilles led, pre-

senting his naked torso to the bite of the sun; in the middle bulged the robust frame of venerable Ulysses, with his grey hair blown about by the wind, and, filling the gaps between those three important personages, came Gyger and Schmidt, betraying on their honest, grave countenances their naive satisfaction at seeing themselves on such a lofty platform. We spent a wonderful hour on the summit.

The view was perfect, as only a winter view can be, over all the great ranges mellowed by the winter atmosphere. Beyond them a vast sea of cloud covered the plains of Switzerland and Italy. We lay about hatless, coatless, and gloveless. Not a breath of wind even to make the inviolable quiet audible. Quoth Lunn :—

> " ' It seemed as if the hour were one
> Sent from beyond the skies,
> Which scattered from above the sun
> The light of Paradise.'

" Time stood still, or rather the time we passed on that aerial summit, seemed stolen from the rest of eternity. At such moments the mind becomes a passive instrument for recording external impressions. Old memories arose unbidden; old associations lived again. Familiar ridges, the hills of Grindelwald, the little chalet, just visible, where I had spent so many happy summers, all lent an element of personal romance to the view, all helped to awaken memories of ' far-off things and battles long ago.'

" The view from the Finsteraarhorn is of its kind almost unique. It is the very hub of vast spaces of

eternal winter. Below, the ice-bound cliffs of the
Oberland, scored with the passage of ages, rise from
a waste of glaciers. The Finsteraarhorn is the
culminating point of this rugged chain, and looks
defiantly over a host of lesser peaks towards its
great brethren of the Swiss Alps. From the Dolo-
mites to Dauphiny, from the Vosges to the Apen-
nines, scarcely a peak of any importance was hid.
The winter atmosphere toned down the harsh features whilst rendering the whole flawless panorama
strangely distinct. The mountains were clad in
those wonderful bluish tints peculiar to the winter
months, their crudities had been softened, their
barren places made smooth. The keynote in the
panorama was a dreamy, languorous atmosphere."

The boundless canopy of clouds dragged itself out
lazily, like a huge soft beast, to fill up all the inter-
stices in this rock-bound and rock-studded vista,
shot through with waves of light. There was a
superb suggestion of indolence on the far horizon,
turning pale against a sky of unfathomable blue.
Below us the small wooden hut, perched on its rock,
added a touch of human interest to the view.

The guides went to sleep in the snow, while the
two educated men of the party contemplated and
smoked, smoked and contemplated.

" Nine long summers I had spent as a small boy
in getting to know the remote bye-ways of the
Faulhorn chain. For nine summers we had looked
longingly up to the great cliffs of the Oberland, the
peaks of storm and of dread, the dark Aar peak, the
Maiden, the Monk, and the Giant. Vaguely we

wondered if it would ever be ours to penetrate into their recesses. By the peculiar cussedness of things, I had climbed in other ranges, but till then had never returned to my first love.

"The force of associations formed in childhood has been insisted on *ad nauseam* by Wordsworth and his imitators, but the sentiment is none the less powerful for being somewhat trite. And even now, as this early ambition had at last reached the point of realisation, I could scarce restrain a feeling of regret. Though, in later years, calm reason convinced me that the terrors in which my childish imagination had clad the Oberland peaks were almost non-existent, yet the ease with which we had conquered their monarch had its element of sadness.

"The hour passed like ten minutes. The professor gave the word to return. We roused Adolf and sadly turned down the *arête*. The weaker brother led with great deliberation. On this occasion we lacked not æsthetic compensations for his slowness. It was a unique sensation, sitting astride that vast cliff, watching the afternoon lights spreading tinges of an infinite gradation of tones over the boundless canopy of mist."

We reached again the fantastic little gap of the Hugi-Sattel, overlooking a sheer cliff that drops down to the Finsteraarhorn glacier. We now rested in the afternoon where we had breakfasted in the forenoon. We looked back up the way we had come down. Owing to the ice, we had been forced off the summer route—which keeps some distance below the ridge—on to the very *arête*. There is nothing on the

Matterhorn finer than that sheer cliff that falls away
to the glacier 3,000 feet below.   Drop a stone, and
it falls the entire distance without a bound.   The
climbing, however, both up and down, had been easy
enough.   Good sound hand and foot-holds—no shadow
of an excuse for a slip, not even for Adolf, who
had come up wailing in the forenoon, contributing
to the gaiety of the party by his monotonous : " Ich
komme schon, aber nur nicht so schnell." With a
shudder he beheld the track of the two Norwegians,
who had taken their ski to within a thousand feet of
the summit, and, on their return, appeared to have
gaily descended a slope of soft snow lying on streaks
of ice, at an angle of 45 degrees, bridging several
yawning cracks.

Having rested on the Hugi-Sattel—this part of
Switzerland recalls everywhere the names of its
explorers and scientific investigators—we slowly
retraced our steps to the hut, reaching it at 5.45.

The merry Swiss boys had left everything in
beautiful order.   We had all the room—and all
the raindrops—to ourselves.   Heated through and
through, the roof was letting the water from the
melting snow pass through the shingles.

Once more a perfect sunset gave promise of yet
another day of cloudless beauty.   Our anxieties—we
had none others than those which might come from
eagerness to succeed—were at an end.   We had
done what we had set out to do.   Had we planned
to go to the North Pole—or to discover the Antarctic—
and succeeded likewise (as mountaineers would have
done long ago if they had troubled to) our feelings

could have differed but little from those that now passed in our minds. There is a likeness in all achievements in this. When the past is just putting forward its forefinger in warning of its readiness to withdraw our deed gently from our grasp and from the sight of men, we feel a pang that to have done something means parting with it soon after. Some may have been so ambitious to reach the North Pole that they set about it in a dishonest spirit. Some returning from another voyage of joint and mutual discovery—that generally goes under the name of a wedding tour—carry home with them a melancholy tinge of regret upon their happiness. So did we.

Yet there is in simple achievements a satisfaction which nothing else in the world can give. Most other successes leave something to be desired. The instability of wealth and health is a platitude. But Lunn rightly says that every successful expedition is a permanent asset, bringing in year by year a high rate of interest, an incorruptible treasure in the memories of the past which nothing can destroy.

" Next day we got away by 7, stumbled down the steep rocks below the hut, picked up our ski, our faithful boards, standing all bespattered with snow, and by the light of the moon skied merrily down the Fiesch glacier. As dawn broke we pushed up the long slopes leading to our next pass, the Oberaarjoch. Suddenly an expression of pleasure escaped Professor Roget. Such an unprecedented phenomenon—on the part of the old Cynic—aroused my attention. I turned and saw what, for an æsthetic mind, was probably the most striking view of the whole tour—namely, softened and subdued by the magic of the winter atmosphere, the perfect pyramid of the Weisshorn flanked by the daring spire of the Matterhorn.

"A little later it was my turn to give vent to some satisfaction, and the professor looked up to see Adolf walking well at the head of the party with his pack trim and neat on his shoulders, like those people who, when approaching the end of their trials, stride forth as if they had conquered the world."

We almost reluctantly took our stand upon this the fifth and last sky-line we were to cut through with the flat of our ski. The last of our five passes disclosed the long arm of the Oberaar glacier, backed by the mountains that overshadow the birthplace of the Rhône. Now the Finsteraarhorn showed us his back view, his shoulder blades, terrace upon terrace of sheer rock.

Indeed, the force that was impelling Adolf back towards civilisation was not of the sort that could make the pace for us. We were going onwards and onwards, but rather drawn by the sun towards his haunt in the east, the common goal of so many pilgrims. But our mood was not devout except that we were nature worshippers who, while marching to Canterbury, were diverting one another with appropriate tales. You might have had pleasure in seeing us advance in very open order up the wrinkled back of the Fiesch glacier. I believe one of us was holding a pipe between his teeth, another strolled with his hands in his pockets, a fourth darted about kodak in hand.

Adolf thought we were slow, and grew impatient at

our tarrying on this astonishing veranda. It has, perhaps, no like in the world in this, that it is a suspended ice-garden of an extent and altitude well proportioned to the physical faculties of man, showing as much of natural beauty under one of its most prodigious aspects as does not exceed the understanding of a well-balanced mind.

I shall never forget the ever renewed delight which I found in skirting the southern buttresses of the Finsteraarhorn range. We did not take a step forward without stopping to look backward through the wide gap formed by the valley down which the Fiesch glacier pours its waters in the Rhône. The whole of the Pennine Alps displayed themselves within this gap.

There they loomed as lifted off the earth, a gossamer, a sea of soft light, a row of pearls looking as frail as a dream, and yet a real world, the key to which is love of the beautiful.

Softly—the ski have a way of caressing the snow— slowly, chatting, then wrapped in silence, we went forward, as on wings. Immersed in light, we might have been borne aloft by an expansive force within ourselves, so much did we rise without any effort. It was barely midday when we stood on the Oberaarjoch. Before us bent and curved the sides of the last glacier which we had yet to follow—the Oberaar Gletscher. Our eyes embraced a new horizon which, surging beyond the Galenstock and the Dammastock, extended further than the Toedi in the north and enclosed the Bernina in the east.

We were not alone on this Belvedere. The

Oberaarjoch hut, high above us on our left, looked like one of those boxes which in a theatre allow the eyes of the occupants to plunge down upon the stage unseen. The platform in front of the hut was occupied by some fellow-runners, whose voices reached our ears almost as soon as we saw them. They were watching us, and we exchanged with them such greetings as ships may send to one another when crossing on the high seas. To-morrow they would resume their course towards the skies we had left behind us, while we pushed our way towards those they had hitherto travelled under.

It would be idle to attempt to reckon up our widely sweeping curves as we came down the Oberaar glacier. The surface, concave at the top, becomes convex at the bottom, with a regularity which is a good example of an unfailing law in glacier pheno- mena. I think we turned to the right, and spun round to the left, and then turned to the left and spun round to the right for about twenty minutes on that sheet of snow without a stop. Our men bowled themselves down anyhow. But the spiral line we looked back upon from the foot of the glacier would have won respect from the most exacting teacher in draughtsmanship.

Lunn says that the top slope was unskiable. So we set our lunch upon it. "Thence some straight running took us over an uninterrupted stretch of snow about five miles in length. The surface was hard and wind-swept, but the gradient was so gentle that we could let ourselves go without thought of possible falls. We turned off beyond the snout of

the glacier and bore away down a gully to our left.
Here the professor supplied an interesting *entre-acte.*

"The guides had, for once in a way, got ahead.
Suddenly Professor Roget fell down at the top of a
steep and trying slope. He did not rise, so I sent
the guides back to help him. Adolf saw his opportunity : a little bit of a tragedy coming in the nick
of time when the perils of the route were over. He
puffed and panted up the slope, leading the search
party with a rush. When at last three hot and
perspiring guides reached the piece of wreckage
stranded on the chilly shore they were not a little
annoyed to see the boat right itself without their
help, and, recovering the use of human speech, the
Professor remarked that he hoped this lesson would
teach them to keep together. It did !"

By four o'clock in the afternoon we had wandered
over the long, flat basin at the end of the Unteraar
glacier, whence we said goodbye to the Finsteraarhorn. Arnold, in high spirits, was bent on making
the most of his last chances. We were on the last
spur abutting on to the flat land in the middle of
which stands the Grimsel hospice, when I saw him
dash to the left over the brow of the last wave of the
hill, exclaiming, "I see a cheeky thing to do !" The
next moment he was sailing along safely on the flats.
We had no thought of entering into the hospice.
Why should we ? We had not a scratch, we did not
feel an ache, our equipment was as complete as when
we had started. We therefore took immediately to
the road.

"Here we at last discovered genuine winter.

Above, on the glaciers, all had been warmth, colour,
and light. Here in this grim gorge all was sombre,
grey, and chill. The hospice seemed to breathe a
feeble defiance to the genius of this abode of frost.
Never have I seen anything more desolate than the
deserted post-road, gagged with old avalanche tracks
and overhung with icicles. Below, the angry gash
of the torrent peered out between cakes of ice, whilst
above the waning light revealed sombre bosses of
grey rock smothered in snow.

" We were anxious to telephone, so I took one of
the guides and made all speed down the road. Some
one had conveniently made tracks, which had iced
during the night and afforded some furious running.
At last, at 6 p.m., twelve hours after leaving the hut,
we pulled up at Guttannen. Here we telephoned to
Beatenberg and Kandersteg and then went in search
of night quarters. The hotel was, of course, closed,
but we found rooms for the night in an adjoining
chalet and were afforded one of those sidelights on
real Swiss life which the summer visitor so rarely
sees.

" We supped in the one room which was warmed,
and here the family were pursuing their various
occupations. The patriarch was mumbling in the
corner over his pipe, attracting, like the majority of
patriarchs, little attention. The father, a guide in
summer, chatted on the winter's work. He appeared
to think that cutting the wood and bearing it towards
the valley left a man little time to grow fat. At the
table a young girl was plying—alas!—not the spinning-
wheel of a previous generation, but an unromantic

'Singer.' In front of her stood some dressmaker's model, a hideous, headless monstrosity on a wire cage. On the stove a small youth slept contentedly. To him entered a bustling little damsel with the maternal instinct precociously developed. With unsuspected tenderness she gently lifted him up, still sleeping, bore him out of the room, and attacked 'with an undaunted tread the long black passage up to bed.'

"Supper over, we lit our pipes with pardonable satisfaction. Our long journey had been carried through without a hitch. Perfect weather, thorough arrangements, every precaution. Seriously, one can scarcely be too careful in winter mountaineering. With every precaution, the entire complexion of things may be altered in one moment. A broken ski, a wrenched ankle, the work of a minute, and the situation becomes charged with painful anxiety. With superb indifference the mountains suffer us for ninety-nine days, and, perhaps on the hundredth— with equal indifference—they strike.

"*Friday, January 8th.*—Up once more before the dawn, to discover signs of bad weather, which had thoughtfully postponed its arrival till we had left the upper snows. One day earlier and we should have been cooped up in the Finsteraarhorn hut for four days, living on stale bread and tinned meat. A sleigh was hired to drive us to Meiringen, but I was anxious to finish the journey on ski, so, with unpardonable sophistry, I ' tailed ' behind the sleigh. This proved far from easy on the icy, winding road.

"At last, six days and six hours after leaving Kandersteg, five happy men stepped on to the Meiringen platform. On lake Brienz the sky was veiled in dark, lowering clouds, and snow fell as we drove up to Beatenberg. On arriving, we were plied with those questions which a certain type of people offer as well-meant flattery: 'Was it not too cold?' 'Wasn't it too, too awfully dangerous?' We could have accepted the heroic *rôle* with greater equanimity, had we failed to realise that any one with decent endurance and a fair knowledge of ski-ing could have accompanied us without risk."

To give satisfaction to so many kind inquiries, I gave two days later my first lecture before a more than crowded audience, and Arnold Lunn supplemented it. The joint address is the common foundation of anything we have since written on the subject.

Let me now wind up with a few final remarks.

1. Winter mountaineering may be more difficult and more dangerous than summer climbing. One often has to face the most intense cold; but with first-class conditions such as we enjoyed, it is scarcely more arduous, and certainly much more enjoyable, than summer work. Our journey in summer would have involved hours of walking through damp, slushy snow. There would have been wearisome tramps up and down *moraines*, tedious stretches of mule paths, dull grinds over grass slopes, and I shudder to think —consider the mileage!—what the last day would have meant in July. As it was, we at no time suffered from the cold, and, strangely enough, though our days were long and mostly uphill, in point of time at

least, we neither of us ever felt tired. This was, to
be sure, owing to good ski technique. "The professor
would never allow us to raise our ski off the surface
of the snow. In that way they were absolutely no
weight, and even the raising of the foot and leg was
replaced by the glide upwards of the ski blade which
provided a resting-point and support, reducing the
muscular action to the same amount of forward
movement as is necessary on level ground, without
any additional force being employed in vertical
action."

Given good weather and normal conditions, a six-
day traverse can be accomplished with very little
fatigue and still less privation. I have done four
such and have never been any the worse. One may
weary somewhat of soup, bread and cheese, but
barring these and similar drawbacks, there is no
reason why any one of moderate physique and fair
ski-ing powers should not follow in our steps.

Somehow the memories of those six days have the
power to impart something of the magical colourings
of a winter sunset to the drab dullness of lowland
evenings. On the mountains we all have moments
when life assumes unsuspected values, helping us to
realise on our return to civilisation, that the things
that are seen are temporal, whereas the things which
for the time are not seen are for all practical purposes
eternal. "The winter Alps are but a vision, a faint
memory intruding itself at intervals when the roar of
the commonplace is for a moment hushed in silence.
If visions were not at times the most solid of realities
this world would be intolerable."

" Just for a moment I have had a fleeting vision," wrote Lunn, when he had once more settled down to the round of daily life, of the silent snows of the Aletsch, as you and I saw them that glad evening on the Loetschenlücke, lit in all the splendour of the January moon. It faded all too soon, and the winter Alps again seem very far away."

2. I append a table of levels, in feet, similar to the table of my vertical displacements, in metres, which the reader has found at the end of the Diablerets to Kandersteg chapter :—

January 2nd.—Kandersteg to Mutthorn hut : 5,700 feet (Tschingel pass).

January 3rd.—Mutthorn hut to Petersgrat (our second pass) : 1,000 feet.

January 4th.—From Kippel to Egon von Steiger hut (Loetschen pass) : 6,000 feet.

January 5th.—From Concordia Platz to Grünhornlücke (our fourth pass) : 2,000 feet.

January 6th.—From Fieschfirn to Finsteraarhorn : 5,000 feet.

January 7th.—From Fieschfirn to Oberaarjoch (fifth pass) : 2,000 feet.

Add 2,000 feet for unconsidered trifles. The total vertical displacement is thus brought out at a little under 24,000 feet.

We paid each of our men a pound a day. Other expenses brought the cost to thirty pounds. It is better to have plenty of men and plenty of food. Plenty of food because one is always liable to be detained some days in the huts by the bad weather— plenty of men, which does not necessarily mean guides, because a party that can be broken up into sections is infinitely safer and handier. A party of six may be expressed by $2 + 2 + 2$, or by $3 + 3$, or

12

by 4 + 2, dispositions which may fit into almost every emergency.

There is no doubt that sealskins are extremely convenient and a great saving of labour in going uphill, because they annihilate back-slip, the bugbear of beginners and of loaded men. Serious trouble may be caused by wrinkled and puckered-up hard snow, or by those extremely slippery patches, either snow or ice, which now and then upset the balance of the High Alp runner.

The remedy to this I have found in a contrivance against side-slip which figures as a permanent fixture on the powerful pair of military ski which I used on all my big traverses. It consists of two blades of hardish steel, about 5 inches long, sharpened and shaped in the fashion of skates. Linked to each other across the upper surface of my ski, they adhere to the sides by lateral pressure only, which is applied by means of a top screw. The edge of each blade stands out beyond the flat of the ski by the merest fraction of an inch, in front of one, and behind the other, foot. This secures straight running on hard snow and ice by biting into it, preventing side-slip when the broadside of the ski slews round to the drop of the slope. The laws of mechanics teach that this contrivance, maintained against the ski by side-pressure only, should get pushed out of place when, the ski being edged, an unduly large portion of the weight of the runner falls to be borne by the ski edge. But, in practice, it is not so, provided you are careful to obtain the maximum of side-pressure that the horizontal binding screw can produce.

ADOLF ON THE FINSTERAARHORN ARÊTE.

To face p. 178.

Studs on the inside of the blade, making impressions upon the wood of the ski, without injuring it in any way, increase the resistance of this contrivance to the vertical pressure caused by the weight of the runner.

3. Within a few years from the date of writing, this part of the Alps will be girdled by a network of mountain railways. The Grindelwald-Jungfrau railway, already completed to the Jungfraujoch (11,000 feet), will deposit the ski-runner within a stone's throw of the Concordia Platz. There he will, as the phrase goes, have it all his own way, with the resources of civilisation and a railway station to fall back upon.

The line of the Loetschberg, on the international railway, now being built to join Berne to Brigue, should be open to traffic by the end of 1913. It will then take but a few moments to run there and back, underground, between Kandersteg and Goppenstein in the Loetschenthal, joining together both ends of the ski route Kandersteg–Gastern–Mutthorn–Petersgrat (or Loetschberg)–Kippel–Goppenstein.

To the east, a line now under construction from Brigue, with a tunnel under the Furka pass to Andermatt, will connect the St. Gothard ski-ing grounds with those we have just described.

Skiers running down the Aletsch will be able to take train at Moerel or Fiesch. These coming facilities are not altogether pleasant to contemplate for those who hold the traditional ideas about the virginity and sanctity of the Alpine Holy of Holies; but to the extent in which it may be possible to work those lines in winter—and to this there is no insuperable physical obstacle—they will greatly contribute to the generalising of ski, and thereby confer inestimable benefits upon young people in Europe, while reducing to the minimum consistent with the zest of manly enjoyment those risks which are the haunting terror of the parents, sisters, and wives of the adventurous winter sportsman.

CHAPTER VI

THE AIGUILLE DU CHARDONNET AND THE AIGUILLE DU TOUR

The aspect of the Grand Combin—Topography—Weather conditions for a successful raid—A classification of peaks—The Orny nivometer—The small snowfall of the High Alps—The shrinkage of snow—Its insufficiency to feed the glaciers—The Aiguille du Tour—Ascent of Aiguille du Chardonnet—The St. Bernard hospice—Helplessness of the dogs—The narrow winter path—The monks' hospitality—Their ski—The accident on the Col de Fenêtre—" Ce n'est pas le ski."

HE Val de Bagnes, the Val d'Entremont, which leads up to the pass of the great St. Bernard, and the Val Ferret are comparatively little frequented by Englishmen, even in the height of the summer season. Why it should be so is not quite clear. There is no finer group in the Alps, from Tyrol to Dauphiné, than the Grand Combin and Mont Velan group. As seen from Lake Champex, or from almost any point of vantage in the Val de Bagnes, the group of the Combins and abutting snow-clad tops forms one of the grandest pieces of mountain architecture that can be imagined, one of a character that is somewhat uncommon, for the breadth and width of the lines are more striking here than in the usual type of mountains tapering up to a peak. The snow-fields and icefalls are magnificent, while the altitude of this group (Grand Combin 4,317 metres, or 14,164 feet) enables it to rank beside Mont Blanc, Monte Rosa, and the Mischabel range, eclipsing the Finsteraarhorn and Piz Bernina.

If the Englishman is not so often seen in summer in that region as he might be, I am sure that in winter none have yet visited on ski the valleys of Bagnes, Entremont and Ferret, with the exception of a party about which I may have something to say in another chapter. The writer of these lines has, therefore, an excellent chance of introducing a novel field to the British ski-runner. He spent an eight-days' week in March, 1907, upon a raid in the valleys above named, ranging from one to another on ski, with two friends, one of whom was a youth of eighteen, and the other a well-known Valaisan ski-runner, Maurice Crettex, from Champex.

A knowledge of topography being absolutely essential to one's safety in High Alp ski-running, even the most expert runner will take care that at least one of his party possesses that knowledge to perfection. The runner who takes the risk of wasting some of his strength—or time on short winter days—upon errors in direction, is little short of a fool. Owing to steep slopes and complicated ground, the slightest topographical mistake may cause a fatal waste of

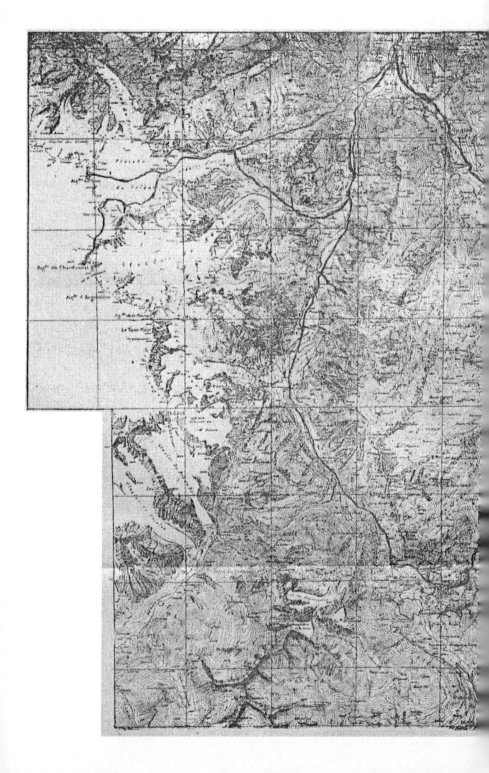

Lourtier

FERRET—ENTREMONT—BAGNES.
(Reproduction made with authorisation of the Swiss Topographic Service, 26.8.12.)

To face p. 181.

precious time—and of a man's useful energy, the fund of which is limited in a town or plain dweller, who only occasionally tries his physical endurance in winter at a high altitude.

A raid on ski is not a raid if it is interrupted by stress of weather. It is then best described as a commonplace misadventure. The intending raider must trust to chance, assisted by a careful reading of the daily reports of the weather issued from Zürich. These reports now very usually distinguish between High Alp weather and the conditions prevailing during the same periods in the lake and river region. When there is a scientific prospect of fog over the lakes and rivers, this means that the air is still, and that the sun shines upon every mountain rising above four, five, or six thousand feet, as the case may be. A wind arising from north or east will not interfere with the raid (except in the matter of cold), but a gale from west or south will bring it to an abrupt end, and be attended with the utmost danger if the warning of a falling glass is not immediately acted upon.

During the eight days that this raid lasted, the weather was absolutely steady, fine, and windless, the sun and moon vying uninterruptedly with each other to extinguish darkness. We suffered at no time from the cold after sunset or in club huts, and basked all day long in the sun's direct heat and in the rays reflected from the snows. The temperature fell at night to 10 or 15 degrees under zero Centigrade, and rose to most extraordinary readings during the day. We were dressed in the warm, tough material used by all competent mountain climbers even in the height of summer, with strong thick boots, and never for a moment suffered from cold feet.

Thanks to the above circumstances and to a happy concourse of every advantage, my two companions and myself were the first human beings who ever smoked their pipes and cigars in winter, and sat in their shirt-sleeves on the top of the Aiguille du Tour, Aiguille du Chardonnet, and Grand Combin. The latter summit was attempted by one of my colleagues at Bâle (Mr. O. D. Tauern, the German gentleman mentioned in another chapter). But the most gallant efforts failed to bring him and his friends to the very top, though the tour was a complete vindication of winter mountaineering on ski. An account of their expedition appeared in the Annual (1908) of the *Schweizer Ski-Verband*.

A ski-raid upon the giants of the Alpine world does not necessarily mean that the raider sets his ski upon the brow of the conquered adversary. Such a pretension would be pedantic. The summits of the Alps may, for the ski-runner, be divided into three classes, strictly according to their conformation, whether they be small or great, Alpine or only sub-Alpine.

There is the class which is inaccessible under winter conditions, because those summits are then led up to by slopes so sharp or insecure that neither ski nor boot can reasonably be used upon them. That class we reject altogether. Another class consists of mountains, such as the Diablerets, Wildhorn, Wildstrubel, the tops of which are led up to by slopes eminently fitted for ski, both upwards and downwards. A third class consists of summits which cannot be reached on ski, because they are rock-pinnacles, but which can be *only* conveniently approached on ski. This class, to my mind, is the best, as it combines ski-running with rock-climbing. The Dufour Spitze of Monte Rosa would be the grandest example in this category.

Grand Combin, approached on the north side from the Plateau des Maisons Blanches, belongs to the same class as Diablerets, Wildhorn, and Wildstrubel. But if the ascent be varied by climbing the rocks *viâ* Combin de Valsorey, a course which I found as easy and comfortable in winter as in summer, the Grand Combin passes into a—to my mind—higher class. The Aiguille du Chardonnet and the Aiguille du Tour, to the tops of which there is from no side a continuous way on snow, are other typical instances.

Any one who would follow in our footsteps and perform, like us, an eight or ten days' ski-running and rock-climbing raid, will find every useful indication as to programme and distribution of time in the following description :—

The raid comprises three parts : First, Aiguille du Tour and Aiguille du Chardonnet; second, Great St. Bernard, and Val Ferret back to Orsières; third, Grand Combin, and back to Martigny.

The ski-runners will leave Orsières at about 7 o'clock a.m., and proceed on their first day to the Cabane d'Orny, or to the Cabane Dupuys, which lies still higher. The Cabane d'Orny being quite comfortable, the vertical displacement from Orsières

(890 metres) to the site of that hut (2,692 metres)
will probably be found a sufficient effort to justify one
in leaving the higher hut severely alone that day.
The Cabane d'Orny may be reached either by following the bed of the Combe d'Orny from Orsières, or *viâ*
Chalets de Saleinaz, from Praz de Fort. We found
both lines of access equally good, but information as
to the best at any given time of the winter season
should always be obtained from those locally
acquainted with snowcraft. The ascent to the hut
being continuous, the ski-runner will save much time,
and save up much energy, in using a contrivance
against back-slip, whichever may be the one he
favours.

There is near the Cabane d'Orny, against a flight
of rocks, a nivometer. This is an apparatus for
recording the height at which the snow may rise
against a rock face. Persons of an observant turn of
mind are requested to read the nivometer (which consists of horizontal bars of red paint, bearing each
a number at regular intervals) and to enter in the
hut-book the date of the observation. This is one
of the many lame devices which have been contrived
to measure the snowfall at a given spot during the
year. It is supposed that interesting data, and
points of comparison from year to year, may thus ɜ
collected. And these, with observations made at
other places in the glacier zone, are digested and
published from time to time.

There is no doubt that the nivometer will show
every day in the year—though it will not be so often
noticed—the height at which the snow stands against

the face of that rock. But how much information can it give about the snowfall? Snow cannot find its true level on the face of a rock against which it is blown about by the wind and where it is interfered with by the temperature of the stone, sometimes heated by the sun and sometimes colder than the air surrounding it.

Snow is not like water or air. It is not an elastic consistent substance or a uniform fluid, like gas, seeking its own level or settling down upon a surface. It falls unevenly upon an uneven ground. It melts or accumulates, shrinks or flies about according to its local situation, and, within a given time, the nivometer will give very contradictory readings. A snow gauge is no easy thing to establish. When rain falls it is easily measured, because, in the course of nature, it is mere water. Not so with snow.

What is measured by the Alpine nivometers is the height of the snow lying at a certain place on a given day. Density cannot be checked. Yet it operates immediately after the snowfall. This mode of mensuration gives no reliable clue. Some of the snow was carried away by the wind that would have remained on a windless day. Some has been blown from elsewhere, in what proportion it is impossible to tell. How much has melted depends on the sun heat, and the amount of this deficiency no instrument is there to record. A storm may have intervened. Another may have blown the snow flat, concentrating the total mass within a smaller compass. Another may have piled it up in abnormal wreaths.

The science of snow measurement is quite in its infancy. When it is developed it will probably be on lines very different from those at present followed, and the results cannot be foretold.

Natural nivometers should be raised above the surface like dovecots and set up in wide - open spaces, in situations exposed to the four winds of heaven. They should be able to receive on all sides the snow moving in the air. They should be in the shape of a cone with long, gently sloping sides. And even then they would not prove much, unless the snow they had collected was gauged after every fall and the apparatus swept clean and prepared to receive the next fall on a smooth surface.

It would then probably be found that the amount of snow falling on the glaciers of the Alps is much smaller than we are apt to imagine. In any case, the depth of the snow that finds a permanent station upon the rock and ice surface of the Alps, till spring, is only a fraction of the depth of snow that would be obtained by adding together each volume of snow that might be gauged after each separate snowfall. Snowflakes form an aggregate which gradually passes into a conglomerate. They lie at first like the pieces of a game of spillikins, at different angles with one another. By degrees the crystals lose their shape. The edges of the prisms die out. The air that circulated between them is expelled. A hard texture takes the place of the flimsy structure of the first moment. In this process of reduction in volume and of increase in density, cracks are gene- rated in the mass. They are at first potential and remain latent till wind-pressure, or the footfall of man, determines the bursting open of the surface, accompanied by a report which sometimes unnecessarily alarms the unwary, and at other times is a sure sign of a dangerous snow-quake.

The depth of the snow is also modified by a process of sublimation which causes it to shrink rapidly. The atmosphere while re-absorbing the air expired by the snow, also re-assimilates some of its moisture, even without the suggestion of a thaw.

The outcome of so many efficient causes may be summed up in one word : shrinkage. But, as snow almost always is wind-driven when it falls, a large portion of the quantity follows in the air a course parallel to the wind, and (when it strikes obliquely the smooth and slippery surfaces—old snow, ice, rock surfaces—over which it travels instead of locating itself upon them) it is impelled forward, and sweeps along till it can find a lodgement against a solid protuberance, or is dropped over the edge of some break in the surface, out of the reach of the wind, when it finds a resting-place and gets piled up. This is another reason why one meets with less snow on the wind-swept, high-lying surfaces than in the middle zone of the Alps.

A third effective cause is to be found in the clouds. Snow-laden clouds do not generally unload themselves at a very high altitude. They form themselves in belts on the lower flanks of each range and pour forth their contents nearer the grazing and forest zone than one would be led to expect when one looks up towards them from the bottom of a valley. We then see the basement and sides of the cloud masses. We project their vertical lines almost infinitely into space. This is the kind of delusion to which we are subject when we look at a house from the street-level or, *vice versâ*, when we look down from a roof on to the pavement. The actual volume of snow whirling above our heads is considerably thinner than we assume. This is the case particularly during the winter season in Switzerland, as winter balloonists may testify.

So, without entering any further into the scientific aspects of this question, we wish here to note provisionally that a properly conducted nivometric survey of the Alps might show that the winter snow storage is quite out of proportion with the quantities required to replenish the upper ice-forming reservoirs to whose function so much importance is attached in the current theories about glaciers.

From the hut try the ascent of the Aiguille du Tour the following morning. On ski, along the easy slant of the Glacier d'Orny, and then by an easy climb, lasting one hour at the most, on good dry rock (3,531 metres = 11,615 feet); this undertaking will be a great delight. The upper reaches of the Glacier du Trient and of the Glacier d'Orny are one of the most magnificent ski-grounds that man can imagine. They can be taken advantage of both before sunset on the day of one's arrival at the hut, which should be reached by two o'clock, and on the next day, for a departure at eight from the hut should enable you to be on the Aiguille du Tour by eleven, which leaves the whole afternoon for runs.

THE VALSOREY GLEN.

To face p. 190.

Your third day can be employed in ascending the Aiguille du Chardonnet (12,585 feet) as follows: ski up to the Col du Tour; ski down the pass facing west, and leaning a bit to your left; then up the slope from right to left (that is facing full south) at first, and then full west, along the foot of Aiguille Forbes. From the moment you have passed that point the ski-runner becomes a climber. You may have to cut a few steps to reach the eastern *arête*, which runs from the dip on the west flank of Aiguille Forbes to the top. The *arête*, of course, requires rope and much skill in manipulating it.

In splendid weather, the rock being free from snow or ice, and, into the bargain, well known to one of the three of us, we did the climb without experiencing anywhere a moment's delay. Time-table: Started from Cabane d'Orny, 5.50 a.m.; reached Col d'Orny, 7.15 a.m.; crossed Plateau du Trient to Col du Tour by 8.15 a.m.; passed foot of Aiguille Forbes by 10.20 a.m.; set foot on *arête* by 12 a.m.; reached top at 1.25 p.m.; completed descent of *arête* by 3.20 p.m.; resumed our ski at 4.20 p.m.; skied back to Col du Tour by 5.40 p.m.; got home by 7 o'clock.

Our rests were: Twenty minutes at 8.15 a.m., twenty minutes at 10.20 a.m., thirty-five minutes at 1.25 p.m., twenty-five minutes at 4.20 p.m., twenty minutes at 5.40 p.m.

For ski tours in the Mont Blanc range, consult the maps by Barbey, Imfeld, and Kurz.

The fourth day of this raid was employed in an easy and very fast run down to Orsières, then on a vehicle to Bourg St. Pierre, whence four hours on

ski bring the runner to the Hospice du Grand St.
Bernard, the gates of which are open night and day
to all-comers. A long night in a most comfortable
bed, after a most substantial meal, and followed by a
plentiful breakfast next day, made sufficient amends
for the nights spent in the Cabane d'Orny.

In summer the hospitality extended by the St.
Bernard monks to passing tourists—one may not
spend more than two nights under their roof—is
somewhat perfunctory, because they are oppressed
by numbers. In winter, on the contrary, they are
left to themselves. Time and solitude are somewhat
heavy and passers-by of some education are the more
welcome.

Within a lap of the hospice we were spied by the
famous dogs. They barked and made but a poor
pretence at coming towards us. They were terribly
handicapped in the snow, which we lightly brushed
with the flat of our ski. No wonder they floundered:
the floury snow was about 6 feet deep. Their fore
and hind quarters went under, and then hove again
into sight, while they swung out of one hole into the
next, as nutshells rising and falling with the waves.

This situation threw some fresh light upon their
legendary life-saving occupation. The tables were
turned. We were much better prepared to save
them from suffocation than they to lend us a helping
paw. In fact, one huge beast's efforts to get on
board my ski somewhat perplexed me.

We had struck out our own line, in coming up,
across the surges of the snow. The farther from any
path, the happier the ski-runner. But we saw

enough of the winter track to understand the usefulness of the dogs. The track is about 2 feet wide. It cuts in and out of the summer road, and consists simply of the narrow footpath which pedestrians and the monks have trodden hard. They manage to keep it open from summer to spring by directing upon it the little traffic there is. The snow hardens after each fall when walked on and raises the pathway by so much, building up by degrees a kind of elevated viaduct on which to remain is the condition of safe progress. Step out to the right or to the left by one inch, you drop down several feet into the drifts.

What this might mean, in the fog or during a blizzard, to those weary, ill-shod, ill-clad, under-fed Italian labourers who still choose that mode of transit to save their railway fare under the Simplon, we could easily imagine. The dogs, on the other hand, would keep upon the track and scent in what snow-covered spot the poor trespasser had missed his footing and strayed. The remainder would be spade and shovel work for the charitable monks.

Easter being early that year, Lent was drawing to an end. The house was wrapped in silence. The bells being hushed, a rattle croaked along the passages instead. But Lenten hospitality may be lavish and fishes must swim at all times, as the capital trout from the Dora Baltea experienced, that was floated on the best of wines down to a worthy home of rest. On the next morning we met a procession ; they were calves being driven up from Italy. They looked sickly against the pure sunlit

13

snow, but they capered and frolicked, and booed with joy. Well might they do so as long as the bells were silent. But after!

Years before this, the monks had been driven to the use of boards for getting about. They invented a rude ski wanting in the essential feature of modern planks, free action for the heel. With them the heel was fastened down to the boards. They sprinted and punted about with the help of a long stout pole, achieving quite a style of their own. With their long robes waving, and swinging their gaffs from side to side, now to steer, and now to propel their unsteady craft, with arms alternately raised and lowered, they cut very picturesque figures against a terribly bleak background, with their dogs pounding after them, till we lost sight of them behind the corner like a flock of mountain choughs.

My next day saw me across the Col de Fenêtre (2,773 metres = 8,855 feet), along the whole Val Ferret, back to Orsières, a most magnificent, perfectly easy and reposeful trip. From point to point, that is, from Orsières up the Val d'Entremont to the Col du Grand St. Bernard, and through the Col de Fenêtre, down the Val Ferret, back to Orsières, the ski-ing is first-rate, these valleys running on parallel lines, downwards, from south to north. The crossing from one col to the other, upon south-facing slopes, is the only unpleasant piece of ski-ing, though quite safe and easy.

A fatal accident befell here a party of runners a few years after. They intended running up the Val Ferret to the hospice when they committed a serious mistake. As the map shows, the summer path winds corkscrew fashion from the bed of the valley to the lakes of Ferret. Now, when a ski-runner is seen upon a steep winding path, or ploughing his way up the sides of it, it often means that he has not reconnoitred the skiers' route on his map. Those young men cut into a snow bulge, the snow ran out through the slit and overwhelmed one of them.

Those bulges are a most treacherous invention of the snow-fiend. They are best likened to an egg-shell full of sand, with some compressed air imprisoned between the shell and the sand. Break the crust, the air runs out with a puffing sound, and the snow, freed from pressure, begins to trickle through the hole, enlarging it. Then the whole mass, blowing itself out and thrown out of balance, comes down.

The study of the map would have shown to the victims of this phenomenon of nature that however much the corkscrew might be the right way up or down for loaded men and cows (the pack and the cow between them determine the lie of every mountain path), such a path was not for men mounted on skiffs that could choose their course upon the country-side with the same liberty of choice as a ship steering upon the open sea.

This brings back to my mind a regulation supposed to have been issued by a certain War Office on the Continent. Some zealous officers had been coaching their men in the use of ski upon open fields, and some trifling injuries had been entered by the army medico in his report sheet.

Next autumn a circular was received in every army corps recommending officers to teach ski-ing on roads only !

Last winter I was trotted up a steepish and narrow winding path by some well-meaning friends who had acquired their ski-ing from a "big" man. Some patches of the road under wood were sunk in deep snow; others, in the open, were ice; others bare earth and stones, and the whole was so well banked in that side-stepping was impossible.

When I mildly remonstrated—after, not before, discipline would forbid—I was politely told that so-and-so always took his parties up that way. No doubt, and quite heroic of him, *mais ce n'est pas le ski.*

In the evening of this day, which I reckon as the fifth, a conveyance carried the three runners, in whom the readers of this chapter may by now have become interested, to Châble, in the Val de Bagnes, and then to Lourtier, a convenient starting-point for an attempt upon the Combin region.

CHAPTER VII

THE GRAND COMBIN

The Panossière hut—Tropical winter heat—Schoolboys and the Matterhorn—Shall it be rock or snow?—The Combin de Valsorey—My third ascent of the Grand Combin—The track home—Col des Avolions—Natural highways of a new character—Twenty-three thousand feet ascended on ski.

N the sixth day of my expedition we left Lourtier shortly before 10 o'clock a.m., knowing full well that we were in no hurry, that we meant to thoroughly enjoy our day's work, and that the hospitable door of the Cabane de Panossière would be no more difficult to open after sunset than before.

As soon as we had passed the last houses of Lourtier, we put on our ski, and, practically, did not remove them from our feet till eight o'clock that evening, allowing for two hours' rest in the heat of the day, from two to four. We branched off from the Fionnay direction to turn to the right at Granges Neuves, crossing the bridge to Mayens du Revers, and hence rising towards the path that leads in summer from Fionnay to the Alpe de Corbassière. We thus reached, by two o'clock, after passing the wooden cross at the point 1,967, and just beyond the chalets of the Alpe de Corbassière, the point 2,227 of the map. We spent there two hours, under a tropical sun. Then we plunged down a gully to the west, on our right, so as to advance on ground which the sun had not softened, and rose again along the side moraine to the point 2,644, whence there lay before us a most romantic moonlit landscape.

The hut was still in darkness when I reached it, the last of the party, in order to enjoy the sensation of seeing the windows dimly lit by the candlelight within, and the smoke curling up out of the chimney. The impression was one of charming " cosiness," in the middle of a more than Arctic landscape, and there was that sublimity above and around which beggars the art of description. A snow and wind-tight Alpine hut, well stocked with fuel and blankets, well supplied with plain food and wholesome drink from the provision bag of its guests, is, in mid-winter, one of the snuggest " ingle-nooks " a natural epicure may wish for, and, strange to say, what he may therein find most pleasurable is the shade and coolness of the shelter, so fairly could I compare our tramp of that day to a trip in the " scrub " under the equator. Forsooth, the prejudice which still prevails against roaming in winter at high altitudes is a remnant of that state of mind which kept early explorers of the High Alps tramping round and round the foot of such hills as the Matterhorn, which

Macaulay's healthy "schoolboy" would now think nothing of rushing at, with his sisters trailing behind.
If it is possible, in sporting circles, to speak of the *Zeit Geist* without pedantry, we should say that the spirit of the time, in matters mountaineering, has undergone a remarkable change since the advent of Macaulay's proverbial schoolboy.

Or is the change not rather a return to a healthier frame of mind?

It is quite true that in few sports is the extreme penalty, death, so constantly near at hand as in mountaineering. But is it not quite apparent, too, that the early lovers of the Alps were full-grown, leisured, and cultured men, whose training, occupation, or temper, had not properly prepared them to see the risk in its true proportions? From them a whole generation took the cue. Then came another, for which the taking of risks exceeding the *modicum* attached to a passive existence was the touchstone of manliness. They sought in the Alps opportunities for strenuous displays, as well as haunts where the harassed soul could take holiday. They are the generation which made of Switzerland the playground of Europe. It is they who brought mountaineering to the present period, when first ascents have become a hackneyed amusement, and schoolboys marvel at the facility of undertakings which, when attempted for the first time in bygone days, rightly called forth the admiration of the civilised world. Is it in the modern spirit that, on the morning of my seventh day, with the grand unconcern of an ever-victorious squad, hitherto

scratchless, bruiseless, and unwearied, we took the
route, well known to all of us, which leads up the
Glacier de Corbassière to the Col des Maisons
Blanches ? On reaching the plateau which precedes
the col, we made up our minds as to the choice
between the two routes to the top of Grand Combin.

The choice lay between rock and snow. Rock won
the toss. From the Plateau des Maisons Blanches
we turned full south, and left our ski at the foot of
the steep snow and ice slope which leads to the Col
de Meiten. The track over this col, dotted upon the
map (Siegfried Atlas, Swiss military survey), crosses
the Combin rocks upon a snow belt from north to
south, where it ends upon the so-called Plateau du
Couloir. The ascent to the col—we were roped—
presented no difficulty. The crusted snow was easily
kicked into footholds.

The rocks of the Combin de Valsorey, which we
ascended from the col, now looking east, were
absolutely free from snow or ice, the only discomfort
being exposure to a hot sun in an excessively dry
atmosphere—just the thing, I should say, for sala-
manders, which, unfortunately, we were not. In
this respect our experience totally differed from that,
already alluded to, of Mr. Tauern and his friends.
Not only did they take to the peak further east, from
the corridor, *via* Grand Combin de Zessetta (this
summit is immediately south of the figures 3,600 on
the Siegfried), using climbing-irons on the steep ice,
but they experienced a cold so intense that they
were driven back.

For my part, being no longer a young man at all,

I felt so overcome with the dry heat on Combin de
Valsorey, that I remembered with complacency how
fully acquainted I was with the top of Grand
Combin, and how useless it would be to bore such
an old friend with another visit at an unusual time
of year. I went, nevertheless, and spent some
minutes of that triumphant afternoon in amicable
nods to Mont Viso, which somehow I had missed on
my previous visits.

The reader will gather from the late hours noted
in the following time-table what confidence a rock-
climber may gain from the knowledge that his ski
are waiting for him below, firmly planted in the
snow, and that a secure track marked on the friendly
element runs uninterruptedly from the spot where
they stand to a trustworthy refuge hut. We cheerfully cut through the loops of our ascending track,
by a perpendicular course, and, as the reader will
see, returned to the hut in an incredibly short time,
enjoying with untroubled mind the afterglow of a
magnificent sunset gradually whitening into mellow
moonlight.

Time-table : Left Panossière hut at 7.15 a.m. ;
reached first plateau by 8.20 a.m. ; reached Maisons
Blanches, 10 a.m. ; reached foot of Col de Meiten,
10.55 a.m. ; lunch, thirty-five minutes ; reached top
of Meiten pass, 12.20 p.m. ; reached top of Combin
de Valsorey, 2.30 p.m. ; reached top of Grand Combin,
3.30 p.m. (14,164 feet); afternoon tea on top of
Combin de Valsorey, thirty minutes ; left Combin de
Valsorey, 5 p.m., resumed our ski, 7.15 p.m. ; back
to hut, 7.45 p.m.

Remember that in runs like this, extending over
8 kilometres (5 miles), the runners must keep
together from beginning to end.

The eighth day of this fascinating circular tour was
an easy one. It is worth noting, as an instance of
many of the same kind, which moderately trained
ski-runners would find extremely remunerative. Our
eight days' work would form the third and last portion of a typical ski trip, such as the Val de Bagnes
enables the intelligent amateur to compose in various
ways, in this instance as follows : First day, from
Lourtier (where night lodging can be had at the
telegraph office), to Cabane de Panossière, viâ
Fionnay; second day, Col des Maisons Blanches,
and back to the hut ; third day, back to Lourtier viâ
Col des Avolions, leaving plenty of time to reach
Martigny by sledge, and catch the evening trains to
Lausanne, Geneva, Milan, or Berne.

The Col des Avolions is an insignificant incision
in the range of rocky heights which run along the
tongue of the Glacier de Corbassière on its west side,
from north to south. From the hut you cross the
glacier very much to the north, though slightly
inclining to the west. In an hour's time you will be
on the col, the vertical displacement from the hut
down to the foot of the pass being about 190 yards
(the difference between 2,713 metres and 2,523
metres is the amount " dipped "), while the rise from
the foot of the pass is 125 yards, approximately.
These 125 yards were practically all the climbing we
got that day. You will ascend with your ski slung
over your shoulders, the most convenient way when

the gullies are steep, short, and full of compact snow.

No man in his senses will attempt High Alp ski-running without strong, heavily soled and nailed mountain boots to his feet. The big nails round the toe of the boot are most valuable for lodging one's feet into steep snow slopes or couloirs, and a broad, flat, nail-fringed heel need never interfere with the running, unless the heads of the nails are uneven. Nails on the sides of the boots are less necessary.

From the Col des Avolions there is a delightful run down, full north-west, to the stream which the path crosses (see map) to lead up to the Chalets de Sery. Keep well to the right (east) of the point marked 2,419. We found the bed of the stream quite practicable on ski, as far as we required it to get round the point 2,419. Then we made for point 2,243, so as to keep on the level (about 2,190 metres), while leaving that point on our left, slightly above us. Then we proceeded down to the Alpe de la Lys, keeping above the tree-line, till we could ski down to Tougne on fairly open ground. Thence, to the bridge that crosses the Dranse to Lourtier, the ground is not complicated, or you may ski down to Champsec. We left the hut at 8 o'clock a.m., sat astride the Avolions saddle at nine, and entered Lourtier at twelve, having in nowise hurried ourselves.

It is a distinctive feature of mountaineering on ski that its votaries look for natural highways of a new character.

The winter snow opens up quite unexpected routes, and it will soon be the business of ski-ing clubs to issue maps revised from that point of view. A well-filled-up steep gully becomes an opportunity for building up a stairway that summer is unaware of. A gorge in which a dangerous stream brawls in summer on slippery rocks may now appear in the guise of an open and straight line of communication between upper and lower reaches separated by impassable shelves of rock. Glacier tails, at other times bristling with spiky *séracs* and riddled with gaping blue pits, turn into smooth bridges thrown over blanks in nature that were a torture to contemplate. Torrents are reduced to the size of tiny transparent rivulets closely hemmed in between narrow banks of solid snow and easily spanned by the long, pliable boards. A frozen-over and snow-wadded Alpine lake, toilsomely skirted in summer by winding up and down its rocky, broken shores, may be crossed from point to point by a smiling navigator. The word snowcraft acquires a new meaning. The runner eyes the country in its broad, general aspect, determines, map in hand, the bee-line leading to his destination, fixes upon the stretches of unbroken snow that will bring him round any unskiable places, and in the end gets home more after the style of birds borne through the air than after the fashion of the clod-hopping kind. Here is, to wind up with, a note of the total vertical displacement which we have shown may be attained, with ski, in the course of eight days. From Orsières to Cabane d'Orny, 1,802 metres; to Aiguille du Tour,

839; to Aiguille Chardonnet, 1,131; from Bourg St. Pierre to Grand St. Bernard hospice, 839; thence to Col de Fenêtre, 228; from Lourtier to Panossière hut, 1,613; thence to Grand Combin, 1,617; Col des Avolions, 125; metres, 8,194. Of course, the measurement on the ground would show a still more significant total, but I do not really believe that more than 600 yards need be added on that score. On the other side the following items may be deducted, as done on foot, climbing: Tour, 270; Chardonnet, 500; Combin, 1,000—metres, 1,770. This leaves, as actually ascended on ski, a minimum of 7,000 metres, a trifle under 23,000 feet.

CHAPTER VIII

ACROSS THE PENNINE ALPS ON SKI BY THE "HIGH-LEVEL" ROUTE.

The "high-level" route—Previous attempts—My itinerary—
Marcel Kurz—The wise old men of Bourg St. Pierre—
Maurice Crettex—Guides with bamboos and laupars !—The
snow-clad cliffs of Sonadon—The Chanrion hut—Sealed-up
crevasses—The nameless pass—Louis Theytaz—The Pigne
d'Arolla—The Bertol hut—Why the Dent Blanche could be
ascended—The ladies' maids' easy job—The dreadful
summer slabs—We push past two "constables"—My cane
—We bash in her ladyship's white bonnet—The Ice-Maid
presses gently my finger-tips—The cornice crashes down—A
second night in the Bertol hut—The Col d'Hérens—An
impending tragedy—A milk-pail *versus* ski—Dr. Koenig and
Captain Meade—The real tragedy of Theytaz's death—Ropes
and crevasses—Mr. Moore's account—My comments—The
Mischabel range and Monte Rosa.

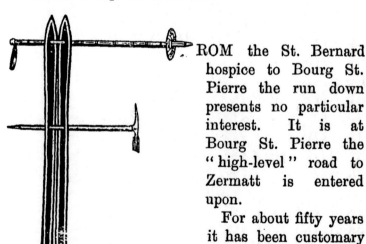

ROM the St. Bernard
hospice to Bourg St.
Pierre the run down
presents no particular
interest. It is at
Bourg St. Pierre the
"high-level" road to
Zermatt is entered
upon.

For about fifty years
it has been customary
to give the name "high-
level route" to the glacier passes which connect

Chamonix and Zermatt—Col d'Argentière, Col des Planards, Col de Sonadon, Col de l'Evêque, Col de Collon, Col du Mt. Brûlé, and Col de Valpelline. All these passes, except the second (Col des Planards), are above 10,000 feet and linked to each other by means of glaciers. This is the high-level route properly so-called, and as followed in summer.

The first attempt to cross the Pennine Alps in winter on ski, from west to east, was made by a party of four from Chamonix, namely, Dr. Payot, Joseph Couttet, Alfred Simond, and the guide, Joseph Ravanel, nicknamed " le Rouge." They started from Chamonix in the middle of January, 1903, and appear to have outlined for themselves the following route, which was intended to bring them in three days from the "Pavillon de Lognan," above Argentière to Zermatt :—

First Day.—Col du Chardonnet, Fenêtre de Saleinaz, Orsières, Châble (in Vallée de Bagnes).

Second Day.—Châble, Cabane de Chanrion.

Third Day.—Chanrion, Glacier d'Otemma, Col de l'Evêque, Col du Mt. Brûlé, Col de Valpelline, Glacier de Zmutt, Zermatt.

Obviously, this plan could not be carried into practice as it was laid down on paper. Into the bargain, the runners were stopped on the Col de l'Evêque by bad weather, and, being short of provisions, they backed down the Vallée de Bagnes, the whole way to Martigny. Thence they went to Evolena, and crossing the Col d'Hérens, they reached Zermatt. From Evolena to Zermatt the day was a long one, and they came down the Glacier de Zmutt at night (see *Revue Alpine*, 1903, pp. 269–284). This first attempt, over ground as yet unknown to the ski-runner, was broken up into three sections.

One month later (in February, 1903), two pioneers, who probably had no knowledge of this first feat, started in their turn upon the high-level route on ski. They were Dr. R. Helbling and Dr. F. Reichert. Starting from the Vallée de Bagnes, they reached with much difficulty the Cabane de Panossière, on the right bank of the Glacier de Corbassière.

After attempting the Col des Maisons Blanches in order to reach the Cabane de Valsorey, they found themselves compelled to return to the Cabane de Panossière, and thence crossed the ridge at Mulets de la Liaz. The descent on the face looking towards Chanrion was extremely trying. They had to carry their ski. Anatole Pellaud, of Martigny, who accompanied them, actually lost his pair, and came home along the Vallée de Bagnes, while the others spent the night in the wretched huts of la Petite Chermontane. The following day was spent in lounging about the Cabane de Chanrion. Then they went on to Arolla by the Mont Rouge, Seilon, and Riedmatten passes. At Arolla they slept in a barn, and next day ascended to the Cabane de Bertol. The last day in this uncomfortable pilgrimage was taken up in crossing the Col d'Herens, ascending the Tête de Valpelline, and descending to Zermatt (see Alpina 1903, p. 207, and following : Erste Durchquerung der Walliseralpen). This is, beyond doubt, one of the finest expeditions on ski that had yet been attempted in the Alps.

THE PENNINE RANGE FROM GRAND ST. BERNARD TO ZERMATT.

(Reproduction made with authorisation of the Swiss Topographic Service, 26.8.12.)

To face p. 208.

In January, 1908, the third attempt took place. Like the first, this caravan started from Chamonix. It consisted of M. Baujard (from Paris), with Joseph Ravanel, "le Rouge," and E. D. Ravanel. Already on the first day this party got off the bee-line. They went down to Châble along the Col des Montets and the Col de Forclaz, then to Chanrion. On the third day they left Chanrion at midnight, and got to Zermatt at 6.30 in the evening, having crossed the Col de l'Evêque, Col du Mt. Brûlé, and the Col de Valpelline (see *Revue Alpine*, 1908, p. 80).

As one sees, these three expeditions partly followed, or cut across, the high-level route. So far as the first three passes are concerned (those of Argentière, of Planards, and of Sonadon), they left them completely on one side. They were right in leaving the first. The best and only rational course is to traverse this part of the Mont Blanc range by the Col du Chardonnet, or the Col du Tour and Orny. Indeed, the Col d'Argentière, on the Swiss side, lands one in a wall of rock, where nobody should think of venturing on ski. The Col du Géant cannot either be used to any advantage.

The Col des Planards (2,736 m.), leading from the Val Ferret to Bourg St. Pierre, is quite skiable, but does not present the same interest as a run on a glacier. Thus if you start from Chamonix, you must, at least once, descend into the valleys. This necessity makes of the "high level" from Chamonix an empty word for the Alpine runner.

If you start from Bourg St. Pierre and proceed to Zermatt from pass to pass, you will travel along an

14

almost unbroken ice route, which may be compared
to that which leads across the Bernese Oberland from
the Lötschenthal to the Grimsel. Chanrion, at the
altitude of 2,400 m., is the only downward bend of
some depth on this road, the only place where one is
not surrounded by ice.

" Mr. F. F. Roget, of Geneva," says a newspaper,
" who in January, 1909, with Mr. Arnold Lunn,
explored the high-level route from Kandersteg to
Meiringen, planned out as follows his exploration of
the Pennine high level in January, 1911 :—

" *First Day.*—From Bourg St. Pierre to the Cabane de Valsorey
on the Sex du Meiten (3,100 m.).

" *Second Day.*—Col du Sonadon (3,389 m.), Glacier du Mt.
Durand, Cabane de Chanrion (2,460 m.).

" *Third Day.*—Col de l'Evêque (3,393 m.), Col de Collon (3,130
m.), Col and Cabane de Bertol (3,421 m.).

" *Fourth Day.*—Ascent of Dent Blanche and a second night in
the Cabane de Bertol.

" *Fifth Day.*—Col d'Hérens (3,380 m.), Glacier de Zmutt,
Zermatt.

" Mr. Roget was lucky in being able to carry out
this programme from point to point, with the
exception of a delay of one day in the Valsorey hut,
where the atmospheric conditions compelled him to
spend two nights. This disturbance in the weather
was in itself an additional piece of luck, as a fall of
snow, driven by a violent north wind, laid a fresh
carpet of dry stuff over the old, making the run,
the whole way to Zermatt, a perpetual delight.

" Mr. Roget had asked Mr. Marcel Kurz, of
Neuchâtel, to be his companion, and had engaged four

guides, all of whom did duty as porters, namely :
Maurice Crettex, Jules Crettex, Louis Theytaz (of
Zinal), Léonce Murisier (of Praz de Fort). The two
Crettex are natives of Orsières, and form probably
the strongest pair of ski-ing guides that the Canton
du Valais can now produce."

Marcel Kurz had been my companion on the
Aiguille du Chardonnet and on the Grand Combin.
He is the youth of eighteen alluded to in a
preceding chapter. He began his career as an
Alpinist in 1898 and, since, he spent every
summer in improving himself, Praz de Fort being
the usual summer quarters of his family. In 1906
he became acquainted with the Grisons ranges and
particularly with the Bernina peaks. The following
summer finds him in the Mont Blanc range, in 1908
he was in the Pennines. His first Alpine expedition
on ski was when I took him up the Chardonnet.

From that time he fell into my way of preferring
winter tours to summer climbing, and intends, in the
end, to publish the skiers' way up and down every
mountain in Switzerland to the top of which he may
be able to get on ski. For two years he presided
over that extremely distinguished society of young
climbers, the Akademischer Alpen Club, at Zürich.
Next spring, on leaving the Polytechnic University
of Switzerland, he will enter the Federal Topographic
Bureau in Berne as surveying engineer.

As a soldier, he was first a private—like every
able-bodied young Swiss—in the corps of machine
gunners attached to our mountain infantry. He
served his term as non-commissioned officer and is

now doing his officers' training course at Lausanne. I would not in this way offend Kurz's modesty and tax my reader's patience by giving here so many particulars about a life career which after all is only at its inception, and is not so very different from that of many young fellows of the same age, did I think it out of place that a sample should appear here of the manner in which mountaineering sport, professional studies or occupations, and military obligations are crowded together in the Switzer's youth.

The journey from Bourg St. Pierre to Zermatt was performed from Monday, January 9, 1911, to Saturday night, the 14th. It might have been done in half the time, but such was not the purpose of the expedition.

At Bourg St. Pierre we met with one of those quite trifling but somewhat unpleasant incidents with which mountaineers may be harried in those remote Swiss villages where winter sportsmen are quite a novel apparition. We fell upon a nest of those obsolete and retired guides who fill the emptiness of their lives with nothing and find in the idle habits they have acquired an excuse for passing adverse comments upon the new mountaineering. We could not but go about collecting victuals from the village shops, and did our packing in the public rooms of the hostelry known under the name of Déjeuner de Napoléon. This started the tongues of those who would talk. Buonaparte, indeed, seems to have bequeathed to those big-mouthed villagers, whom he astonished by breakfasting like any other mortal, a distinct capacity for bluff.

Three old guides sat, hours before midday, with a glass of kirsch huddled between their thumbs, eyeing our goings and comings and scanning all our doings. Then they consulted each other and began bragging of the wonderful exploits they had performed in their day. Having thus employed half an hour in impressing us, they proceeded to call our attention—simply by making much of it within our hearing—to the enormous risk we were about to incur by entrusting ourselves to such inexperienced men as those young madcaps whom we had brought along with us, and who had no share in the vast knowledge and weight of authority that had by degrees been amassed in Bourg St. Pierre.

When they thought they had successfully filled us with suspicion towards our men, they asked Maurice Crettex, in my presence, whether he had fully recovered from an accident he had met in the summer when running a cart-load of hay into a barn. The hay was toppling over and he had been badly squeezed between the wall and the cart while holding up the unsteady mass with his pitchfork. Little did they know that I was fully aware of that and had purposely wished to be Crettex' first employer since the accident.

All their sly dodges having failed, their vindictive jealousy and self-conceit, when we had left, ran into another channel, and of this a few words will be heard at the end of our chapter. The jolly old villain of Kippel was sterling gold as compared with that ugly crew.

First Day.—Fine warm weather, foehn wind.

From Bourg St. Pierre to the Chalets d'Amont
(2,192 m.), the ski-runner's track falls in with the
summer route ; but instead of climbing the chimney
over which stands a cross, the ski-runner keeps on
to the south, and enters on the left the gorge through
which escapes the water of the Valsorey glacier.
This glacier is thus reached, then the Grand Plan,
whence one discovers the hut standing on the Sex
du Meiten. Starting from Bourg St. Pierre at 11
o'clock, it was quite easy to reach the hut by
sunset.

I noticed that the guides were provided with
sealskins, light bamboos, and laupars. There can
be no question about the utility of sealskins on
long Alpine expeditions ; but a light, short bamboo
is certainly not the right weapon for a guide, and
laupars, with a few nails driven in, certainly are
most unsuited for glacier work. In other respects
the men were perfectly equipped. There were three
ice-axes in the party, two ropes, and everybody was
provided with climbing-irons.

Second Day.—A violent wind during the night,
then snow till midday, when the north wind gained
the upper hand, clearing the sky after 2 o'clock.
Beautiful sunset, clear night, 18 degrees Centigrade
under zero.

Third Day.—Weather beautiful ; quite half a foot
of fresh dry snow on the old wind-driven snow.

There is on the way from Bourg St. Pierre to
Chanrion over the Col du Sonadon a difficulty
which may have turned the earlier runners away,
and no doubt induced them to go round that range

THE SONADON CLIFFS.

To face p. 214.

from the north rather than go across. This obstacle
is the wall of rock which runs as an unbroken,
fortified line from the shoulder of the Combin on
the north to the Aiguilles Vertes in the south, and
divides the Glacier de Sonadon into two basins—the
upper and the lower. The old editions of the
Siegfried Atlas show a dotted line which passes
close to the Aiguille du Déjeuner (3,009 m.), but
it has been recognised that this route is exposed
to falling stones. Caravans now prefer to ascend
to the Plateau du Couloir under the shoulder of the
Combin, and to descend upon the Glacier de Sonadon,
and thus reach the pass of that name.

We were quite successful in traversing the snow-
covered rocks, along which ran in former days the
usual route. In case any runners should feel called
upon to prefer the new route, owing to the state of
the rocks and of the snow, here are some indications
as to how to strike upon the right course. From
the Valsorey hut one should climb straight up, on ski
or on foot, till one is on a level with the Plateau du
Couloir. If the snow is good it will generally be
found to be hard; if it is powdery, avalanches are
likely. From the Plateau du Couloir one may slide
down to the glacier and put one's ski on again,
getting gradually on a level with the Col du Sonadon.
I do not say that this track is better than the old
one which we took. The conditions of snow and
rock should each time be considered in the choice,
because open snow slopes on hard ice-worn rock are
the happy hunting ground of the avalanche fiend.

At 10 o'clock, having crossed the small Glacier du

Meiten, my party was standing on the edge of the high wall which overlooks the lower basin of the Glacier de Sonadon. For ski-runners the situation was somewhat ludicrous, and was not one in which to remain for any length of time. The party removed their ski, put on their climbing-irons, and the Crettex brothers, carefully roped, went forward as scouts. The snow was in capital condition (newly fallen powdery snow, very light and dry on the bare rocks, and in the couloirs old snow of great consistency). Progress was possible along a kind of ledge, which dropped slantingly along slopes whose angle of declivity was about 45 degrees. One's foot rested occasionally in the compact snow, and sometimes on the rock itself. This ledge presented an extremely narrow surface, and if one did not know that it is in use in summer one might question in winter whether it existed at all. It is very irregular, zigzagging across the couloirs and hanging on to the spurs which separate them, but extremely interesting.

When once the Col de l'Aiguille du Déjeuner had been reached, the snow showed a continuous surface on to the Glacier du Sonadon. The ski were once more put on, and the party " tacked " its way, first down, and then up, on slopes on which the sun brought trifling avalanches into motion. At about 3 o'clock in the afternoon the caravan was seated in the full glow of the sun on the Col du Sonadon (3,389 m.). An hour later began a rapid descent on the Glacier du Mont Durand—one of the many of that name—with one's face turned towards the sunset on the mountains above Chanrion (Ruinette,

Glacier de Breney, &c.).   One should avoid running
too low down on the glacier.   The thing to do is
to cross over to the north-east *arête* on Mont Avril,
and to descend full speed, pushing on to the Glacier
de Fenêtre, describing thus a vast semicircle on to
the tip of the tongue of the Glacier d'Otemma.
Hence by moonlight to Chanrion on the opposite
slope.   The hut was reached at 6 o'clock.   There
was but little snow in front of the door, and no snow
at all inside.   By that time the moon shone through
a damper atmosphere; the glass was somewhat
lower, though comparatively high (it remained so
throughout the expedition), but the cold had considerably abated since the morning.   This meant
the gathering up of mists during the night.

There is a serious drawback to the Chanrion hut.
Its situation marks it out as a most convenient resort
for Italian smugglers in the dull autumn and winter
months when the tourist traffic has ceased.   Those
smugglers cross over from Italy in large numbers,
bringing in farm and dairy produce, and then return
to their homes laden with heavy packages of tobacco,
sugar, and every kind of grocery that is heavily taxed
in their own country.   They are not above lifting
such things as spoons, forks, tin plates, and sundry
useful kitchen utensils, nay, even the blankets with
which the club huts are furnished.   Such movables
are therefore almost entirely removed from Chanrion
at the close of the summer season when the caretaker
comes down.   The six of us had to be content with the
barest necessaries out of the always very scanty club
furniture : six spoons, six forks, six plates, six knives,

six blankets : quite enough, you see, whether smugglers or no smugglers.

Fourth Day (January 12th).—As foreseen, the weather was dull. Departure at 8.30. Considerable masses of snow had filled up, or at least completely closed, the huge crevasses, which in summer are open at the junction of the Glacier d'Otemma with the Glacier of Crête Sèche. Not the slightest fissure could be detected.

There are at the outlet of the Crête Sèche glacier some interesting engineering works to regulate the outflow and obviate floods which have repeatedly visited the Dranse valley, owing to the collection of water in glacier pockets and their bursting when the weight is too great for the ice walls to bear. Of these not a sign could be seen.

As a long and wide avenue, the glacier stretched itself out before the runners, and out of sight. Grey mists, rising from Italy, hung loosely over the southern rim of the glacier. But when near the upper end, at an altitude of 3,000 m. or thereabouts, the mist melted away and the sun reappeared. Three passes had to be crossed on that day in order to reach the Bertol hut by night. At that time of year those passes were nothing more than slightly marked elevations in the snow-fields. The first opens between Petit Mt. Collon and Becca d'Oren. This pass, as yet nameless, and which it will be convenient to call here Pass 3,300 m., affords a much more direct route than the Col de Chermontane, or any other. Messrs. Helbling and Reichert had swerved away from the continuous snow-highway to the north. Messrs.

Baujard and Ravanel had taken refuge from the crevasses upon the rock passes south of the Bouquetins range. In our case the choice was determined by the requirements of ski technique. From Pass 3,300, gentle downward and upward slopes led us on to the Col de l'Evêque (3,393 m.), which was reached at 2.30 in the afternoon.

In the direction of Italy the sky had remained dull. To the north the mountains shone (including the Bernese Oberland) in a blue sky, in which floated a few clouds. The glass on that day, as before, gave very fair readings. There was but little wind, and the cold was not sharp.

On that day I conversed much with Louis Theytaz. It was with me a set purpose that he should accompany us on this expedition, since I had read in the Alpine Ski Club Annual, and otherwise heard, of his High Alp runs with Mr. W. A. M. Moore and some of that gentleman's friends. I wrote to Theytaz from Les Rasses above Ste. Croix. He joined me at Martigny. He was what one would call " a nice, jolly chap."

But was he in for bad luck ? He had hardly placed his things in the net of our railway carriage, going to Orsières, when his climbing irons fell from the top of his rucksack upon his head, badly bruising his forehead with the prongs. I had engaged him to carry my own pack, as I had made up my mind that I was now old enough to have a personal attendant all to myself. My luggage was particularly valuable to the whole party, as it contained all the spirits I allowed them, namely, in two large flasks, the contents of

four bottles of whisky, the proper allowance for six
men during six days in January weather at a minimum altitude of 10,000 feet. Theytaz surprised me
when, on arrival at the Valsorey hut, he violently
threw my pack upside down upon the bed planks.
The stopper of one of the flasks flew out, and then I
had the pleasure of seeing the floor streaming with
whisky. We got through to Zermatt very well on
the contents of the other flask. But the head of an
expedition so serious as this, when he has forbidden
wine and limited spirits to the supply which is known
to be in his possession only, does not like to see half
of it spilt on the first stage of the journey by an act
of sheer carelessness.

Anyhow, I viewed Louis Theytaz in the light of
what I had read and heard in his favour. Knowing
that he was again to accompany, within a fortnight
of leaving me, Mr. Moore and friends to the Pigne
d'Arolla, that mountain gained much interest in our
sight, as, with the searching eyes of ski-runners, we
examined its slopes dipping into the higher reaches
of the Glacier d'Otemma. We photographed it a
little later in the day in its eastern aspect. Seen
from the south and west it presented the most attractive appearance. From the east, it would have been
out of the question. What it might be from the
north we could suspect from its ominous hang
that way.

Recollecting that Messrs. Helbling and Reichert
had struck the Glacier de Seilon from the west, I
advised Theytaz either to lead his party down south
to the Col de Chermontane, or to take them back the

way they had come, and reach Arolla in the same
manner as the eminent gentlemen whose route was
on record. But I did not at the time attach any
particular value to my opinion, having learnt from
experience how much better things generally turn
out in practice than they appear likely to do when
considered by an over-prudent man in a pessimistic
mood. Louis Theytaz was swallowed up by a crevasse on the Glacier de Seilon.

From the Col de l'Evêque to the Col de Collon the
snow was hard for half a mile or so ; but as soon as
the northern slope of the latter was reached the snow
resumed its excellent quality. Thus the three passes
were crossed. Wide curves brought the party down
the gentle slopes of the Glacier d'Arolla to the level
marked 2,670 in the map. From that point we made
towards the right bank of the glacier, and landed on
the very steep slopes which rise between it and the
Plan de Bertol. Some of the party removed their
ski rather than run along the top of this ridge.
When we were well above the Plan de Bertol we
were careful not to dip into it, but turned in to the
right, and this move brought us to the foot of the
Glacier de Bertol, in which the six runners opened a
fairly deep track while tacking with geometrical regularity in the direction of the Bertol hut. They
gained about 25 metres in each tack. The moon lit
up their march. In the higher reaches of the glacier
the slope stiffened, but the snow remained excellent.

Let it be noted here that from one end to the
other of the trip we were entirely spared hard and
wind-beaten snows, except at the Col de Collon, as

above specified, this being the result of the day's delay in the Valsorey hut, during which it snowed so nicely. Moreover, the high-level route presents on its whole length a belt of comparatively low summits on the south side—low because the route is situated so high. This almost continuous parapet considerably interferes with the view upon Italy, but it is a protection from sun and wind, and no doubt assists in keeping the snow in good condition.

At seven o'clock in the evening the foot of the Rocher de Bertol was reached. The ski were hidden in a niche for the night. We climbed on foot, like dismounted dragoons, up the wall, the rocks of which form a kind of ladder. The rope which is permanently fixed there was available, though partly buried in snow. This hut, perched as an eagle's nest above the glacier, looks as if the Neuchâtel section of the Swiss Alpine Club (to whom it belongs) had wished to underline with a stroke of humour the Swiss Alpine Club regulations, which say that, in the first instance, huts are intended for the accommodation of the sick and wounded. The door was blocked up with snow, but the windows gave quite comfortable access to the kitchen.

"On that evening," says the newspaper already quoted, "the party became more confirmed than ever in Mr. Roget's resolve to attempt the ascent of the Dent Blanche. The condition of the mountains and the weather seemed to justify his anticipations. In forming that bold plan Mr. Roget had taken his stand upon the successful experiences he had had before in his winter ascents of the Aiguille du Tour,

the Aiguille du Chardonnet, the Grand Combin, the
Finsteraarhorn, the Diablerets, the Wildhorn, the
Wildstrubel, &c. It could not but be, he thought,
that the Dent Blanche, like all the foregoing peaks,
would present itself in January in such a good condition that its ascent by the south *arête* would be quite
possible. It was Mr. Roget's belief that the *arête*
would show in its fissures but a thin layer of dry and
powdery snow. He was convinced that the cornices
would show a full development, with their faces to
the east and south-east, but without any hem of snow
on the west side of the *arête*, where the ascent is
practically made. The slabs, he thought, would be
entirely covered with ice, but this ice, in its turn,
could not but be covered with an adhesive layer of
old snow, with fresh snow on the top of it, and this,
having fallen in comparatively mild weather, must
have cemented itself on to the old snow, so as to
form with it a reliable surface, at whatever angle a
footing might have to be gained. After a spell of
fine weather, the Dent Blanche could not be more
difficult in winter than in summer. In fact, he
thought the rocks had been shone upon by the sun
till they were dry and free of snow, the couloirs had
been swept clean by the wind or clothed in a firm
crust. That the cornices might come down with a
crash was evident, but this would be into the abysses
on the east slope, which was immaterial. On the
western slope the snow would be firmly enough
attached to the ice to leave but little opportunity for
the ice-axe to come into play."

Those forecasts, brought to the proof, were borne

out by reality. The snow, which had fallen three days before (a light, powdery snow, coming down in whirls), had gained no footing, nor could it, upon such an *arête* as that of the Dent Blanche. The little of it which the sun had not had time to melt we swept away with our gloved hands. It was an easy job, as that of ladies' maids brushing away the dust on their mistress's sleeves, and we certainly did not complain of having some little tidying-up to do.

Fifth Day.—At six in the morning some early mists were trailing slowly on the ice and snow-fields between the Dent de Bertol and the Dent Blanche. The light of the setting moon broke occasionally through the clouds. The weather might be uncertain—and it might not, for the glass was at fair. The mists turned out to be, as on the preceding days, such as herald a beautiful autumn sunrise. A start was made in the direction of the Col d'Hérens. Slowly the day dawned, and found the party on the Glacier de Ferpècle. By that time we could make out which was the real direction of the wind in the middle of those mists which seemed to drift about aimlessly. It actually blew from the north-east, then from the north, with a steady but moderate strength, which abated entirely only at sunset. The *impedimenta* were, for the most part, left on the northern side of Col d'Hérens, keeping but a few victuals, the three ice-axes, the climbing-irons, and two ropes. We turned the heads of our ski against the north wind, skirting the foot of the big southern *arête*, so as to reach a small terrace situated above the spot

marked Roc Noir on the map. On this terrace the
ski were firmly planted in the snow. Dismounting,
we fastened on our climbing-irons. Three ski sticks
were kept along with the three ice-axes.

Among the first rocks the party halted in order
to take some food. It was 9.15. By means of the
ropes two caravans were formed, and these soon
started, exchanging a cheerful *au revoir* in case some
incident should separate them.

The brothers Crettex and Marcel Kurz were on the
first rope; on another myself, Louis Theytaz, and
Léonce Murisier, this last carrying the bag of
eatables.

The fairness of the weather, the capital condition
of snow and rock, and the fitness of the party would
have made it quite possible to reach the top of the
Dent Blanche at one o'clock in the afternoon. But
there was no good reason for any hurry. A quick
march might bring on some fatigue, or at least some
totally unnecessary tension of mind and physical
effort. This would entail some slight additional risk
to no purpose whatever. The climbers had the whole
day before them, and need not make any allowance
for difficulties when returning to the Bertol hut, for
they would follow their own tracks (which they knew
to be safe) back across the glacier, whatever time of
night it might be. Consequently this ascent of the
Dent Blanche was deliberately carried out, and
almost without any effort. It was accomplished in
such leisure as not to need any quickening of the
pulse.

Maurice Crettex and Louis Theytaz were fully

15

acquainted with every peculiarity of the Dent
Blanche, and treated her with as much familiarity as
though they had been babes sitting on the lap of
their own grandmother. The Crettex section of the
caravan got on to the *arête* at a trot, and began to
ride it (the expression is false, but picturesque) at the
point 3,729. Lunch was relished at point 3,912.
Thence the two sections kept about 50 yards apart.
Up to the first Grand Gendarme the *arête* is
undulated rather than broken up, and quite comfortable to follow. There are fine glimpses on the
Obergabelhorn to the right and on the Matterhorn ;
the cornices of the *arête* formed round those pictures
magnificent frames with an ice fringe.

I had long been curious to ascertain what might
be in winter the condition of the famous " plaques "
or " dalles " (slabs), which have acquired such an evil
reputation in summer. No such thing was to be
seen. They were pasted over with excellent snow,
in which Maurice Crettex dug a few steps when the
ice came near to the surface. He seemed to do it as
a matter of form : assuredly it would have been an
irregular practice to do otherwise. It is true that
without our excellent climbing-irons we might have
been much less at ease. In point of fact, it was
enough to dig out the snow with one's boot-tips and
to stand firmly in the holes on one's climbing-irons
in order to skip over those formidable slabs.

The *arête* offered the best means of progress
immediately after passing the Grand Gendarme.
This appellation is bestowed upon the turrets, which,
constable-like, bar one's progress along a ridge. On

the rock of the *arête* there was the merest sprinkling
of fresh snow, so dry and light that it could easily be
brushed aside, and nowhere prevented one's gloved
hands from securely grasping the rock. The
scramble was quite interesting, and the hours passed
by so agreeably while proceeding up this magnificent
staircase, that nobody felt in a hurry to shorten the
pleasure of the climb. There was occasionally a bit
of a competition between Louis Theytaz, leader of
the second rope, and Maurice Crettex, leader of the
first, as to who should lead the van, but Crettex
would not yield his place, and stormed on.

Here I left my stick planted in a mound of snow
on the *arête*. We might, or might not, pick it up
on the way back, and I took my chance. This stick
was worthy of being planted and left there. It was
a beautiful bit of cane, smooth and white as ivory,
which I had picked up from a heap of drifted wreckage on the Cornish coast, in the preceding summer,
while bathing. What scenes it might have witnessed
upon the deep I did not like to picture. Yet, but for
its suggestive power, I should not have brought it
the whole way from Watergate bay.

It has always been my fancy to unite in one sweep
of vision the ocean and the mountains, the deepest
with the highest. My Dent Blanche might be one of
a school of whales stranded on high when the waters
withdrew, and my harpoon was well placed, sticking
in one of the vertebræ of her petrified spine.

At the time of writing, I understand that it is
there still, respected of the eagles and of the gales.
The summer thaw has left untouched the fleecy

patch of snow. The lightning has drawn in its forks before the unaccustomed wand. Now and then a guide writes me that he has seen it, that so-and-so could not believe his eyes when he led up the first party of the summer season and found an ivory staff shining on the ridge. In wonderment, he reported the matter to some colleague of mine who had heard in our club-room my first account of this ascent.

For my part, I am content to look upon this incident as confirming my views. A frail stick, planted in the middle of a patch of snow on the most exposed and weather-beaten *arête* in the Alps, appears here as the needle showing how nicely balanced are the scales of Nature.

In due course the rock came to an end, and the *arête* showed itself under the appearance of a white-hooded crest. It was the final pyramid. On that day, Friday January 13, 1911, the small, conic snow-cap which surmounted the brow of the peak was brought down by a blow from an ice-axe, at 3.30 p.m. A short time was spent on the summit. The view was now and then obscured by a cloud sailing rapidly down from the north and skirting the watch-tower on which stood the onlookers.

On the way down, each section, in its turn, with feet deeply embedded in the snow, reached again the bare rocks of the *arête*, having resumed the footprints made on the way up. But when leaving the snow that covered the terminal pryamid, the party did not continue on the *arête* the way it had come up, but wheeled to the right—that is, westward—and began ploughing in a downward course the slopes of the

Dent Blanche facing Bertol, which had the appearance of being all snow. In spite of the extreme steepness of the slope, the party, with heels and climbing-irons well wedged into the snow, advanced with great security and speed, though the irons did occasionally impinge upon the ice. The slope getting sharper and the layer of snow thinner, it became necessary to substitute a lateral or horizontal course for the vertically downward course. A few steps had to be cut before a footing could again be gained on the *arête*. But, by that time, the caravan had proceeded beyond both Gendarmes, and, though it was night, we could hop along quite nicely.

During this bit of traverse, being without a stick I rested my left hand upon the snow each time I moved forward, digging in my bent fingers to relieve the foothold from some of my weight. The Ice Maid then kissed my finger-tips very gently. The bite was so timid that the kind attention escaped my notice at the moment. But late that night, before the stove, in the hut, I struck a match upon the hot iron plates with my right hand, to light my cigar, while holding up some garment to the fire with my left. The heat made the mischief apparent. It caused almost no pain, only giving an earnest of what the Ice Maid could do if pressed too hard.

Through the mists of this January dusk the moon threw a gentle light, which made it easy to discern the footprints made in the morning on the snow. The few steps which had been cut here and there on the ice were quite visible, and the rope made it a simple matter to descend the rocky parts. So, from that moment, the descent consisted simply in repeating in the opposite direction the moves of the morning.

The cornices on the left hand were made more beautiful than ever by the play of the moonbeams through the icicles. Now and then some fragment of the cornice came down with a crash, and a cloud of dust arose from the abyss and sent minute crystals across the faces of the men. It was 8.30 when the party stood again beside their ski. An hour later we picked up our heavier luggage. Sitting on our rucksacks, we took an evening meal. Then, ropes and all being packed, the six strolled back across the Glacier de Ferpècle at pleasure, and, as fancy bade, each chose his own way. The night sped on, and half its course was almost run when we reached for the second time the hospitable nest on the Bertol rock. We might have been shades moving in a dream rather than men. Our task being successfully accomplished, we might claim a right to vanish away, like dissolving views thrown for a moment upon a screen.

Sixth Day.—The morning was long and lazy. At eleven o'clock, after a good rest and full of good cheer, we entered upon our last day's work. The sun shone brilliantly, and, thanks to his kindness, and thanks also to the smooth and sparkling snow, this last day, more than any of the foregoing, if possible, gave rise to one of those rambles on ski which are the delight of the Alpine explorer. On approaching the Col d'Hérens, the track of the preceding day was departed from where it had bent away towards the Dent Blanche, and the party

ON THE DENT BLANCHE, WITH MATTERHORN.

To face p. 230.

turned their backs upon their conquest. The rocks, which on the Col. d'Hérens divide the Glacier de Ferpècle, on the north, from the Stock glacier to the south of the Wandfluh, could just be seen emerging from the snow. The ski were removed for about ten minutes while descending those rocks.

It may be said that from that point to Zermatt the run was practically continuous. No obstacle of any sort ever came to interfere with the downward flight. Whenever the party came to a stop, it did so for its own pleasure and convenience. After the rush down the sides of the Stockjé came the run down the Glacier de Zmutt, with the icefalls of the Matterhorn glacier on the right. Fragments of ice studded the snow surface, and the ski occasionally grated against them. On the moraine, where in summer the surface is stony and the climber's brow wet with perspiration, we slid along as borne on by wings, rushing through the air. When we reached the Staffelalp the sun was begining to set. Over the tops of the arolla pines stood forth in a mighty blaze many friends visited of old —the Rimpfischhorn, the Strahlhorn, the Allalinhorn, the Alphubel; the beautiful mouldings of the Findelen glacier were bathed in rays of purple fire. On approaching Zermatt the snow proved heavy and deep. The ski got buried in it and shovelled along masses of it, somewhat delaying the running. Zermatt was reached by five o'clock at night.

The village was in a hubbub, and we arrived in the nick of time to ring the necks of I do not know how many birds of ill omen ready to take their flight.

The Bourg St. Pierre dunderheads had had six days in which to rouse the journalists. They had stuffed them with fusty words of ignorant wisdom. Reporters had telegraphed and telephoned, to make sure of their quarry. A column of guides had been warned by the head of the Zermatt relief station to be in readiness. They were to leave on the next morning for the scene of the expected disaster.

They might do so yet, for all we cared. By looking about carefully they might detect the tip of one of Mr. Kurz's ski, which had snapped off against a stone, at the moment when, entering the village at a quick pace, he had suddenly come upon a milkmaid with her pail balanced on her head. There was nothing for it but to go gallantly to the wall. This was more courtesy than the ski could stand. Its point came off, and this the rescue party might bring back as a trophy.

Joking apart, Zermatt gave us a grand reception, seasoned with steaming bowls of hot red wine and cinnamon.

Thus was accomplished the first successful ski-run from Bourg St. Pierre to Zermatt. Luck was good throughout; indeed, if an attempt to ascend the Dent Blanche on a Friday and on the thirteenth day of the month could not break the weather, nothing would.

The Crettex brothers went back by rail to Orsières. Louis Theytaz got out of the train at Sierre. He returned to his avocations at Zinal, looking with well-founded confidence to his next engagement, a few days hence, with Mr. Moore.

The Crettex' had no sooner reached home than a telegram reached them from my friend Dr. König of Geneva, one of the pioneers of the new mountaineering school, enjoining Maurice to expect him at once for a repetition of the successful expedition, news of which had meanwhile been carried to Geneva. Dr. König and Maurice found our ski track generally undisturbed, but the wind and sun had done their work upon the fresh snow, hardening it and covering it with the usual icy film. The running was fast and uncertain, for want of side support for the ski blades. On the way they climbed the Grand Combin, as I had done in 1907. Imitation by such a distinguished mountaineer was the most flattering form of appreciation I could look for. I met him some time after at our Geneva Ski Club, when he observed that he wondered not so much at what my party had accomplished—in which he was quite right, as I proved by producing the table of our very easy hours—as at the bold practical thought that had inspired and helped us.

Like me, Dr. König had noticed from the Zmutt glacier how practicable the Matterhorn would be. In fact, Maurice would have tackled the Zmutt *arête* on the slightest provocation. Meeting at Zermatt Captain Meade, who had just achieved the Zinal Rothhorn, Dr. König communicated to him his observation concerning the Matterhorn. As was soon made public, Captain Meade succeeded in making a January ascent of the Matterhorn. Unfortunately he suffered very severely from exposure.

I had returned to my ordinary occupations in
Geneva, when I was startled one morning by a note
in the local papers. On the very day on which
Captain Meade was "doing" the Matterhorn—
January 31st—Louis Theytaz was perishing on the
glacier de Seilon, an occurrence which changed an
otherwise successful trip into a dreadful ordeal.
The cold may be gauged from Captain Meade's notes
in the *Alpine Journal*. The thermometer down at
Zermatt at 7 a.m. showed 27 degrees of frost
Fahrenheit.

The fatal accidents to ski-ing parties that I so
far know of in the Alps have proceeded from one
or another of three causes : avalanches, exhaustion
ensuing upon stress of weather or losing one's way,
and crevasses. For no accident yet can ski be
made responsible, a rather remarkable exception,
when one reflects how easily a ski blade may
break or a fastening get out of order.

Theytaz's accident was caused by a crevasse.
He was one of four able and well-known guides
accompanying a party of three gentlemen who put
implicit faith in their leadership and in whom
they had every confidence.

The third on a rope of three, Louis Theytaz
followed the two leading over a crevasse which,
after the event, showed itself about 7 feet wide,
and of which the party had become aware before
launching themselves across it. It was unfortunate
that the leading guide "took" the crevasse obliquely
to its width. The moving rope, too, compelled each
man in succession to bring his weight to bear on

TOP OF DENT BLANCHE.

To face p. 234.

the same spot. The rope could not be of much use for want of stable supporting points. A man advancing carefully on foot breaks his speed at every step. Not so a runner on ski.

The gentleman preceding Theytaz made a stopping turn on the further side of the crevasse, and waited to see him over. By that time Theytaz's brother Benoît, who was leader on the rope, might have been ready. Anyhow, the snow broke. Theytaz was hurled down and the rope snapped.

I was on the very rope when ascending the Dent Blanche. It was an old rope, but perfectly satisfactory. Why are the best of ropes liable to snap? After this accident, which roused his personal interest as it did mine, my friend Kurz instituted experiments on all kinds of rope material on the market. The results showed conclusively what rope material, under tension, was the best, but no light was thrown upon the supposed greater liability to snap when frozen, either when dry or after absorbing moisture. All we know so far about the breaking-point of mountaineering ropes, is that they may break under a shock which will leave a man unmoved in his steps though, on trial, they may resist a tension far greater than can be put upon them by the dropping suddenly into space of a man's weight.

An athlete may burst a taut chain by muscular effort. A horse may burst his girths by a little inflation. What about a slack rope?

Popular imagination, baffled by such obvious but unexplained contingencies, at once suspects foul play. The strangest stories may be heard in the Val d'Anniviers about Theytaz's broken rope.

Mr. Moore's own account appeared in the Alpine Ski Club Annual for 1911, and runs as follows :—

"On January 28th last, a party assembled at Martigny, A. V. Fitzherbert, A. D. Parkin, and myself, with four guides : Félix Abbet and the three Theytaz brothers, Louis, Benoît, and Basile, all of Zinal. Next morning we walked up to Fionnay, where a small hotel had been opened for us. The snow was in perfect condition, and as we had an hour or so of daylight to spare, we enjoyed some practice runs on an excellent slope just outside the village. Here we made the acquaintance of three ex-presidents of the Geneva section of the Swiss Alpine Club, who were learning to ski in this deserted retreat. They had a comfortable chalet, where we spent a most pleasant evening, surrounded by Alpine paintings and old Swiss wood-carved furniture.

"At 8 a.m. on the 30th we got off, provisioned and equipped for a hard two days, and started up the valley to Chanrion. It was easy-going as far as Mauvoisin, but beyond that the summer path was quite impassable in places, owing to the overflowing and freezing of streams. We lost much time over these, and finally had to descend to the bottom of the gorge, which afforded much better going."

May I break here the thread of the narrative to insert an observation. Louis Theytaz had got information from us as to this passage, and had

been told that the summer path was known in the
Bagnes valley to be impassable in the winter,
particularly with ski. The gorge is the right ski-
ing route.

"A steep and trying couloir brought us up to
Chanrion. We left next morning at 6.30, and
made for the Glacier de Breney, where we were
able to put out the lamp. It was pretty cold.
Near the top there must have been nearly 50
degrees of frost. The glacier presented no difficulties, the only obstacle being an ice-fall, up
which we had a little step-cutting.

"The trouble began about an hour below the
Col de Breney, where we were met by a piercing
north-east wind, which struck us in gusts, sweeping
up clouds of powdery snow, through which one
could hardly see. The snow was quite hard under
foot, and all, except Louis, took their ski off on
reaching the col. Half an hour's walking brought
us to the top of the Pigne (12,470 feet), where we
got the full benefit of the gale. The view, however,
was magnificent, and fully justified the struggles
of the last few hours.

"We stopped on the top about five minutes, and
then returned to our ski and began the descent to
the Glacier de Seilon. For half an hour we
descended on foot over wind-swept slopes, at
first gentle, and then steep and crevassed, till we
at last got out of the wind and into the sun, when
a short halt was made. At this point I became
painfully aware that three fingers had been tempor-
arily frost-bitten. Parkin also had lost all feeling

in his toes, but did not realise how bad they were till later on. We were soon off again on ski, and on perfect running snow, in the following order: Benoît, Fitzherbert, and Louis on the first rope, myself and Parkin on the second, followed by Félix Abbet and Basile unroped.

"As we approached the ice-fall which gives access to the Glacier de Seilon, there occurred the sad accident which cost Louis his life, depriving us of an old and tried companion, and the Valais of one of its best guides. We were running down and across the glacier when the leading three came to a small depression and ridge running straight down the slope parallel to the sides of the glacier, evidently a crevasse bridged over by snow. The first two crossed safely, but apparently loosened the snow, which gave way under Louis. He fell back into the crevasse which was about 8 feet across, and as the rope tightened, it snapped, and he was gone. Basile was running on to the bridged crevasse a little higher up, at the same moment, but although it gave under him, his pace carried him over, and he fell clear. Abbet was just behind Louis and saved himself by throwing himself down."

Mr. Moore next gives a sketch of the crevasse and of the position of each inrelation to it. Then he continues: "This journal is no place to describe the half-hour which followed, the memory of which is only too fresh for those who were present. It is enough to say that we could not reach Louis with 130 feet of rope, and had to tear ourselves

L.M.C.

ON THE STOCKJÉ, LOOKING EAST.

To face p. 238.

away. It was a great relief to know from subsequent examination that, although we had heard him answer for about five minutes, he could not have lived longer, and in all probability felt nothing. The search party of guides that went up next day found the body 160 feet down, and as we had only 80 feet of reliable rope, we could have done nothing."

The sketch shows—and its accuracy cannot be doubted—that Messrs. Moore and Parkin were keeping a course that led them past the crevasse without touching it; that Basile Theytaz showed less discretion, and escaped because, being unroped, he came singly on the bridge, in a place where the crevasse was narrower and when he was sufficiently under weigh. Abbet escaped simply because he approached the crevasse in the wake of Louis Theytaz, and took warning in time, for he was about to cross the gulf at its widest.

One may say—in all kindness and with every sympathy—that the roped party which met with the accident was badly led, and one may say so the more confidently, as the leader seems to have been fully aware that he was heading for a formidable crevasse.

When planning my traverse from Bourg St. Pierre to Zermatt, I had it in my mind that an expedition across the Pennine Alps from end to end would not be complete, unless I pushed on over the Mischabel and Weissmies ranges to the Simplon pass, beyond which begin the Lepontine Alps.

The weather was so fine and our powers of endurance had been so slightly taxed that we might easily have pushed on. In fact, in respect of weather, circumstances remained so favourable that we might have continued till the end of February without experiencing a check. The weather report was so perpetually : Still and warm in the High Alps.

Unfortunately Marcel Kurz had broken his ski, and it might be just as wise to go home and nurse my frozen finger-tips. There are other things in life than ski-running. So we came to the conclusion that we had done enough for glory.

However, Marcel Kurz took this spring (1912) his revenge over the misadventure to his ski and, with some friends, completed our interrupted programme.

I append here his notes, as the Mischabel range is about to be an object of great interest for British runners who will find that Saas Fée has become a nursery of excellent ski-running guides.

At the moment of writing (August, 1912), the Britannia hut on the Hinter Allalin, as already pointed out in this volume, is about to be formally inaugurated. It opens up to the ski-runner a magnificent field for exploration on account of which the English ski clubs liberally contributed to the erection of this ski-runner's hut *par excellence*.

The map entitled Mischabel–Monte Rosa shows one of the numerous zigzag tracks for which the district will become famous.

Mr Kurz's notes show also what an incredible

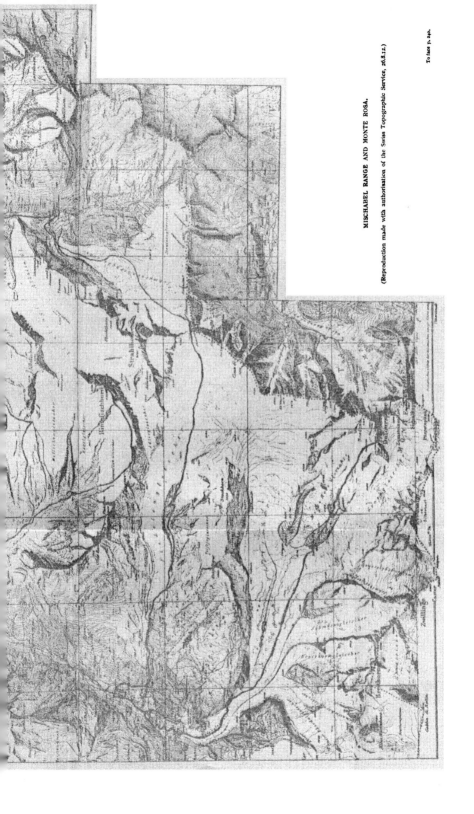

MISCHABEL RANGE AND MONTE ROSA.

(Reproduction made with authorisation of the Swiss Topographic Service, 26.8.12.)

To face p. 240.

amount of stiff mountaineering can be crowded easily into a short time by ski-runners, including the ascent of Monte Rosa, the highest peak in the Alps next to Mont Blanc. The latter is not a ski-runner's mountain. The gradients are too sharp and exposed. Monte Rosa, on the contrary, is an ideal runner's mountain. I lay no stress on the fact that Mr. Kurz's raid was guideless. I have endeavoured elsewhere to show how much this term is a misnomer when applied to perfectly competent mountaineering parties that dispense with professional guides.

March 27*th.*—We started three from St. Nicolas for the Mischabel hut up the glacier of Ried and over the Windjoch pass. The weather was very fine, extremely warm at about three o'clock in the afternoon. The glacier was extremely broken up, presenting the same appearance as in autumn. Would do very well for ski in a normal year, particularly on the higher *névé*. The last 300 feet of the Windjoch should be done on foot. On the top of the pass there rose an unpleasant west wind, and the snow being most unpleasantly hard, we elected to leave our ski on the spot, intending to come back for them on the next day and to ascend the Nadelhorn by the way. We spent the night at the Mischabel hut.

March 28*th.*—Very uncertain weather ; too much wind to attempt the Nadelhorn. We walked down to Saas Fée in two hours on very firm and very reliable snow.

March 29*th.*—On hard snow and dry rocks we

walked up to the Gemshorn and thence along the
snow *arête* to the Ulrichshorn, coming down on to
the Windjoch to pick up our ski. We then ran
down the Riedgletscher till within a few hundred
feet of Gassenried, and thence walked to St. Nicolas,
first on hard snow and then on wet snow.

March 30th.—We walked from St. Nicolas and
then skied to a fairly hospitable hut on the Untere
Taesch Alp.

March 31st.—Along the Untere Taesch Alp and the
Langefluh glacier, our ski carried us up to the *arête*
rising above the Rimpfisch Waenge and along that
arête to the altitude of 3,600 metres. Then on foot
along the ordinary route we reached the top of
the Rimpfischhorn (13,790 feet). The ascent took
seven hours, the descent four hours. The rocks
were absolutely dry, as "summery" as possible.
This is a very interesting ski tour and had not yet
been attempted.

April 1st.—The weather is bad; we come down
to Taesch and go to Zermatt to get fresh supplies.

April 2nd.—Weather splendid with a furious
north wind. We return to our cabin on the
Taesch Alp. One of us returns to the lowlands and
two only are left to continue the campaign.

April 3rd.—The weather is very cold and we
make too early a start. We cross the Alphubeljoch
to Saas Fée, leaving the Alphubel unascended on
account of the fury of the wind. A pass somewhat
steep from the Taesch side and somewhat crevassed
on the Saas side, from the runner's point of view,
but magnificent with respect to scenery.

FOOT OF STOCKJÉ, LOOKING EAST.

To face p. 243.

April 4th.—Weather magnificent. North wind not so strong. We ramble most delightfully on our ski from Saas Fée to Mattmark, which is a deadly place in other respects.

April 5th.—From Mattmark to Zermatt by the Schwarzberg Weissthor. Weather mild, foehn, rather cold on the top, magnificent outlook over Zermatt. The snow hard throughout allowed us to ski up very quickly (four hours from Mattmark to the summit, 3,612 metres). At Findelen we enjoyed an afternoon nap under the arolla pines. Amid regular flower-beds we descended to Zermatt, where we met two other friends.

April 6th.—From Zermatt to the Bétemps hut on Monte Rosa, following the Gorner glacier from the beginning and employing half an hour in crossing the *sérac* zone on foot. The heat on the upper reaches of the glacier was most overpowering.

April 7th.—Monte Rosa. Snow quite hard here, and everywhere else, throughout this fortnight. Weather beautiful, slight north wind. We left the hut at six o'clock, reaching the top at 12.35.

April 8th.—Not a cloud in the sky all day long. We take sun baths all day about the hut.

April 9th.—We intended to ascend the Lyskamm, but bad weather came and punished us for our idleness on the preceding day. Foehn and fog. There was nothing to do. We ran down to Zermatt in two hours along the whole of the Gorner glacier.

This laconic record is extremely instructive. It bears out the contentions already formulated in other parts of this book. The snow surface was hard, reduced in volume, and as cemented by the wind. The *arêtes* were bare of snow, free from ice, and perfectly dry. The crevasses were either plainly visible or firmly crusted over. Ski were throughout useful in preventing the surface from breaking underfoot, perhaps still more in going uphill than when rapidity of movement lightens one's weight flying downhill. The summer of 1911, as one knows, was one of the two driest on record in the preceding half-century. The glacier snow was therefore worn down to its thinnest when the winter snows began to pile themselves in layers above them. These too remained comparatively thin, affording admirable running surfaces when sprinkled over with fresh snow.

CHAPTER IX

THE PIZ BERNINA SKI CIRCUIT IN ONE DAY

Old snow well padded with new—Christmas Eve in the Bernina hospice—The alarum rings—Misgivings before battle—Crampons and sealskins—A causeway of snow—An outraged glacier—The Disgrazia—A chess-player and a ski-man—Unroped!—In the twilight—The Tschierva hut—Back to Pontresina—Hotel limpets—Waiting for imitators.

T the close of 1910 Marcel Kurz was at Pontresina. I had occasion to draw up certain reports upon the winter aspect of the district, and he kindly undertook the inspection of the glacier routes for me. A few glorious days seemed about to efface the memory of many previous gloomy ones. On the day on which this account begins, a little snow had fallen in the morning, the skier's welcome *quotum*. Nothing affords such excellent sport as old snow well padded out with about a foot of new floury stuff. The ski blades sink nicely through the top layer of rustling crystals. The ski-points pop out of the snow like the periscope of a submarine. The sparkling prismatic flakes stream past each side of the lithe, curled-up blade, like silvery waves parted by the prow of a fast motor canoe.

"The north wind," writes Mr. Kurz, "was now clearing the sky of every cloud, leaving the dazzling snowy heights and the forests below steeped in sunshine and brightness. It was our last chance, and, in a few minutes, our minds were made up to accept it. Half an hour later we were in the train on our way to the Bernina pass.

"The exact itinerary of this expedition I published in the *Alpina* (Mitteilungen des Schweizer Alpenclubs) number of February 1st, 1911, p. 22. The following only being intended as a short sketch, I will not describe the route too minutely. The principal landmarks are : Pontresina, Bernina pass, Alp Palü, Palü glacier, Fellaria glacier, Upper Scerscen glacier, Fuorcla Sella, Sella glacier, Roseg glacier, and back to Pontresina.

"'Grützi Herr Staub! Grützi Herr Kurz!' These first words of greeting, uttered on our arrival by our little friend at the hospice, showed her evident pleasure on seeing us so soon back again. It was, in fact, our second visit to the hospice within the week, but this time we came firmly intending at last to carry out our plan.

"Here was the same low-ceiled, comfortable room in which we had sat before, while the landlord and his friends talked the whole evening away, with a big dog snoozing by the stove. We had taken supper at this very table with Casper Grass, the Pontresina guide, on Christmas Eve. Here had huddled together an Italian couple, busily writing endless cards of Christmas greetings. The landlord, ever to be remembered, his bead-like eyes looking out from behind his spectacles with a malicious twinkle, stood up at times, munching a long ' Brissago,' to see that all was right, while talking volubly in Italian. A maidservant sat at the corner table, pen in hand and with vacant look, evidently stuck fast in the midst of her literary endeavours. Not a star was to be seen outside, and the howling wind, rattling the shutters with every gust, made us feel how rash it was to have come at all. To drown the sound of the storm we set the phonograph going, which cheered but little our drooping spirits. Still, we started on the morrow, but on arriving at the Alp Grüm, the violence of the wind made it impossible to go further—a disappointment we had anticipated.

" But now we were out on our second attempt, and would not go back. This time our friend Grass had unfortunately been obliged to remain behind at Pontresina, in spite of his longing to join our expedition. The weather was fine and cold, intensely cold. Our chances of success were great ; the reconnoitring done on Christmas Eve had sharpened our appetite for the unknown beyond.

* * * * *

" The alarum had rung long since, and our candle had been alight some time. The window-panes, white with frost, shut out the black night and the piercing cold ; never had one's bed felt so comfortable. If our bodies remained motionless, our thoughts wandered forth, trying to pry into the secrets still lying concealed in the lap of the coming day, just as the watchman's lamp pierces the darkness of the night.

"There is a delightful thrill of impending battle hazards in being the first to break upon new ground, as when a troop nearing the line of fire eagerly questions the dissolving morning mists and doubtingly greets the light that will expose it to the enemy's strokes. What unkind shafts might Fate have in store? What bolts might the glacier be preparing to fire off, when we should pass under the portcullisses of its castellated strongholds? With what pitfalls might the snow desert not be strewn under the winning aspect of its rustling silken gown?

"If we wished to reach the Roseg glacier before nightfall, we must cross the Fuorcla Sella between four and five o'clock that afternoon. This, supposing that we should have passed the Palü glacier by midday. All that, and back to Pontresina, in one day! Would it be very hard work? That was the question, for nobody had yet ventured there in winter, and on ski.

"Thus did our thoughts travel till we finally dropped off to sleep again, only to wake a few minutes later with a start, and leap from our beds to make up for lost time.

"At 6.30 we left the hospice. It was pitch dark, though numberless were the stars shining overhead, so the lantern was lighted which had already guided many travellers. A cheery voice, from one of the

PIZ BERNINA CIRCUIT.

(Reproduction made with authorisation of the Swiss Topographic Service, 26.8.12.)

To face p. 248.

windows above, wished us good luck, and with this pleasant sound in our ears we started on our way.

" Having reached Lago Bianco, we went due south, the wind at our backs. Looking down, we saw the valley of Poschiavo sunk in the mist. We rapidly crossed the lake and the level ground beyond, when dawn began to break. By the time we had passed Pozzo del Drago it was already broad daylight. At the steep wooded slope above Alp Palü we took off our ski and put on crampons. The ten- or eight-pronged crampons fit very well on to ski. They are wide enough—being calculated to enclose the heavy-nailed sole of mountain shoes—to embrace the blade of the ski, and the bands are long enough to be buckled conveniently over one's boots.

" To the left appeared Le Prese, with its lovely lake among forests of chestnuts, while to the right began to tower the threatening mass of the Palü glacier, which formed part of our route. We were again running on our ski when, at this point, the snow proving very slippery, we attached our sealskins.

" These should be fitted with a ring to throw over the point of the ski, and should stretch down to the middle of the ski, where they should terminate. Here they are fastened to the ski binding by a proper mechanical contrivance. They may be taken on to the back end of the ski, but then they are difficult to stretch and fix over the heel of the ski. It is quite unnecessary to carry the sealskin so far back. The clamp under the beak of the ski completes the arrangement and tightens or loosens the skin *ad libitum*.

" We continued thus till our arrival at the first fall
of the glacier, when, to reach the opposite side, we
passed along a narrow strip of snow we had noticed
and marked to that effect some time before. The
slope became so steep that our sealskins failed to
adhere, and we were beginning to skate about on the
hard crust of snow. Above our heads hung the
séracs, which forbade our venting our wrath in loud
vociferations. We strengthened ourselves, therefore,
with the additional safeguard of our crampons, and
proceeded comfortably, taking care to have a firm
grip of the hard snow. On arrival at the first table
of the glacier we stopped for breakfast and enjoyed
the sun. Before us stretched a long causeway of
snow to the top of the glacier ; near us Pizzo di
Verona, its ice cascades resembling a shower of
glittering emeralds, cast a shadow on all around.
The weather was glorious. Stäubli introduced me to
several of his old friends towering on the opposite
side. Far beyond appeared the majestic Ortler
group.

" We continued our ascent round the western side
of the glacier, roped this time. At the foot of Piz
Cambrena we took the direction of the col opening to
the west of Pizzo di Verona, and from thence an easy
way opened up through wonderful *séracs* all aglow
with the morning sun. *Va piano, va sano.* A few
more gaping crevasses had to be carefully avoided,
then the *névé* became even, and we finally reached
the col, leaving behind us the Palü glacier, moping
over its mysteries now unveiled. It was midday.

" We could not restrain an outburst of admiration

at the new world before us, with the Disgrazia as the culminating point. Stäubli, mad with delight, began a wild dance on the edge of the precipice. One of the many slabs of stone which surrounded us served well for a table. While the kettle was boiling we could have had time to ascend Pizzo di Verona, but we preferred to remain where we were and enjoy the wonders before us, taking an occasional photograph. A great stillness reigned everywhere. We did not talk. We understood each other just as well, perhaps better. But why should there not have been more than the two of us to enjoy that glorious sight? Would that I could have transported all you city people to magic scenes like these!

" I cannot help thinking of one who, regularly every day, at Zürich, comes to the restaurant where I dine to play his game of chess at a table near me. He salutes his partner, the small glass of cognac is brought, the cigars are lighted, and then the game begins and continues to the end, without a single word being uttered, and this each day of his life. Poor wretch, how I pity you! How shall we repay our fathers for showing us the mountains and their glory?

" We were roused from our motionless ecstasy by a sensation of cold, and upwards still, continued our way along the Italian frontier towards the Piz Zupo, and lazily skid over the frozen ice-waves of the Fellaria glacier. How shall I describe the fairy-like scenes met at every step? We came to the foot of the huge buttresses of the Piz Zupo and Piz Argient. What a contrast between those awful, dark, jagged *arêtes* and the snowy robes flowing round their feet ? Further on we came into a fresh region of glaciers, dazzling in their brightness, with the mass of the Disgrazia in the background, sunk in shadow.

" ' Man wird verrückt ! ' exclaimed Stäubli, my dear little friend Stäub.

" Having unroped and relieved our ski both of crampons and sealskins, we once more glided softly over those lovely snow deserts which run along the border on Italian territory. A cry of ' Youhéé ' fills the air. Stäubli was flying over an enchanting lake of ice, and though the snow was not of the best, we enjoyed our run to the full. Soon we were half-way across the Fellaria glacier, directing our steps towards the western side, where a new region was about to open before us ; a black *arête*, however, hid the other side still from view. It was a solemn moment. We began to descend and fly over the ground, when, turning the cornice of rock, we suddenly stopped to gaze on the wonderful sight before us. The two Scerscen glaciers stood out bathed in light at the foot of the Gümels and Piz Roseg, the whole suffused with the soft mauve tints of the ebbing twilight.

" We soon reached the Upper Scerscen glacier, in the midst of a formidable amphitheatre of mountains. The king of them all, Piz Bernina, was at last revealed to us, towering above Piz Argient, Crast Agüzza, and Monte Rosso di Scerscen. The Italians showed their good taste in erecting the Rifugio Marinelli in this very Eden. We could stop at this little stone hut for the night. We preferred, however, continuing our run. From here to the Fuorcla

To face p. 258.

UPPER SCERSCEN AND ROSEG GLACIERS.

I. M. G.

Sella we roped, and made a large circuit to avoid the region of crevasses as much as possible. Soft clouds of snow were raised by the wind, and sparkled like diamonds in the sun.

" By twilight we began ascending the last slopes to the Fuorcla Sella. We reached the col, and, leaving the sunny Italian slopes behind us, entered into the shadow of the Sella basin. It was 4.30 p.m.; we still had three-quarters of an hour of daylight left, which would exactly allow us to reach the flat of the Roseg glacier. We enjoyed a lovely run over the soft, powdery snow tinted with mauve, the reflection from the rocks of Piz Roseg all on fire in the setting sun. We knew our way here by heart, and skimmed over the snow without fear, 'yodling' frantically.

" By the last ray of the setting sun we left the Sella glacier, and passed on to the Roseg glacier. There were still a few traces left of our expedition three days before on our way to the Piz Glüschaint. Far in the distance we could see the lights of Pontresina brightly shining. We seemed quite near already. We stepped over the back of the glacier in long strides, and on nearing the Tschierva hut, where two friends were to meet us, we began to yodle. However, our calls remained unanswered, and no lights could we see. We were not astonished on learning later that those two distinguished mountaineers had been enjoying luxurious couches at Samaden all the time !

" One difficulty remained, in the shape of the Tschierva moraine. I asked Stäubli for some light.

He tied an electric lamp on to his belt, leaving me in complete darkness!

"A little later we started on a splendid run, descending from the Tschierva hut, where we flew over the ground like phantoms. This run was cut short on arrival at the bridge of the Roseg Restaurant, where the road is completely spoiled with the deep ruts made by the sleighs. We took advantage of this stoppage to rest awhile and finish some cake left from our morning's repast. After this, we passed through the beautiful Val Roseg, a lovely spot, but wearisome after a long night run.

*   *   *   *   *

"In the hotel, brilliant with many electric lights, we are sitting at a table with our friend, the guide Grass, and some welcome bottles of wine. Stäubli, the pink of neatness, is giving the guide a long account of our trip. Around us the usual set of well-dressed people laugh and talk. For them it is like every other evening; for myself, I find it difficult to realise that all I have seen and felt is not a dream. A glow of happiness fills my heart that not all these lights could surpass, and the wish comes to shut out all around and rest once more in those glorious solitudes. What a gulf seems to separate me from those who have not seen the wondrous mountains, those who have not shared our vision of the silent snows!

"Life is made up of contrasts, and I take pleasure in recalling them to my mind in order to perpetuate their memory."

*   *   *   *   *

Strange it is, on reading over those lines written by Marcel Kurz, to have to add that the idea of the Piz Bernina ski circuit did not germinate in a Pontresina mind. Forsooth it was reserved for the Swiss to conceive and execute. But how strange is that apathy, that subjection to routine on the part of an otherwise bold and enterprising people! And how strange too that out of the number of foreign sportsmen congregating every winter in the Engadine, not one could brace himself to " get up and go " from Pontresina to the Bernina hospice, thence to the refuge Marinelli, thence to the Tschierva hut and back to Pontresina, in three days, if he so pleased!

CHAPTER X

FROM AROSA TO BELLINZONA OVER THE BERNARDINO PASS

The Arosa Information Bureau—The hospitality of sanatorium guests—The allurements of loneliness—Whither the spirit leads—Avalanche weather—The Spring god and King Frost —The source of the Rhine—The post sleigh in a winter storm—The Bernardino pass—Brissago.

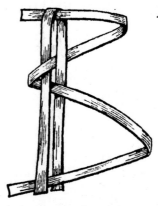

ADEN in Aargau is a flourishing watering-place, whence I was glad to make my escape a few years ago in the last days of March.

I had wired to the information bureau at Arosa, asking how long I might expect to find good snow. The answer came: "Till the middle of May," which sounded boastful, in fact rather alarming, by promising so very much. But why should I malign those good people? I found heaps and heaps of snow, enough to satisfy all reasonable requirements till the middle of June.

My little daughter kept then a small paper box, in which she stored up all the fine weather I might wish to apply for. On fair terms of purchase she "let out" a certain number of fine days—as many as she thought I might be allowed—to take me to Arosa and thence to Bellinzona, where I was to join her and her mother on the way to Brissago on Lago Maggiore.

There certain open-air orange and lemon groves I knew of awaited us and a blossoming aloe near by on the way to Ascona.

To swoop down the Bernardino pass upon Mesocco on ski and land a few hours later on the banks of Lago Maggiore, after crossing the Rhaetic Alps from Arosa to Hinterrhein, tickled my fancy. My line would be from Arosa to Lenzerheide, along the Oberhalbstein valley to Stalla, otherwise called Bivio, thence to Cresta Avers, and somehow along the Madesimo pass to the Splügen road, and then east to Hinterrhein, and across the Bernardino pass through the village of that name to Mesocco. The whole thing could be done on ski. It would nowhere take me over glaciers. I should do this alone, carrying my pack, sleeping every night in a comfortable bed, and tramping by day on ski like any ordinary summer vagabond wasting his shoe-leather on the hard high road.

I could imagine nothing pleasanter. I should not take off my ski till the last strip of snow sticking to the edge of the Mesocco road gave way and should bring my navigation to a standstill upon the characteristic mixture of mud and gravel found on postroads during the spring thaw. There is no small charm in slithering upon snow getting thinner and thinner till it is from two to three inches deep and

tapering in the end to the bare inch, which is enough
for the expert runner.

Spring has a delightful way of creeping and sneak-
ing up the Alpine passes, using against King Frost
every seduction that a soft, tender heart can devise
to disarm a fierce, unrelenting spirit. It threads its
way delicately from one warm, protected nook to
another, and throws out feelers that stretch forth
tremblingly from the rock crannies into the rough
air.

Flowerets peep out here and there. The eggs of
frogs float about in slimy masses upon pools of warm
water banked in with snow. The released springs
and waterfalls throw off their transparent scarves of
iridescent crystal ice. The blackbirds hop about
from branch to branch piping upon bare trees that
are still sunny through and through, but do not yet
venture to chill their feet by touching the ground
still encumbered with deep snow.

The hard winter god, gradually coaxed into a
softer mood, relaxes his hold upon the crust of the
earth. What more delightful than this mixture of
two seasons ? Under one's feet all is winter still.
Above, spring skies, a scented air. Within one's
breast a heart yielding gently to the suggestions of
a new atmosphere. To enhance the contrast and
accelerate its phases, the spring god artfully turned
the head of my ski full south straight in the face
of the sun.

Thus it is within any one's power to rewrite in this
way for himself Hesiod's "Book of Days," and he
will do it best if alone.

It was a peculiar thing to pass from Arosa, still lying under six feet of snow, over the south brim of the cup and to swoop down upon Lenzerheide, while the steamy fog of incipient spring hung over the moving, thawing masses, and the man who had brought me up so far shrank back. There were cracklings round about and dull thuds. A roar and clang came up from the bottom of the gorge as the snowbanks crashed in upon the stream whose reawakening had soaked and eaten away their supports. Something had gone wrong with a ski-binding. Thus a kindly word may be spoken in time by the mountain fiend before he strikes. He plays fair. Go away, he says, unless you know that you have the luck of the Evil One. The brim of that snow cup was a parting line. One pair of ski carried its man back the way he had come. The other carried its man forward whither the spirit led.

I left Arosa with a pang of regret. I had lived there some perfectly happy and health-giving days in an abode reserved for so many who are sick beyond human help. I was alone, and went from table to table as a guest bidden to dinner. My hosts would, if I may apply this figure of speech to a moral attitude, seek me out for my strength, and I found, in the proximity of their illness, the shadow of our common human plight falling across my path, bringing with it a kind of excuse for my rude temporary immunity from physical ills in which in time we all share alike, but which seem to create such unfair contrasts.

Some were there, so to say, for a last throw of the dice in this Monte Carlo of consumptives. On the

return of some to health depended the future of
a home, wife, children, awaiting anxiously the
physician's verdict upon their chief, for whose cure
the last moneys of the family were now being staked
upon the double card, Arosa Davos.

A powerfully built Englishman, among others, I got
to know. On the next day he was to be told whether
he could go home or not. He was writing to his wife
in the last hour of that day, about that hour of the
next which would hail his return to life, duty, and
love, or bring down upon his head another of those
blows for which there is no other remedy than the
infinite serenity of the children of God.

Then he came up to me, spoke of the impending
interview and of all that was at stake.

I looked at him and said, " You are as sound as a
bell." The words were magnetic. They were posted
to London that night, and the next day the happy
father and husband, released by the professional
man's verdict, prepared to pack.

There are two tragedies that to my mind are
particularly pathetic, both Alpine—that of the lung
patient whom the Alpine sun cannot save, and that
of the Alp worshipper in bounding health for whom
the Alps have become as a car of Juggernaut.

I have seen dead, handsome young men, for whom
the avalanche had woven a shroud of snow, and I
have beheld wasted frames for whom the sun could
not weave fresh physical tissues.

Of the Arosa scenes I carried a keen remembrance
as I passed, safe and sure, from ice-cold slope to sun-
baked slope, whether the northern blast froze my

moustache, or the Ausonian breeze loosened the rigidity of the air into balmy wafts. But Arosa was not without its moments of fun. There was a parson there who gave me his Christian name to guess. It began with B, and that was to be the clue. But I suggested Bradshaw, Bradlaw, and Beelzebub before his obliging wife put me on the way to the right spelling, Bible.

Of all places that suggest Chaos, a poor bare beginning of things, that place is the desolate spot in which the Hinter Rhine takes its rise. It is called Paradise, and if ever man required to cheer himself with a euphemism, it might be here. From Splügen to Hinterrhein extends a flat tract of country on every inch of which nature has left an impression as of exhausted powers. And yet, under those external marks of sterility, lurks the beginning of a great thing, the Rhine, its fruitful valleys, its grandeur, its world-renowned towns. You may "tail" behind a post-horse from Splügen to Hinterrhein for an hour in the gathering dusk, and wonder whether the next moment will not drop you over the edge of the world.

But a comfortable inn will open its homely rooms. You will tumble among children learning their lessons around the stove. A place will be made for you beside the young mother with her youngest hanging at her breast. The father will walk in with the proud gait of him who bears himself with grace and kindness in his sense of manly power.

"Crossing the Bernardino," he says, "to-morrow, alone!"

"Why not? I am on ski; the post-sleigh does its service in all weathers."

"Yes, but two men go together with the sledge and the horses."

Indeed, I saw them the next day. I left at a reasonably late hour, and they left still later, catching me up along the flat. Then I passed them up the slope. They took all the windings, I cut across. It was a terribly bleak day. The wind blew the snow in wreaths, and these laid themselves across the old hard wreaths. Sleigh and horses cut through them, throwing out the two men. They rose again, and got back into their seat to cut through the next wreath. This time the sleigh was overturned. The horses—harnessed tandem fashion—plunged, reared upon their sinking hind-quarters, ploughing the snow with their breasts, while their hoofs pawed about for a footing. Then they came off with a rush, once more taking the sledge through. It was a long, narrow sleigh, just wide enough to hold two men, with the mail bags boxed in behind them—more like a torpedo than anything else.

It seemed impossible to distinguish the causeway under the wreaths of snow, in the snow dust blown up by the wind and with strips of fog flying and curling about. Yet the horses kept to the winter track, and all that plunging and kicking was the ordinary business of every day. The *Cantonieri* stationed from league to league in stone sheds all along the pass, kept guard in the worst places, and came out with spade and shovel to expedite the mail.

I saw all that, hovering about like a stormy petrel,

unable to make out whether my hoverings were looked upon as of bad or good augury. I expect the latter, for if there is a gift that mountaineers seldom lack, it is that of jovial good humour. To talk and exchange impressions would not be the question, till we might "foregather" in Bernardino village, where horses would be changed and men might rest. But long before the mail came down I was swinging through the empty village, between its deserted hotels, leaving the storm behind me and opening my coat to the sun-rays that brought the snow down in trickles from the roofs.

On and on I went, staying at last my course on the edge of a wood above Mesocco. There I sat on the corner of a stone wall, riding it as a lady's saddle, with one ski dangling and the other hanging down as a stirrup, lost in contemplation. The contrast was so complete, so wonderful, knotting together as it were in one bow the most opposite aspects of nature.

There I rested, snow-man and sun-man in one.

A peasant came slowly and stolidly by, making a mess of the thin snow with his heavy boots. He looked at me with great sympathy, stopped, and let out that one word in the Italian tongue, "*Stanco!*" ("Tired!")

A few hours later my ski were stowed away in an attic room at Brissago. Their time was up. But I would take them out again on the return of the appointed hour. "Jamais pressé, toujours prêt."

CHAPTER XI

GLACIERS—AVALANCHES—MILITARY SKI-ING

A legacy from the past—The formation of glaciers and atmospheric conditions—Forests and glaciers—Our deficient knowledge—The upper ice and snow reservoirs—What is the annual snowfall and what becomes of it?—How glaciers may be classed—Mechanical forces at work—Moraines and *séracs*—Avalanches—Periodic avalanches—Accidental avalanches—The general causes—The statics of snow—What happens to winter snow—*Strata*—How steep slopes may be classed—Excusable ignorance of strangers to the Alps—Those who write glibly in home magazines—Unsafe slopes—Avalanches when running across slopes—The probing-stick—Avalanche runs—Military ski-ing—The St. Gothard and St. Maurice districts—Military raids in the High Alps——The glaciers as military highways—Riflemen on foot as against marksmen on ski.

N the whole the Mid-European glaciers are a legacy from a distant past.

Their former size and extent corresponded to general meteorological conditions which have long ceased to exist.

They might—and no doubt did — alternately increase and decrease within historical times.

They nevertheless must be viewed as a bequest, a kind of heirloom coming from a prehistoric ancestry. They are the survival of a phenomenon which, in its former compass and intensity, is no longer compatible with the meteorological *régime* of Central Europe.

The temperature most suitable for the formation of ice in nature is the temperature which remains the most steadily around the freezing-point of water. Extremes of temperature are not favourable to the formation of snow, which is the form in which water generally passes into glacier ice.

It stands to reason that the oftener the atmosphere can be saturated with moisture in circumstances which allow a frequent discharge in the shape of snow falling upon surfaces that are iced— or such as will retain the snow, assuring the transformation of some of it, ultimately, into ice—the more will the thermometer readings show a temperature rising and falling only moderately above and below the freezing-point of natural water. There is no use in further emphasising this obvious truth.

Everybody will understand that moisture formed in hot tracts of the atmosphere has little chance of being converted into snow, and that, while a warm atmosphere may generate water—destructive of ice and snow surfaces—a very cold atmosphere cannot assist in glacier formation—on high land, at any rate—for want of vapours to condensate and precipitate, and for want of water masses to consolidate.

It follows that, within historical times, the Alpine glaciers have undergone variations according to changes in the quantity of moisture contained in the atmosphere, theirs being such altitudes and such climatic conditions as might allow the Centigrade thermometer to swing pretty steadily between 20 degrees above zero and 20 degrees under, all the year round and in the course of a day.

These conditions existed more fully in periods when the Alps were well wooded. Such a period pre-existed the first historical epoch of Switzerland. Under the Romans, say from 50 B.C. to 500 A.D., this first historical epoch was marked by the wholesale destruction of forests—the usual price to be paid for civilisation—and the glacier world retreated in a ratio commensurate with the process of denudation.

Then came the Early Middle Ages, which for about six or seven hundred years show a distinct retrogression in Swiss civilisation. The glaciers now regained some of the ground they had lost, because the wooded surface, which is the most favourable to the condensation of moisture, underwent a considerable increase.

In modern times the forest area has again undergone such shrinkage that it has reached the minimum when artificial means have to be devised for its preservation. Glaciers have gone back again.

We may therefore define glaciers as ice and snow reservoirs formed under prehistoric conditions which no longer exist. They are kept alive on a reduced scale, in a direct ratio to the moisture yielded by the atmosphere as often as it is conveniently a little above and a little below the freezing-point of natural water.

Our knowledge of the glacier world in its formative processes is as yet extremely deficient. What

THE SONADON GLACIER.

To face p. 266.

proportion of the year's snowfall—within the glacier region—is actually converted into ice ? What proportion melts away on the surface and passes directly into water, to be carried away, carrying along with itself some of the ice ? What proportion is, by sublimation and evaporation, returned to the atmosphere, to become again the toy of winds, in the shape of snow or rain-clouds, never feeding the glacier at all on which it first fell ?

On the other hand, who can tell how much ice is formed on the glacier surface by the direct absorption of the air moisture collecting upon such a condensator ? And would it be alien to our subject to ask what effect may have on the present glaciers the loss of pressure consequent upon the enormous reduction in bulk and height which they have undergone ? Is the glacier ice formed under the present rate of pressure capable of offering anything like the same resistance to disintegration as its prehistoric congener ? What are its powers of self-preservation under the vastly inferior pressure which it experiences in the very places in which ice was once packed to a height and in a bulk we should not like to express in figures, even if we possessed competent data ?

The broad fact seems to be that as much snow as falls on the glaciers throughout the year is taken back into the atmosphere, and that the snow congealed and fixed in the upper basins is as nothing compared with the quantity of water that evaporates or runs away at the nether end of the mass every summer. What is the capacity of the ice-forming *firn* of the Aletsch basin compared to the extent of its melting surface? And how much snow does the *firn* receive every year from the atmosphere? And how much of that snow is incorporated?

There are now so many approaches to the glacier world of Switzerland that it should be easy to determine, at the outlet of a few typical glaciers, the amount of water thaw conveys to the valleys below. According to the season, it is quite easy to distinguish between rain-water, water from springs, and glacier water. Such observations would lead to results reciprocally verificatory.

My provisional conclusions are that :—

1. The snow falling on the Swiss glaciers is a mere fraction of the quantity wanted to assure their stability.

2. The average snowfall of any year returns to the atmosphere.

3. The source and means of congealation are not proportionate to the exigencies of ice-formation, even for the maintenance of the *status quo*.

4. The glaciers, regressing as they are now doing, are not being replenished to any appreciable extent from the so-called everlasting snow storage, and certainly not at all in proportion to their wastage.

In other words :—

1. In a number of years X the whole glacier mass of Switzerland is dissolved and reconstituted in proportions that are less than in the preceding X period.

2. The snow fallen during the period X—if present conditions are accepted—is pumped back by the atmosphere during the same period.

3. The quantity of water flowing from those glaciers in the time is greater than the means of glacier recuperation.

4. Yet the glaciers do recuperate in some proportion to their former size.

5. Consequently the condensation and congealing of atmospheric moisture must be much more effective an agent than hitherto suspected, for there is no reason why, upwards of 9,000 feet, snow should be less liable to thaw on ice than on rock surfaces. Rock and ice areas are conterminous.

Glaciers may be classed, according to their physical conformation, under the following headings :—

1. *Circular Schema.*—They are then enclosed in a basin more or less irregular in shape. The enclosed mass of ice remains concave as long as it is lower than the rim of the basin. But it becomes convex in the centre when it rises above the horizontal line joining the opposite rims of the basin.

2. *Longitudinal Schema.*—A. On the flat, or approximately, those glaciers show convex surfaces.

B. When resting on a slope they are concave in the upper basin, which feeds them and become convex as they reach lower and wider channels.

This second type is the normal glacier type.

A diagram or section of the convex portion of the glacier—an ideal diagram of course—would show the mechanical and static forces at work in a fan-shaped formation radiating from a point on the not geometrical, but mechanical, centre line of the glacier, this point being situated on its bed, where the side-pressures converge and annihilate each other's progress.

From this point the bottom ice works its way up to the melting-surface—but obliquely, being the whole time carried down by the slope—and throws up side moraines and one or several spinal moraines in the process. The spinal moraines always rest on pure ice. The ice seams have been thrown up from the inside.

Crevasses may occur in an outward, open, surface-formation, as in *séracs* when they are grouped together, or else they are the result of accidental deflections or temporary oppositions in mechanical and static forces at work in the ice.

We said a while ago that there was no reason why, at the height of 9,000 feet and upwards, snow accumulations should be more stable and constant on ice surfaces than on rock. The cause for this is simply that rock and ice are too near to each other and at altitudes too closely alike for serious differences in temperature.

Let us now pass to the matter of avalanches. If snow is utterly unstable on rock, so it is on ice. Rock and ice constitute an avalanche area, which in winter extends down so as to include all steepnesses on which snow may lodge and whence it may be dislodged by the forces of Nature.

Avalanches may be periodic or accidental.

A periodic avalanche is the kind that comes down regularly at a known spot, each time sufficient cause is brought into play. Maps of the Alps exist on which those periodic avalanches are noted.

Almost every Alpine village has a periodic avalanche
on its territory. The peasants know when and
where to expect it. It is called *the* avalanche of
so and so, and your business is to find out, each
time you propose going out on an expedition,
whether it has come down or not, and all
about it.

An accidental avalanche arises from general causes
taking effect fortuitously.

The general causes are :—

1. A quick rise in the temperature.
2. A sudden fall of the barometer.
3. A change of wind.
4. A fresh fall of snow.
5. Slopes of a certain angle and conformation.
6. Differences of density, moisture, and consistency
in superposed layers of snow.

A study of the statics of snow is the royal road
to the understanding of avalanches.

On a slope snow is in a state of more or less
pronounced instability.

A first fall of dry winter snow upon dry slopes is
extremely avalanchy, provided it be heavy enough.
If it be a fall of wet snow on a porous surface—that
is, neither frozen ground nor hard rock—the snow
will as it were flop together in a slithering mass,
but is not likely to form itself into a dangerous
compact floe.

As soon as a second fall of snow comes to adhere
to what is left of the first, it may happen that the
second layer does not get properly welded to the first.
The thoroughness of the attachment depends on the

adhesiveness of the snow and on weather conditions. A foundation is therefore laid for the slipping of the new snow upon the surface of the old.

In the course of the winter the snow gets con-solidated in one mass, but the process takes each time from two to three days, during which caution is necessary. A homogeneous layer of snow, hardened from the outside by wind pressure, or freezing over after a slight thaw, may then break up into slabs which slide down on the older snow, should one with ski, or in any other fashion, cut that snow away—at any point—from its support.

A *stratum* of snow on a steep open slope is like a piece of cardboard balanced on your finger. There is a limit to the inclination of the cardboard beyond which it will slip off its pivot. So it is with snow.

Newly fallen snow soon ceases to be an amorphous mealy mass. Its bottom layer models itself on the surface on which it lies and, if turned over, would show that surface *en relief*. The next *stratum* adheres to the first more or less, and finds points of support for itself, such as rocks protruding through the first *stratum*, trees, shrubs, fences, dykes, &c. Every ensuing layer is less shored up than the one beneath. Should there be a rise in the temperature, an increase of moisture brought on by a change in the wind, the snow becomes heavier and may start down; as a dry sponge on an inclined board, gradually absorbing water, must slide down when the inclination of the board and the quantity of water reach the critical point.

Our illustration from the cardboard balanced on a

finger-tip, and from the sponge on an inclined plane, makes it clear that it is impossible to state at what definite angle the equipoise of a snow *stratum* must be lost or is sure to be kept. That angle depends on the finger-tip, on the weight and size of the cardboard, on the sponginess of the sponge, on the slipperiness of the plank, on your holding your breath, or mischievously blowing upon the suspended object, &c. When about to capsize, the cardboard may meet some external point of support, such as your raised hand, which, in the case of the snow *stratum*, would be a pre-existing prop and maintain an otherwise impossible stability.

A fall in the barometer almost always means an increase of moisture which is unfavourable to the steadiness of old snow. A dry, hot wind—such as *foehn*—is worse, because its heat penetrates the snow to the very bottom and sets it moving throughout its thickness.

New snow is dangerous till it has had time to set —that is, for two or three days.

Runners are generally agreed to call steep the slopes on which avalanches may occur.

Steep slopes are either concave, convex, or straight.

They are concave when the slopes converge towards a central dividing line lying deeper, to the eye, than their sides ; these are scooped out of the hill.

Concave slopes are :—

1. Funnel-shaped, when the funnel may be either upright or upside down.

If it is upright, the wide opening is at the top. If the slope affect the shape of a reversed funnel, it

18

opens out at the bottom, but it may also be choked up in the middle, opening up again above, like an hour-glass.

Concave slopes are quite safe if strewn with rocks, overgrown with shrubs, or wooded. They are untrustworthy if the sides have been planed down, as it were, by what we may call natural wear and tear.

The reader sees here how the indications of nature may be properly interpreted. It is quite clear that a gorge which is a natural shrubbery, for instance, has not been visited by avalanches for a time at least as long as the plants took to grow to their visible size.

The trouble here is that Londoners, for example, having to deal with a gorge which they have not seen free from snow, cannot be expected to tell whether it is safe or not. The local man alone—a permanent eye-witness—possesses the information required, and failing actual acquaintance with the place, a practised mountaineer alone can form an opinion.

Slopes are convex when the centre line, to the eye, rises above their sides. These stand out from the hill, diverging from its top.

Convex slopes should be ascended and descended along the dividing-line. This line, as a dominating centre, will always be sought out by the good High Alp runner. It is both the shortest and surest path from point to point, and great is the delight to see at one's feet the avalanche runs. If the coping is occupied by rocks, the runner will keep to the snow near to the rocks, but he has no business there at all if the rock ridge is considerable enough to harbour avalanche snow. A practised eye sees at a glance whether snow in excess of the capacity of the gullies is still suspended above the runner's head, or whether it lies in cakes and balls at his feet. Here again the native will know. It would help you but little to say that you have found him out to be an unconventional runner, that he is slow and not at all the handy man you expected. However much you may be entitled to fancy yourself or your skill as a conventional runner, he is the better mountaineer, and should your conventional style leave you in the lurch, he is the fellow to do the right thing for you. It is then just as well to remember, when one writes in a home magazine, that, on the spot, one was the incompetent person of the party. "He of the ice-axe," your guide, would do that second job, too, far better than you, if the use of the pen in that periodical was not inconsistent with his inferior social standing and extremely imperfect education.

The straight slope is the slope on which every point is on the same plane as another. These slopes are safe when they abut on to ground which obviously is locally viewed as not exposed to avalanches : vineyards, potato-fields, woods, haylofts, &c.

They are unsafe when undermined by a trickle of water—springs, for instance—and when the layer of snow next to the ground has melted away without affecting the upper layers ; or when the slope rests upon a protruding ledge over which it bulges out; or when it is cut by longitudinal ribs of blown-out snow which you may break open unawares, letting out the mealy contents upon yourself.

All slopes may be traversed—that is, you may run across them obliquely.

When about to traverse, look to the foot of the slope, and then look to the head of the slope. If all is right, sound the snow with your stick and glance into the conic hole made by it. In time you will acquire an ability to tell by the feel whether the snow is mealy, or set, or damp, and how many layers your stick breaks through before coming to a standstill upon frozen ground, or against rock, or before sinking into the hollow space that may exist between the nethermost layer of snow and the soil.

Of course, all this you cannot do with a short, light bamboo, conveniently fitted with an osier disk within three inches of the point! To go forth so simply equipped means that you are leaving your brains at home on that day—a thing I often do myself—but, I assure you, only when out for mere play!

A stick that cannot be used on an emergency either as an anchor or as a sounding-line to take castings with, is a poor friend. It is instructive to look curiously into the hole made by one's stick. What would be the use of a sport practised simply as an opportunity for being scatter-brained with impunity, so long as luck lasts?

On the hill-side, slopes—concave, convex, and

straight—are joined to one another by linking surfaces varying in shape and inclination, but of too limited a development and too irregular a build to offer to avalanches any opportunity of spreading over them ; or else slopes are separated from one another by breaks in the ski-ing surface, such as ravines. In these, masses of snow gather most conveniently. The longitudinal gaps opened up by landslips, torrent beds, or even only the slides made by wood-cutters through forest and pasture land to launch felled trees into the valley, are very distinctly avalanche runs. Efforts are now being made to bar such runs by artificial plantations, fencings, or walls.

The centre of military ski-running in Switzerland is in the environment of the permanent Alpine forts which defend the St. Gothard knot of trans-Alpine and sub-Alpine (railway tunnels) lines of communication from Italy into Switzerland, betwixt the sources of the Reuss, Ticino, Rhine, and Rhône. Another centre is situated in the Rhône Valley, at the point where a natural defile bars the line of communication between the upper Rhône Valley, at St. Maurice, and the Lake of Geneva, commanding to some extent the roads converging upon that point from Northern Savoy and leading to it from Italy over the St. Bernard pass or through the Simplon tunnel.

The opening of the Loetschberg tunnel on the new short railway route between Berne and Milan will, however, make it advisable to erect some kind of additional works about Brigue.

The Gothard and St. Maurice guards use ski, and ski-ing detachments are about to be attached to the brigades of mountain infantry located all along the range of the Alps.

Many junior Swiss officers have made themselves proficient in the new mountaineering by joining military ski courses. Military patrol competitions meet with much favour at the large ski gatherings.

For all that, the adaptability of ski to military purposes is not very great in the High Alps. Still they are called upon to become quite a consideration in border defence or attack. Small troops of skiers could pass easily from one side to another of the Alps, occupying flying posts of observation, and even raiding places where the defence would have preferred to put its own outposts, had it not allowed itself to be forestalled. The Alpine Club huts afford sufficient shelter for summarily equipped detachments numbering from twenty to forty men.

Bodies of troops crossing the Alps in winter by the passes available for considerable military transport would enjoy a distinct advantage if the outlet of the passes had been previously occupied by half or quarter companies of bold ski-ing infantry pouncing, as it were, from the skies upon small snow-bound places with summer hotels ready for occupation and better stocked with means of subsistence than one would at first be led to expect. In some Swiss Alpine villages particularly, large supplies are often accumulated for the next summer season, and in others much merchandise is stored up to accommodate the Italian smugglers

AT THE FOOT OF COL D'HÉRENS.

To face p. 279.

whose "exports" from Switzerland are all the year round a source of profit to their purveyors.

Swiss ski-runners, by expeditions like my own, have proved that the glaciers may be used, within strict limits, as highways for rapid and unexpected military movements. Till now it was assumed that crevasses, iced rocks, and piles upon piles of corniced snow would offer insuperable obstacles to any military action. But the crevasses—as the reader now knows—are most hermetically sealed. To the expert and wary runner the snow opposes no greater barrier than to the pedestrian in summer. Does not history teach how foot-soldiers have *en masse*, with artillery and baggage, been moved to and fro across the Alps ? Henceforth, military runners may be trusted to scour the ranges, undetected, cutting communications one day at the St. Bernard hospice and opening fire three days later upon the Simplon hospice, hanging alternately on the only two military roads joining Switzerland and Italy between the St. Gothard forts and French Savoy.

Those raiding parties could be followed by considerable parties of transport men, carrying fresh ammunition and supplies.

Such places as Bourg St. Pierre, Fionnay, Arolla, Zinal, Zermatt, Saas, would be, from the Italian point of view, worth seizing and manning at the outset of a winter campaign. From the point of view of a Swiss advance aiming at laying hold of the southern outlets of the military roads before the enemy could move up its advanced columns, those places would be valuable bases for the auxiliary services waiting upon the raiding detachments.

Hitherto forces crossing the Alps in winter could expect to be safe from attaok on their flanks. Henceforth there might be a very different story to relate. The few experiments hitherto made show that an attack by skirmishing ski-runners upon columns on the march could not be met by dispatching against them rifle-men on foot. Across country a man on foot will take about an hour— on flat ground—to cover a distance which an average runner on 2 feet of snow will overtake in one-quarter of the time. Uphill, the advantage of the ski-man is still more marked, and he may continue much longer. Moreover, he disposes of the whole hill-side, and may take cover exactly as he pleases, by crossing snows over which the pedestrian can make no progress at all, and becomes a most convenient mark. The ski-runner may force his pursuer into any ground he chooses. For a force developed across an expanse of snow, it is extraordinarily difficult to carry out an attack upòn ski-runners firing from behind shelter. They occupy probably the higher position, and their field of vision is absolutely uninterrupted. Rushes from point to point across the zone of fire are quite out of the question in the absence of any screen whatsoever.

As for the rifle-men or sharpshooters on foot in charge of a village, sallying forth to dislodge a party of runners firing into their position and then withdrawing out of the reach of adversaries firing from opened-up tracks, spaces, or houses, the idea is not plausible. A dismounted horse-soldier might just as well advance sword in hand against marksmen manning rifle-pits, or an infantry man, short of ammunition, might just as well trust his bayonet to reach a horseman galloping away out of sight.

Ski-ing patrols of mountain infantry with portable machine-guns could defend such passes as the Furka or the Grimsel against forces pushed forward in vastly superior numbers.

CHAPTER XII

THE MECHANICS OF SKI-BINDINGS

The shoe—The original bindings—The modern bindings—The foot—The hinge in the foot—Different functions of the toe-strap and heel-band—The parts of the binding—Faulty fasteners—Sketches of faulty and correct leverage—A schematic binding—*Critique* of bindings in use —Suggestions—Cheeks and plates—A whole blade—Cause of strained feet—Steel wire in bindings.

N choosing a suitable binding for the high-level routes in the Alps—as in thinking out or devising such a binding—the runner's commodity is the main consideration. There is human anatomy. There are the possibilities of leather, metal, and wire. And footgear, and ski, and binding have to work together.

Runners who run for sport alone have a preference for the boots known in the trade under the name of laupar boots. They are thick-soled, flat-heeled, box-shaped above the toes. The Lotus boots, made on an American shape, are a good type also. But are they good Alpine boots?

Runners in the Alps for whom ski are a means to an end, as well as an object in itself, generally wear an ordinary mountaineering boot of a large size, carefully nailed on heel and sole. This for two reasons :—

First, there is frequently some distance to be travelled over, in order to get across the rough, broken, or wooded ground before reaching the high snow-fields.

Second, it is practically impossible to dispense with nails in one's boots when crossing, above the snow-line, rocks and icy patches. On these ski are useless. They have to be carried for awhile or left behind, till called for. The runner is then thrown upon his boots and climbing-irons. Should his boots be laupars, the climbing-irons have to be fitted on to the bare soles. This is an inconvenient process, partly because the bands are liable to freeze, partly because it may take more time to don and doff the irons than the emergency will be kind enough to allow.

Those who speak of injury done to ski-blades by boot-nails carry too far their sympathy for an excellent servant. In point of fact, a symmetrically and regularly nailed boot makes upon the ski-blade and plate a harmless impression. The lodgement of each nail-head is clean. It even affords an additional support when turning, or breaking, or swinging.

The characteristics of a good running boot are, as one sees, few and definite.

With ski bindings, or fastenings, the matter is altogether different.

The popularity of ski-running burst forth so suddenly upon the sporting world that the invention of new bindings—of which there is no end—soon proceeded even beyond the boundaries of common sense and reason.

The original Scandinavian and Lap bindings, with bent twigs, twisted cane, or long thong, were quite sufficient for their purpose and in their place.

Of the new bindings a large number are of a commercial character only. Others, brought out on the score of mechanical perfection, come forward with purely academical credentials.

The early Scandinavian or Norse fastenings had a distinct quality. They were not invented, but grew. They were made of one same material throughout, showing the essential feature of a sound binding : uniformity of texture. But the ski-blade was directly fastened to the foot, more particularly to the toes, by the binding.

The defect of these original bindings came to light when they were put to more athletic uses. They then proved too weak, and not sufficiently durable, in the hands of Germans, Austrians, and Swiss, practising the Norse sport in their own countries.

Iron and steel, in varying degrees of hardness, were pressed into service. The uniformity of material was thus brought to an end.

To make a long story short, the Huitfeldt and Ellefsen bindings are generally admitted to be the most useful. The former is distinguished by a clamp for bolting down the heel-strap. The latter obtains rigidity—which is considered indispensable—by binding the heel of the runner to the ski-blade by means of a stiff sole.

Whatever the binding, the mechanics controlling the linking together of limb, boot, and ski in common action, need some explaining. Even the lay-reader may gain some benefit from a short and easy excursion in the domain of *technique*.

The foot consists of toes, ball, and heel. The point of play is the same, whether one walk or use ski. It lies across the ball of the foot. It is determined by the structure and articulations of the foot, from the extremity of the big toe to above the ankle-joint. But the line of play does not lie *along* the foot; it lies athwart. On this line turns or hinges the foot, as though a rod were run through it, whether the motion be up and down — that is, vertical; or horizontal (right and left); or oblique (foot sideways and edgeways), as in turns, swings, &c.

There is thus an axis of rotation through the foot. This axis need no more be horizontal than, for instance, the wheels of a motor-car when one drives over an obstacle.

The foot should sit at ease in the binding. It must not be fretted, chafed, galled, or pressed by the material of the binding when the work to be done puts a long and enduring strain on the boot. To that effect, the binding should be such that the pressure will, as it were, cancel itself by an equal application and even distribution, whatever may be the movements and position of the foot.

In other words, the heel-strap must have its point of attachment on the axis of rotation across the foot, the point on which it revolves to describe some portion of a circle in the vertical direction.

But this attachment must be mobile throughout in the horizontal plane. It should not be fixed on to the side of the ski-blade, or upon the ski in front of the foot, or anywhere else. One should bear in mind that, in mechanics, a heel-strap adhering to the ski at the centre of revolution acts like a rigid arm. The balance of the body is upset by sudden shocks which may react injuriously upon the foot, whenever there is a rigid connection brought into play, if only for one instant.

It is the business of the toe-strap to establish a connection (a close and immobile connection) between the foot and the ski, which it is the foot's function to propel. To the contrary, to perform its office, the heel-strap requires no fixed points of vertical support. In a mechanically perfect binding, the foot of the runner would be free to revolve, as on a pivot, in the horizontal plane, spending thus forces of lateral origin, while the ski continued upon its course. As it is, a good runner surmounts disturbing, incidental forces (the ordinary cause of accidents arising from ski-structure) by passing them up along his body and neutralising their effect by shooting himself upwards, as if to fly.

When twigs of twisted cane were used they broke away under the strain. The long leather thong was stronger, but it froze, or imbibed water with too much alacrity.

A ski-binding is essentially composed of four parts :—

First : A ring, or toe-strap, in which to adjust the point of the foot, and which is the *fulcrum*.

Second : A heel-band, which, passing round the foot, presses its fore-part against the *fulcrum*, in the ring, or toe-strap.

Third : A fastener, either clamp, bolt, buckle with eye and prong, sole of appropriate length, lever, &c., wherewith to regulate and adjust the pressure of the heel-band upon the *fulcrum*.

Fourth : Side-supports, or cheeks, for the ball of the foot, generally placed on each side of the *fulcrum*.

It is under number three (clamps, buckles, and levers) that all fastenings are at fault. They would have to be self-adjusting, so far as quick adaptation to changing weather conditions and sudden running strains is necessary. But such cannot be automatically obtained yet. The best fasteners are approximate in their action. The worst are clumsy mechanical contrivances. Most, good or bad, link the heel-band with the ski blade. Some fasteners are placed on one or both cheeks.

We have already made it plain : the heel-band, when stretched out round the foot, should be free to revolve in the same plane as the flat of the ski, as set forth in the following sketches :—

FAULTY LEVERAGE.

Here lateral impulses or checks are transmitted through the point of attachment of the heel-band.

CORRECT LEVERAGE.

A. Oblique View.

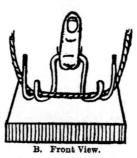

B. Front View.

Here none but the pressure exerted by means of the heel-band fastener upon the *fulcrum* (toe-straps and cheeks) controls the ski.

If the reader will kindly remember what we said about the axis of rotation lying across the ball of the foot, he will now understand that the heel-band has to describe " some portion of a circle " on the apex A, as follows :—

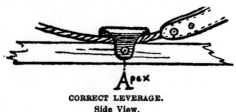

CORRECT LEVERAGE.
Side View.

each time the foot moves up and down in the vertical line.

Consequently the principles of a schematic binding work out in this way :—

First : That the heel-band be free to move in a horizontal plane, and be made to run through the fastening lever instead of being itself attached to the ski by an extremity.

Second : That the heel-band run loosely through a loop or sleeve placed on the apex of the foot axis on each side of the ball of the foot. The band will hinge on the loop, else it would slacken and tighten as the foot rises and falls.

Third : That the heel-band be of the nature of a continuous rope, or closed circuit, passing through the handle of the lever which, when opened or shut, releases the foot, or presses it down into the toe-strap.

Fourth : That the heel-band hang upon each apex of the rotatory axis instead of being tied there.

There are many reasons for accepting the above remarks. For instance, the point of rotation works out too high in many manufactured bindings. The heel-strap then cannot adhere as it should to the boot. Its radius and that of the heel do not coincide. In the case of a well-known Norwegian binding, the strap, on the contrary, starts from a point of attachment which, on each side of the ski, is placed lower than the toe-line. Thus the heel-strap is wrongly centred again. The boot undergoes irregular pressure, a cause of additional fatigue and a waste of mechanical power.

19

Most makers have been led into this fault by
the bulk and thickness of the material ordinarily
employed—namely leather. Leather does very well
for circling the heel, a flat band being there the
proper thing to be used, but it is less useful to
the front, where tension is called for.

The fore part of the heel-band might perhaps be
replaced by a rope of fine strands of wire, with a
breaking strain equal to, say, six hundred pounds, by
far exceeding the strength of the stoutest ski-thong.
At the point of rotation, the strap, in which is
placed the heel, would meet the wire. Thus the
connecting-point between the heel-strap and its
wire extremities to the front would coincide with
the pivots on which the heel revolves in the axis
of the foot.

Under those conditions, when lifting from the
ski the heel of the boot, the tension of the heel-band
remains uniform in every position.

This part of the binding apparatus may be practically autonomous. Free from any direct connection
with the wood, it ceases to be a medium through
which shocks may disturb the balance of the body.
The foot then is free to exercise unhindered its
own balancing power and to obey its spontaneous
"statics."

When cheeks are used, they generally consist of
two steel plates, with turned-up sides or ears, and
frequently provided with holes at suitable distances.
Hammered into shape, the plates usually overlap
each other on the centre line of the ski. Sometimes a pin driven through any two holes in the

superposed plates (by means of a spring, to which it is attached) maintains the plates at such a distance from each other as may fit the boot of the runner.

Plates need not be inserted through the wood of the ski, as is the case with most bindings with cheeks, but they may be laid on the flat of the blade, quite on a level with the rotatory axis of the foot. A steel spring may then be adjusted along the middle line of the foot-rest. It may be raised with the greatest ease, bringing the pin with it.

To the usual practice of boring a hole through the wood of the ski should be preferred an arrangement such as we have just described, preserving for the runner that on which he most justly may pride himself: a whole and uninjured ski-blade.

The writer has always used in the High Alps a binding fulfilling the conditions here laid down. He found his binding both safe and strong.

Elasticity and uniformity of pressure are so well secured by the severance of the heel-band from the body of the ski, that a fall forward is not accompanied by an awkward strain, such strain being almost always brought about by the reaction of the weight of the ski upon the muscles or bones of the foot. It is now generally recognised that strains and breaks are not caused by the firmness of a binding, but by an unequal and jolting application of pressure to the bones and muscular tissues.

A binding, the whole of which may be detached from the ski-blade by taking out a pin and removing a lever, is handy to travel with, as instruments to fit on a new binding instead of an old or broken one, are inconvenient adjuncts.

The weak points in steel rope bindings are :—

1. That the rivet connecting wire and leather may give way. The splicing should be most carefully seen to.

2. The metal cheeks may turn out to be brittle, if too hard or too thin, as in any other binding with cheeks.

3. The soft steel wire being made of strands, the very condition of its pliancy, this also means that the strands may be too soft, or too hard, or that they may be broken or unwound by coming into contact with hard edges. To obviate this risk, an oiled leather sleeve through which the wires might run, would protect them against friction and provide them with a lubricant.

The lubricant should be applied also on the bends of the wire.

The leather sleeves are placed outside each cheek by means of a rivet with the loop upwards and free. This provides a non-rigid " focus " of soft material, through which the fine wires, though tense, run loosely. The section of the wire thus enclosed lies at a varying angle with the foot as it rises and falls, and adjusts itself to this in its every position.

The lever by means of which the tightening of the wire heel-strap is managed, is best placed across the ski-blade in front of the foot. The wire runs freely through this lever to which, as mentioned before, it should not be attached. Thus, in case

of a wrench, or should the runner fall, the whole
of the wired heel-band may yield to the foot and
shift it just a little to one side or the other,
instead of jerking it, as is otherwise common,
either against or out of the binding.

Be this as it may, and taking things at their
best, the modern ski-runner's desideratum—a binding of uniform material, adaptable and elastic
throughout—has yet to be met.

An occasionally rather heated warfare was, a few
years ago, waged in words, all about ski-bindings.
The shape, length, breadth, and grooving of the
ski-blades were also drawn into the field of con-
troversy. Such debates are a positive relish for
enthusiasts and fanatics. But, though angry words
break no bones, violent talk is apt to be vapid
and, save for the sake of exercise in vituperative
wit, can serve no useful purpose.

CHAPTER XIII

RUDIMENTS OF WINTER MOUNTAINEERING FOR SKI-RUNNERS

The new "Alpinism"—A re-statement of elementary principles—
Ski-runners *versus* summer pedestrians—The experiences of
an eminent physician—How to walk in snow—Put not your
trust in sticks—Keep your rope dry—Stand up on your feet
—Ski-sticks as supports—Winter clothing.

TILL within the last one hundred and
fifty years mountaineering as a sport
was undreamt of in Europe. The high
Swiss valleys were then visited by a few
scientific and geographical explorers or
by people whose means of livelihood
and business occupations stood in some
connection with the valleys, their produce and inhabitants.

During the nineteenth century, poetry
and literature fostered summer mountaineering, and commercial enterprise was not slow
in following in the wake of the intellectual and
emotional admirers of mountain scenery. The High
Alps were frequented by others than mere trans-
Alpine travellers.

But it was reserved for the present generation to

invent winter sports. By them, the Alpine winter
has sprung into international life. Thanks to them,
winter mountaineering is now fast adding a new
branch to Alpinism.

In the light of this new age, even the most elementary principles of the mountaineer's art have to
be re-stated. Within the compass of the most
modest pretensions, the present chapter aims at so
doing—for winter sport lovers of either sex, whom
the perusal of the foregoing chapters may further fire
with zeal. General readers—ladies particularly—we
would not rudely expect to be at pains to supplement,
by incurring a course of severe trials, their deficient
opportunities and brevity of experience. They will
not regret their patience if they read these pages,
which, roughly speaking, cover a ground beyond
which few of them ever are likely to push their
investigations.

None can safely and properly use ski in the Alps
but they who have become acquainted with a
mountainous country as summer pedestrians. But
many now visit the Alps in winter only. As these
have no previous acquaintance with the conditions of
mountaineering, let them here take heed and be
warned.

For want of minding these hints, you might fare
like a famous physician of our acquaintance who,
coolly, in mid-January, after an early breakfast, left
his hotel, at Beatenberg, with a sandwich in his
pocket, a few drops of whisky in his flask, and
accompanied by his son, lightly clad and lightly shod
like himself.

They went merrily along in the snow, on gently sloping ground bathed in the rays of the sun, till they found themselves by midday above a somewhat tall and far-stretching wall of rocks. The heat of the day and the weariness of the flesh promptly brought about the disappearance of the whisky and sandwiches. But the sun would continue to burn above and the snow to be deep below. Hot heads, icy feet, worn limbs. To trudge back seemed uninviting. So the tourists at sundown took to the steep rocks with trembling legs. Their hands were numb. They slipped on wet snow. They got no grip on the ice. They fell into snowdrifts. Their heads were dizzy. Their feet froze. To reach quickly the happy end of a sad tale, it was three o'clock in the morning when they were snatched from the edge of the grave by a party of peasants bearing lanterns and drawn to them by their despairing cries.

Like cases are well-nigh of daily occurrence.

So, if you would be a mountaineer, you may learn here a few things which probably you think you know already, but perhaps do not :—

1. *How to Walk in Snow.* Wear heavy socks and stockings, put on boots of stout leather with nailed soles and broad low heels.

To go uphill, set your feet down lightly but firmly in the snow, putting your weight upon the ball of the foot. Then raise yourself on your foremost leg by a forward swing of the body, to bring it well above your bent knee. This will set your hindmost foot free to step up in its turn, quite lightly. You must not raise yourself by means of a push away from the ground, you would merely glide out of your step, backwards.

To go downhill, put your foot flat in the snow, heel and all, keeping your heel straight, to build a foundation. But do not thump your foot down. There is frequently, under the snow, a slippery surface of stone or ice.

Put not your trust in sticks. As you do not know very well where the point will rest when thrust through the snow, it will often cause you to stumble. Your body should be well supported and well balanced on your legs alone.

2. If you use a rope in snow do not let it drag. Insist on your guide keeping it dry by coiling it up in his hands when it would be inconvenient to keep it taut. A rope that has over and over again been frozen and wetted is slippery under any condition and may snap under sudden stress.

3. When climbing rocks or steep grass slopes in winter, it is safest to assume that they are frozen over. Wear strong gloves and use them to hold on with, but do not lay your full weight, through your hands, on to jutting pieces of rock. Such supports are indispensable in climbing, but likely to break away. So use them as supports only. The weight of your body must rest on your feet and be raised by your legs to its next resting-point. Frozen ground, frosted grass, iced rocks are always extremely dangerous.

When letting yourself down frozen rocks, as a rule with the help of a rope, stand upright and in most cases with your back to the rise of the hill. You may then let yourself down on your bent elbows while your feet settle in their next hold.

4. The winter mountaineer has such a preference for ski-running that he has but little opportunity to use the instrument called *pickel*, *piolet*, or ice-axe. However, when compelled to remove his ski and sling them across his shoulders to pass a difficult piece of ground, he will hold his sticks together and use them in guise of an ice-axe for support.

When going down a sharp incline on foot, hold your sticks together, with both hands resting on them. Let the point end rest on the high ground well behind you, but do not lean back. You would find your feet running away from under you. When going uphill, plant the point ends of your sticks somewhere on the ground in the middle of your stride, but somewhat higher on the rise of the hill than the ground you stand on. It is a common mistake to plant one's sticks down the slope, a sure way of running into danger. In case of a slip, the place of hands and sticks is on the higher ground, while it is the business of the feet to seek alone a fresh hold lower down. They are thus partly relieved from the weight of the body, and this is kept upright.

5. The clothes of the winter mountaineer should be strong and warm. When moisture-laden, the air is more trying than when it is dry, though colder. Thaws are not unknown in winter, and rain in the valleys is an experience to be prepared against. Boots and leggings should be weather-proof. One should wear wind-proof knickerbockers or breeches, a

chamois leather waistcoat, a short but wide and easy coat. Rough woollen material collects the snow. Such should be reserved for underwear. Outer garments should present to the snow a smooth, closely woven surface.

CHAPTER XIV

WINTER STATIONS—WINTER SPORTS—HOW TO USE SKI

The awakening of the English—Switzerland the ice and snow rink of Europe—The high winter stations and the low—Principal sporting centres — Insular delusions — The Continental network of winter sport associations—Winter sports on ice—Tobogganing—The winter climate varies with the altitude—A classification of sporting centres according to altitude—The ski-runner is monarch of the Alps —How to keep one's ski in good order—How to learn the gentle art of running on ski—Precepts and practice—The turns, breaks, and swings—*Point final.*

T is strange to have to acknowledge, that while in the high-lying valleys of the Alps the Swiss have basked for centuries in hot Christmas sunshine, the English, till within the last twenty years, remained ignorant of Alpine winter sports. Enlightened medical men first recommended the tonic properties of the Alpine climate in winter. Then came the spirited promoters of the Public Schools Winter Sports Club. Now Sir Henry Lunn's winter stations stud the Alpine ranges from end to end.

These stations are typical of the best organisation hitherto devised to connect winter games known in England, such as skating, curling, and hockey, with the magnificent scenery and inexhaustible opportunities afforded by the Swiss winter climate. As compared with regions situated further north, the sporting advantages of Switzerland over, say, Scandinavia, consist in its central situation in mid-Europe, the closeness of its population, the immense accommodation for visitors, the short distances from station to station, the compactness of the road and railway system, and above all in the abundance of sunlight throughout the winter months. We need say nothing on the benefits of altitude. If air, sun and snow are ideal winter conditions for modern men and women, the higher we go, the more completely will those benefits be secured.

Be this as it may, stations under 5,000 feet are not so reliable for steady, continuous frost, as those situated above that level. This is a pity, because, from a social point of view, the lower stations are largely patronised. The winter sportsman likes to rise quickly. He knows that high peaks and deep valleys are nowhere so closely and attractively interwoven as in Switzerland. The two highest points permanently inhabited by a sedentary community are, in the valley of Cresta Avers, between the Maloja and Splügen passes, and at Chandolin d'Anniviers above Sierre, both at an altitude of about 6,000 feet. These places are above the forest zone and should in time become the flourishing winter sport stations which their situation entitles them to be. At the other and lowest extremity of the scale, but in the vicinity of Mont Blanc, and wanting but little energy to raise its potentialities to the level of the very best, should rank Megève, above Sallanches in the valley of the Arve. Unfortunately there has been hitherto in that part of the world but little disposition to act in an enterprising spirit.

The most important stations, so far, are those situated :—

1. In the Engadine and adjoining valleys (St. Moritz, Pontresina, Kampfer, Silvaplana, Sils, Maloja, Fex, Davos, Arosa, Klosters, &c.).

2. In the Bernese Oberland (Grindelwald, Beatenberg, Wengen, Mürren, Grimmi Alp, Kandersteg, Zweisimmen, Adelboden, Gstaad, Lauenen, &c.).

3. In the Vaudois Alps (Chateau D'Oex, Comballaz, Les Ormonts, Leysin—this latter with many sanatoria—Caux above the lake of Geneva, &c.).

4. In the Rhône valley (Chesières, Villars, Gryon, Morgins and Champéry, Montana and Vermala, Louèche les Bains, in German, Leukerbad), &c. Zermatt is accessible and may be most comfortably lived in in winter, but cannot be said to be as yet a properly opened up station. The same may be said of Saas Fée, to which the new Britannia hut of the Swiss Alpine Club, a gift of the British members of the club, should draw henceforth a large number of English ski-runners. The Simplon and St. Bernard hospices are open throughout the year.

5. In the St. Gothard district (Andermatt, &c.).

6. In the Jura range (St. Cergue sur Nyon, Les Rasses sur Ste. Croix, Mont Soleil sur St. Imier, &c.).

7. In the Mont Blanc district (Chamounix, St. Gervais, Le Planet, Finhaut, &c.).

The offices of the Federal Railways at Regent

L.M.C.

THE BRITANNIA HUT.

To face p. 302.

Street, 11B, London, S.W., deliver gratis an illustrated winter list of Swiss mountaineering resorts. Many of these have been founded by local enterprise only. Such, though quite commendable and moderately expensive, do not often afford the first-class skating facilities found in the Engadine, at Grindelwald, and in stations under English management.

Stations which may boast of a large and well-kept skating rink, a curling pond, well-laid toboggan and bob-sleigh runs, a rink for hockey, and plenty of good ski-ing slopes, with hotel accommodation for an unlimited number of visitors of either sex, are a modern achievement of no mean order in primitive out-of-the-way Swiss mountain villages, buried under anything from 3 to 9 feet of snow.

There is a marked difference between the stations patronised by the English—or visitors from the capitals, whatever their nationality—and the stations frequented by the local people for sport or holiday purposes. Those two classes avoid each other very effectually, though unconsciously for the most part, and without any pointed intention so to do.

The former class depends on " central heating " for comfort. So exclusively do they depend on this and so steadily do they flock to the best accredited stations, that they often fondly imagine themselves to be the only sportsmen active in winter. How often has the writer been asked, at Villars, for instance : How is it that we English are alone seen on ski in Switzerland ? This mistake is easily accounted for, because those who get that impression do not go far enough afield to correct it. If they did, they would soon find out what an extremely small proportion of those who run on ski are English. A little thought will show that this is quite natural.

Ski-running facilities stretch, as it were, in an unbroken line from Scandinavia through central Europe straight down to the Maritime Alps, and from the Vosges and Dauphiné in the west to the Carpathians in the east. The number of ski-runners recruited over this immense area is immeasurably larger than anything the British Isles (where there exist no ski-ing facilities worth mentioning) can produce.

The whole of Central Europe is, as it were, caught up in the meshes of a huge net of Alpine associations and skiers' clubs. These hold periodic competitions and meet in international congresses, commanding a degree of public attention and drawing to themselves an interest the magnitude of which passes quite unnoticed in the United Kingdom.

In a rather ill-considered manner, winter visitors to Switzerland like to crowd the resorts which have become famous for their suitability in summer. This is not quite the way to set about the thing. Winter stations should be sought out for their own characteristics. Several low-lying centres are not nearly so suitable in winter as in summer. Besides, many which could be favourably reported upon by specialists, have hitherto failed to be introduced to the public.

Winter sports may be divided into two classes:—

1. Those which depend upon nature alone.

2. Those which depend upon nature artificially aided.

Among the latter class, skating and curling are foremost. Running on ski ranks first among the former.

It would be out of place here to dwell upon skating, curling, and hockey. These are most congenial pastimes under the blue skies and amid the magnificent scenery of the Alps, but they are distinct from mountaineering. Scottish and Swiss curlers vie with each other in such stations as Kandersteg. Curling stones are imported from London, and ponds are now made in all centres favoured by players of the game.

Skating rinks are a much more costly affair than curling ponds. Patrons of the sport are apt to forget how valuable and extensive is the land that has to be purchased and prepared in the vicinity of the hotels. A staff of professional skating rink builders is in request, with an army of sweepers under their orders. In the middle of the day the great heat of the sun has often to be kept down by filtering the rays through huge pieces of stretched-out sacking or canvas. As the supply of electricity for lighting purposes is seldom scarce, night *fêtes* are a great feature upon the Alpine rinks.

The social life is indeed sometimes a little excessive, and may interfere with the steadiness of one's nerve. When Englishmen, by way of amusement, use the Swiss military rifle at the local range in friendly rivalry with the peasantry, the Swiss team has hitherto been invariably victorious, no doubt because

20

the British marksmen are called out "for social duty on the station" at too close intervals.

The toboggan, or *luge*, and the sleigh are usual vehicles with the Swiss. A sight deeply indicative of manly power and grace, is that of Swiss woodmen steering heavily laden sleighs round jagged corners and down precipitous ice cliffs. A run on one of these is an introduction to a new set of sensations.

But the "common herd" toboggan and bob on well-defined roads or tracks, or buzz down runs purposely laid out for their use. According to the lie or curve of the land, and with a view to accelerated speed, artificial runs are scientifically built up in lines and bends carefully designed beforehand. The banks are made of snow piled up with a shovel, and often hardened into blocks by pouring water upon the snow.

The Alpine climate, whether the Swiss, French, Italian, or Austrian Alps are considered, varies with the altitude. It is at its worst in the region of towns, lakes, and rivers, wherever the altitude is under 1,500 feet.

The winter months begin to wear their characteristic aspect in places ranging from 3,000 feet and upwards. But climate must not be confused with general suitability for sport, and stations between 3,000 and 4,000 feet, however excellent in every other respect, are not yet high enough to show a thoroughly reliable winter climate. South-west winds, recurrent thaws, rain, and fog may affect sport seriously in such places for the whole of any one week out of three.

But, upwards of 4,000 feet, a steadily dry winter climate sets in early in December, and may be relied upon to last until the end of March. There is sure to be some thawing now and then, under the influence of mild weather or as an effect of long exposure to the sun, but the dry, cold air, and the torrid rays of an almost tropical sun, are the prevailing features of the sporting season.

As, upwards of 7,000 feet, no winter stations have as yet been thrown open, the useful range of Alpine climate is as follows:—

1. Under 3,000 feet (such as Mont Pélerin, above Vevey, and Ballaigues, above Vallorbes).

2. From 3,000 to 4,500 feet (these stations are the most numerous and the most frequented).

3. Between 4,500 and 6,500 feet (at this altitude some people begin to experience breathing and heart troubles, mental excitability, and insomnia).

Stations situated in this last and highest zone afford excellent sport. Such are, for instance: Mürren, Montana-Vermala, the whole of the upper Engadine, Arosa, Davos, &c. They are the ski-runner's paradise. Pontresina, particularly, is one of the very finest centres for long excursions on ski. But, while some other parts are rather too flat, the Pontresina district does not abound in short, easy runs.

At from 7,000 feet and upwards, the climate is that of a glorified North Pole; alternative spells of beautiful blazing sunshine, and of stormy, snow-laden, piercingly cold winds. In winter the temperature of the air is always low and, practically speaking, there is frost above the snow-line every

night even in summer. But, in the coldest January
weather, the sunbeams are poured forth in such
arrays, for weeks at a time, from cloudless, windless
skies, that one's sensation of bodily heat, between
sunrise and sunset, may be quite overpowering.

All those allurements would perhaps, as in former
days, still count for little, but for the transportation
of the ski from their dull, northern home to that
house set on high which opens its southern frontage,
as a balcony 200 miles long over the plains of
Italy.

This chapter would not be brought to a fit conclusion if its last lines were not the means of
enabling the reader to make himself proficient in
the bare rudiments of the ski-ing craft which brings
the High Alps in their winter garb within reach of
human gaze.

The beginner should purchase ski made of ash, and
somewhat shorter than the reach of his arm when
extended above his head. He will find the Huitfeldt
binding most convenient, with the improved Ellefsen
clamp patented under the name of Aspor.

Previously to using your ski, oil them repeatedly
at intervals of a week, and give the oil (if possible
hot linseed) plenty of time to sink into the wood.
Then rub lightly some dry paraffin-wax into the grain
of the wood. Each time after using your ski, clean
them and rub them down with an oily cloth or
sponge.

Warm feet are the royal road to health and comfort: there must be room enough in your boot to
leave freedom of motion to each toe.

First learn to move about on the flat, without any support of any kind. If you have followed our advice as to oiling and waxing ski, the under surface of yours will be perfectly smooth and very slippery. So, next, choose the most gentle slope you can find to glide upon. Let it be an easy slant leading on to a flat piece of snow.

Practise going down steadily and slowly, holding in each hand, if you like, a light bamboo or hazel-wood stick. These are to be used only to pick yourself up. Never practise with a single stick, or a stout, heavy stick, or a long stick.

Put the right foot foremost, then the left. Then go down on one foot alone, alternately using the right and the left.

Go through these preliminary exercises with extreme patience. In nothing so much as in ski-running is it fair to say "The more haste the less speed."

The beginner who raises his ski off the snow surface falls into a serious mistake. He should glide his ski along the surface of the snow when moving uphill as well as on the flat. Ski were not made to be lifted, like feet, but to be pushed along, like a drawn-out wheel. A sensible learner never forces his way up a slope, but, as soon as he feels himself sliding back, he eases off to the right or left. He should always keep his ski close to each other, whether his course be upwards or downwards. The knees, too, should be held close together when descending. The body should not stoop from the waist but lean forward from the ankle-joint, so as to be well balanced over the middle of the ski, the limbs remaining loose and easy throughout.

The whole secret of straight and easy running may be further summed up in the following simple golden rules :—

1. Stand upright on your ski, keeping your body at a right angle to the slope down which you run.

2. Keep ski, feet, and knees together.

3. Then practise lunging with each foot alternately, with the forward knee bent each time as far as it can go.

4. While lunging bring the weight of the body to rest alternately on each ski.

5. Practise thrusting back each leg alternately as far as it can go, with your body resting on the forward bent knee.

6. Then bring both ski close to each other again, and let yourself be borne downwards along hangs of increasing steepness.

7. Then let yourself fly down the whole length of a long slope, first on one foot, then on the other, till you can move along on each ski, without bringing the other into play.

8. Practise dragging each ski alternately behind the other, setting the hind ski free from your weight, then raise the front ski in the air and transfer all your weight to the back ski.

Having got so far one may begin trying swings to the right and left.

1. To do a Telemark swing to the right, push your left ski forward, and bring the weight of your body well above your fully bent knee. If you then

incline your body slightly within the curve you wish to describe in the snow to your right, the forward ski, left, will begin to glide in sideways. The inner ski (the right ski) will follow within the curve, provided you keep your right leg well extended behind, and keep the weight of your body off it.

2. To do an Alpine swing to the right, turn the beak (or head) of your left ski towards the right ski, while laying the weight of your body on the left ski, placed lowest on the slope. The left ski will then swing downwards and sideways, and, under the pressure of your foot, come round the head of your right ski, accomplishing the turn. In this swing the heels (or back of the ski) fly apart.

3. To do a Christiania swing to the right, start with ski even and close together. Advance slightly the right ski, get up speed sharply and then throw your weight somewhat backwards by a side thrust inward, ranging from the left hip to the right. The heels of the ski will slip together away from your body, behind you, to the left, and the heads of both ski will point to the right.

The Christiania is reputed a difficult swing, but here is the " straight tip " : Old ski, with edges worn down at the heel, feather round beautifully.

Beware of learning those turns in deep or heavy snow, lest you sprain or wrench an ankle. Hard, ridgy snow is even more dangerous.

This is not the place to teach how, at the altitude of 7,000 feet and upwards, begins High Alp ski-running, in which the Swiss are past masters, because this phase of sport is not for beginners.

On the other hand, consummate runners with good guides and inured to every kind of hardship, might well be trusted to add to this book many a page showing, much better than the present writer can, how the High Alps in winter have infinite pleasure in store for the bold, cool-headed, and strong.

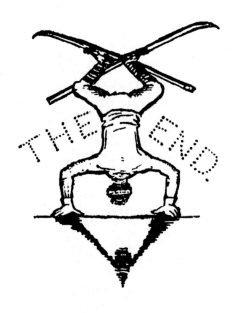

Printed in the United Kingdom
by Lightning Source UK Ltd.
117690UKS00002B/205